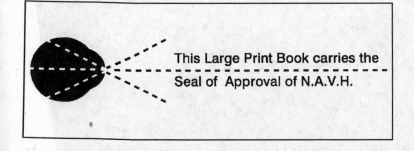

This Large Print Book carries the
Seal of Approval of N.A.V.H.

# RUN, DON'T WALK

# RUN, DON'T WALK

## THE CURIOUS AND CHAOTIC LIFE OF A PHYSICAL THERAPIST INSIDE WALTER REED ARMY MEDICAL CENTER

## ADELE LEVINE

**THORNDIKE PRESS**
*A part of Gale, Cengage Learning*

GALE
CENGAGE Learning®

Farmington Hills, Mich • San Francisco • New York • Waterville, Maine
Meriden, Conn • Mason, Ohio • Chicago

**GALE**
CENGAGE Learning®

LIBRARY OF CONGRESS CATALOGING-IN-PUBLICATION DATA

Levine, Adele.
   Run, don't walk : the curious and chaotic life of a physical therapist inside Walter Reed Army Medical Center / by Adele Levine. — Large Print edition.
     pages cm. — (Thorndike Press large print inspirational)
     Originally published: New York : Avery, c2014.
     ISBN 978-1-4104-7074-4 (hardcover) — ISBN 1-4104-7074-1 (hardcover)
     1. Walter Reed Army Medical Center—Anecdotes. 2. Amputees—Rehabilitation—Washington (D.C.) 3. Physical therapists—Washington (D.C.)—Biography. 4. Disabled veterans—Rehabilitation—Washington (D.C.) 5. Disabled veterans—Medical care—Washington (D.C.) 6. Disabled veterans—United States—Anecdotes. 7. Iraq War, 2003-2011—Veterans—Medical care—United States. 8. Afghan War, 2001- —Veterans—Medical care—United States. 9. Single women—Washington (D.C.)—Biography. 10. Washington (D.C.)—Biography. I. Title.
UH474.5.W3L48 2014b
956.7044'37—dc23
[B]                                       2014011755

Printed in the United States of America
1 2 3 4 5 6 7 18 17 16 15 14

*In memory of my hardworking, eccentric, passionate, kind father, Richard J. Levine. Dad, I was always going to dedicate this book to you. I miss you so much, my friend.*

*And to Ashley*

# CONTENTS

Difficulties are just things to overcome,
after all.

— ERNEST SHACKLETON,
polar explorer

■ ■ ■ ■

# PART ONE

■ ■ ■ ■

# COSMO

The phone rings in the amputee clinic and it is one of Darcy's patients. He is on a ski trip sponsored by Disabled Sports USA and wants to tell Darcy that he just went down the ski slope on a mono-ski (seated ski). It's his first trip away from the hospital since an improvised explosive device (IED) in Iraq blew his legs away four months ago.

His exhilaration is reflected in Darcy's face. She downplays it when she hangs up the phone, but I can tell she's secretly thrilled. Getting these phone calls, hearing these stories, are huge victories. It is what we live for as physical therapists — whether it's seeing a patient head back to the ski slope, or, because we work for the U.S. Army, back to combat. It's what makes the long hours and the physicality of our work worth it.

"Wasn't that sweet?" she says to me. "That was Joe Davie calling to tell me how much fun he was having skiing."

All of Darcy's patients seem to pick up her good nature and cheer.

"You're lucky," Sergeant Hernandez jokes. "If any of my patients call, they'll be calling to yell at me. *'I'm falling on my face over here! What the hell did you teach me in PT? I can't walk. I can't ski. This trip is a total joke!'* "

It was spring 2009 and I was a physical therapist in the most famous military hospital in the world: Walter Reed Army Medical Center. I'd been there for four years, and I'd go on to work there till its preplanned closing in 2011 — part of a congressional budget base realignment and closure (BRAC) decision. In the amputee section where I worked, there were ten physical therapists and, in the course of the day, more than a hundred patients. We were squeezed into a disproportionately small, glassed-in gym on the top floor of Walter Reed's Military Advanced Training Center.

It was a strange idea, putting us under glass. On display for the rest of the world, but otherwise leaving us to our business. The glass wall allowed the tour groups to walk by without disrupting the patients. Three to six groups came by every day, often with celebrities in tow. But nothing distracted a patient more than looking up to see Angelina Jolie or an openly weeping congressman staring at him through the glass. My coworkers and the patients would joke that this must be how it felt to be an animal at the zoo.

I spent most of my evening hours swimming, so to me our facility felt like an aquarium. We were fish in a bowl.

That day began like any other — at 0700. We gathered in the Fishbowl to go over the medevac list with our supervisor, Major Tavner.

Maj. Tavner looked over the list of new patients and then asked, "Okay, guys, who's ready for a new one?"

The other PTs and I skimmed the names as fast as we could, clamoring to see over her shoulder. Some of my colleagues wanted the big, complicated cases. They'd gone to graduate school specifically for this purpose — to serve as physical therapists to the nation's war wounded — and no challenge was too great for them: triple amputees, open abdominal wounds, fractured spines, broken pelvises. No problem.

Some wanted the prizes — the Special Forces patients, the West Point officers — patients who had been overachievers before and, they hoped, would carry that motivation through their upcoming rehab.

15

And some of my colleagues wanted a certain type of amputation.

"I'll take the double AK!" my friend and co-conspirator Darcy passionately volunteered. When she saw that I'd burst out laughing, she added for emphasis: "I love double AKs. They just can't cheat."

. A "double AK" is a person whose legs have both been amputated above the knee. They can't "cheat" because they literally don't have another leg to stand on. And because both of their legs are amputated at the thigh, they won't have an easier amputation on the other side like a BK (below-knee amputation) to favor. Darcy had worked with these challenges many times before and considered herself something of a specialist. I made fun of her for it, but to a certain extent, we all played favorites, especially in our morning sports medicine sick call clinic. "Oh, I got an elbow. I hate the elbow! What'd you get, an ankle? I'll trade you."

Darcy is tall and thin and, no matter what the situation, always looks like she is about to dissolve into uncontrolled laughter. Her mission every minute of the day is to uncover the hilarity in random scenarios. Once, when the colonel who was in charge of the PT department held a long staff meeting on finding functional goals for our patients to achieve before discharge, Darcy had suggested with perfect comedic timing that they try to cross Georgia Avenue, a busy four-lane road outside the hospital. This was a preposterous suggestion, as just the week before, a Walter Reed nurse had been hospitalized after getting hit by a car while trying to cross Georgia Avenue. The only person who heard Darcy's comment was me. This had been deliberate on Darcy's part, as she knew I would fall completely to pieces.

Usually, though, Darcy can't keep a serious look on her face to save her life, and her laughter is completely infectious.

I knew for a fact that an AK/BK (above-knee and below-knee amputee) is Darcy's least favorite type of amputation. I teased Darcy that I was going to pick out an AK/BK for her. "Don't you dare!" Darcy said dramatically, before exploding into laughter in spite of herself. "They are such cheaters."

As for me? I just wanted someone easy. My dream patient, the one I crossed my fingers for, would have just one leg neatly blown off by a rocket-propelled grenade. No shrapnel injuries to the other side. No brain trauma from a huge explosion.

Unlike some of my colleagues, I'd never

felt it was my calling to be here in Walter Reed. I'd put myself through physical therapy school after several depressing rounds of unemployment. My ambitions were fairly modest. I just wanted a straight job, a job with regular hours, and nights and weekends off. And I wanted a Ford Mustang. I thought after PT school I would have it made: decent pay, a steady paycheck. But student loans were expensive. I never got that Mustang. But I lucked into a cheap apartment, a basement apartment, on Alaska Avenue. Walter Reed was across the street, so I sent in my résumé. Convenience: that was my calling.

Every day for the past few years, I'd pretended to be ambitious at these intake meetings, scanning the list and supposedly looking for a challenging patient, when in reality I was so paralyzed with indecision that I just picked out the patient with the most interesting name in the group. It was the same reason I ate oatmeal every morning in the hospital cafeteria, after first doing my usual inspection of the eggs, bacon, and waffles. I couldn't make a decision to save my life. If I wasn't so worried about my coworkers figuring out my secret, I would have selected new patients in alphabetical order. Luckily I had my system. I'd find the

18

most unusual name, shout it out, and hope for the best when it came to his injuries. Lately, however, there really *hadn't* been any "bests." Thanks to ever deadlier IEDs in Afghanistan and Iraq, the soldiers were coming in looking worse and worse. We'd admitted our first quadruple amputee in 2009, and four more had followed in quick succession.

I was still laughing with Darcy when I realized that everyone but me had picked a patient. Bright red, I turned back to the list. Injuries, ages, and ranks jumbled together in my head: They were all severe, all complicated. It was a miracle that any of these men had survived — indeed, a testament to their strength, as well as recent advances in combat medicine — but all of their roads would be long and trying from here.

That's when I caught sight of my unusual name: Cosmo. In addition to losing a leg above the knee, Cosmo had multiple spinal fractures, a dislocated elbow, a femur broken in two places, and a smashed tibia. *Terrible,* I thought, *but just another typical Walter Reed patient. You'll be fine.*

Our new patients usually arrive from combat to Walter Reed within seventy-two hours. They are able to survive devastating

19

injuries that would have otherwise killed them because they carry tourniquets into battle, and because they have access to immediate and aggressive medical and surgical care.

Each soldier carries two tourniquets and is trained in applying them to their comrades and, in many situations, to themselves. In addition to tourniquets, the medics carry special blood-clotting powder and blood-cauterizing gauze bandages that can be packed into open wounds to quickly stop the bleeding. The injured are swiftly transported from battleground to combat support hospitals (CSHs) located close to the front lines, where they are stabilized and prepped for flight back to the United States on huge cargo planes that function as flying surgical hospitals. It sometimes happens that the flight nurses and surgeons are strapped to the stretchers as the plane is coming in for a landing so they can continue working on an unstable patient.

They land at Landstuhl Regional Medical Center in Germany for continued medical and surgical care and to prepare for a long air evacuation to Walter Reed. From Germany, an email is sent to Walter Reed listing the number of incoming wounded and their injuries. Walter Reed preps the operating room suites and gets hospital beds ready.

Landing at Andrews Air Force Base in Maryland, the patients are loaded into army ambulance buses for a lights-and-siren-screaming ride around the Beltway to Walter Reed.

Awaiting their arrival, a lone figure stands in front of the hospital. The chaplain.

Behind the hospital doors a small army of medics holding stretchers are standing ready to carry the wounded off the ambulance buses, the last leg of their long trip, into the receiving arms of the hospital.

The bus pulls into the loading dock, and the medics explode through the hospital doors, whisking the patients off the buses, rushing them past the chaplain and waiting family members, and straight into the operating rooms.

It's the first of at least a dozen surgeries for these soldiers. Explosions are dirty and blow infectious residue deep into the body. Once at Walter Reed, the patients spend their first month on a dizzying surgical schedule, getting rotated in and out of the operating room as frequently as every other day to clean the infection and dirt out of their wounds.

Physical therapy begins immediately and continues daily.

My work with Cosmo began with a physical therapy consult from the physician managing his case — a short note in the electronic medical chart titled "PT Consult." I replied electronically that I had read the consult and then I scanned through the rest of Cosmo's chart. In his case, as was common in our patients, his amputated leg was the least of his injuries. There was also the dislocated elbow, the spinal fractures, and his remaining mangled leg. With at least six fractures, a sciatic nerve injury, and big chunks of soft tissue loss, I knew that remaining leg was going to be a real problem.

No combat details were presented in the chart, with the exception of noting that Cosmo was an "AD 22 yo M OEF 11B s/p dismounted IED." Translated, Cosmo was a twenty-two-year-old male, active duty 11 Bravo (infantry) soldier with injuries sustained in Operation Enduring Freedom from an improvised explosive device. A device he had triggered by walking across it.

Deep in his bed in the intensive care unit, Cosmo was wrapped in so many bandages and casts he was barely visible, but I could see a shock of bright, curly red hair rising above it all.

From the pillows I heard a soft whisper. I leaned closer. "Cosmo?"

"I'm getting fuckin' piles lying here in this fuckin' bed."

People coming off of anesthesia don't remember much, so I repeated the refrain heard all down the hallways of Wards 57 and 58 — the wards tasked with receiving most of the war wounded: "Do you know where you are? You are at Walter Reed. You are at Walter Reed and you are okay."

"Just don't tell me where the fuck I am again," Cosmo replied. "I fucking know where the fuck I am. In fucking Walter Reed, that's where. What's up with this fucking hospital? Do you know where *you* are?" For someone who was just out of surgery, he was surprisingly alert.

Taken aback by Cosmo's unusual ICU presentation, I hurried through his initial examination. It wasn't a long exam. I was just checking to see how much motion he had in his remaining joints and how well he could move himself around the bed — if at all. Could he lift his leg, the one with the metal frame on it? How about his stump? Could he bend his remaining knee? Roll onto his side? Pull himself into a seated position? Any injuries to his hands? How strong was he? Could he sit without falling over?

Cosmo's eyes were bright green and semi-wild. He was a Colorado boy. As I evaluated him that first day, he told me he liked fucking adrenaline, the fucking outdoors, fucking hunting, and fucking Sonic milkshakes. All he wanted was just to get fucking outside again.

A few days later, Cosmo was transferred out of the ICU to Ward 57, the Orthopedic Floor, where he became famous for his colorful vocabulary, consisting of really just one word, repeated over and over. *Fuck.*

"Oh, it's fucking physical fucking therapy coming to fucking force me into a fucking fuck back brace. Come the fuck on in."

Until a patient's pain is firmly under control, I see the patient at bedside in his or her hospital room, where we practice bed mobility: rolling onto one side, scooting up in the bed, and sitting on the edge of the bed. Sitting unsupported without falling over can be a challenge for a new amputee, even for a soldier who's lost just one leg. Your body's center of balance has shifted. Without the leg on that side to balance you out, a simple task like leaning over to pick something off the floor is a good way to topple out of your chair.

For those who have lost both of their legs at thigh level, it's harder still. For a soldier who has lost a leg at the hip joint, or for those unlucky enough to lose both legs at the hip joint or part of their pelvis, sitting can be a real workout. There's very little to balance on. And without the counterweight of your legs, it's a heavy abdominal workout.

While soldiers are confined to their beds, we also do simple strengthening exercises. I helped Cosmo lift his shattered, steel frame–encased leg up and down. And, since Walter Reed is a military hospital, modified one-armed push-ups. Later, when his elbow had healed further, we would do pull-ups using the overhead bedframe as a pull-up bar.

Cosmo dutifully did his rehab exercises, but without much enthusiasm. He didn't seem interested in getting strong — he just wanted to get outside again.

"Fuck this. I need to get me some fucking sun. Can you help me out of this fucking bed?"

What Cosmo really wanted was a cigarette. I was merely a vehicle to help him get into a wheelchair so he could roll himself out to the courtyard, park blatantly beside the NO SMOKING sign, and defiantly chain-smoke.

While the front of the hospital was drab

cement, the interior had an open courtyard containing a landscaped garden. Because of the open center space, regardless if a patient's room was on the inside or outside of the building, they all had a window facing out. It gave Walter Reed a light, greenhouse feel to it, as you were always looking through a window at a flowering garden.

The center gardens were sectioned off by ward. Some of the gardens had a fountain. The garden outside Ward 54, the Psych Ward, had a volleyball court. Carrying a walker and staring down at the courtyard from the sixth floor, I was always taken aback to see patients playing, what was that, *volleyball*?

The garden that was shared by Ward 57 and Ward 58 had several flowering dogwood trees with stuffed-animal monkeys hanging off the branches. I'm not sure who did this. But I sure thought it was funny. I'd been at Walter Reed five years before I noticed them. I had been waiting impatiently for a patient to get off a bedpan and had wandered out to the courtyard to check the weather. Looking up at the sky for clouds, I saw the monkeys way up high in the branches — yellow, orange, and red monkeys. I had stared at them in disbelief before laughing appreciatively.

Regardless of a patient's true motives to get out of bed, I always applaud on the inside. That's what physical therapy is all about. To get them out of bed. To coax them down to the rehab gym. To do their strengthening exercises. To buy into the program. All in order to prepare them for the day they will eventually walk again. But I downplay my enthusiasm at a soldier's pain-tinged request for fear he'll figure out that's what I've been trying to get him to do and rebel. It's always better to make it seem like it is their idea all along.

Cosmo couldn't get out of bed by himself. His body was cluttered with the typical array of medical devices for a Ward 57 patient. His right leg, laughingly called his "intact side" because it wasn't the amputated one, was inside a metal cage — an external fixator ("ex-fix"), which held the broken pieces of bone together. The rods from the ex-fix pierced into Cosmo's shin and formed a type of scaffolding to hold his fractured tibia together. Sticking out of Cosmo's thigh was another type of external fixator, a long piece of metal that ran parallel to his leg, with evenly spaced metal pins that disappeared into the meat of his thigh. It looked like a refrigerator handle and was frequently used by physical therapy as such, as we usually grabbed the "handle" to move the leg around.

Cosmo's other leg was amputated at the thigh, and wrapped up like a peppermint stick in thick white bandaging. Running out of the end of the amputation was a clear plastic tube, which ran over and underneath Cosmo's bed sheets, down the length of the bed, and into what looked like a small air-conditioning unit: the wound vacuum. The wound VAC ran constantly, sucking infectious fluid out of Cosmo's open amputation to help it heal faster.

His left arm with the dislocated elbow had a long plastic brace on it, courtesy of my rehab colleagues in Occupational Therapy, who love nothing more than to heat up plastic, cut out strips of Velcro, and cheerfully make custom braces for their patients (and frequently themselves, should they somehow manage to sprain both wrists and an elbow playing softball on the weekend).

Dangling haphazardly off Cosmo's bandages like red Christmas ornaments were several small plastic grenades. Or at least, that's what they reminded me of. These were wound drains. They were typically safety-pinned to a patient's bandages, but if you weren't careful, they sure were easy to pull off. I would know. The first time I got

Cosmo out of bed and into a wheelchair, I inadvertently snapped one of those drains off. At first I thought someone had just ambushed me with a paint gun. The front of my shirt, my shoes, and the floor under the wheelchair were covered in purpley-red blood. I called the nurse, and she came in and gave me a long, angry look before asking how many milliliters of blood I thought was in that drain before I carelessly yanked it off.

Like a Dr. Seuss highway system, all sorts of lines and tubes crisscrossed over and underneath Cosmo. Every time I saw him for physical therapy, before we could begin exercises in his bed, or before I could help him slide out of bed and into a wheelchair, I had to first untangle him from his nest of lines and tubes. This had to be done delicately, since it was easy to accidentally yank something out. At least Cosmo was usually in his room alone. It was much more stressful when a patient's terrified, sleep-deprived family watched me run IV poles around, unhook wound vacuums, move drain lines, and fish around the bed for the nerve block. The last thing I wanted was to be another star player in their nightmare.

Thanks to their nerve blocks, new patients at Walter Reed weren't screaming in pain as you'd expect them to be — considering the extent of their injuries. The pain team put portable epidurals in all the new patients, so they were essentially numb from the waist down. These epidurals could be placed directly into the spine or into selected nerves, blocking sensation from that point on. They were very slender and looked like fishing line taped on one end to the patient's skin. But believe me, you didn't want to be the one to accidentally yank the nerve block out.

With his wound VAC, nerve blocks, external fixators, drains, Foley catheter, IV pole, casts, and back brace, it usually took at least one, sometimes two, staff members to slide Cosmo out of bed and into a wheelchair. But after only a few weeks in the hospital, Cosmo mentioned that he had a plan to "Get the fuck out of the fuckin' hospital and catch a fuckin' bus to the fuckin' White House." I didn't take him seriously. Who would have?

Cosmo's pain was under better control at that point. He could be disconnected from his IV pain meds for most of the day and he was spending most of his time, when he wasn't wheeling himself down to the physical therapy clinic, in the Ward 57 courtyard. So he got his first day pass. The day pass was a nod of approval to go somewhere outside the hospital and usually a test run for patients to see how well they would handle discharge.

Most patients didn't go very far. The majority spent the day lying in bed and watching TV with their families across base at the Mologne House hotel. Others went to the Borders bookstore in downtown Silver Spring one mile away, or got lunch at Ledo's Pizza restaurant across the street from Walter Reed. But Cosmo was the first patient I knew of who decided to catch a bus downtown.

Back on Ward 57 that night, Cosmo relaxed in his bed, pleased with his big caper but irritated at Nursing's reaction. He missed curfew and the nursing staff wasn't pleased. They didn't go into any details the next day, but I could tell something was up since they were tight-lipped and looked clearly annoyed when I checked in at the nursing station. According to them, a patient had "gone bad," which was what they always said when something unorthodox happened, as if the patient in question was a piece of fruit left out in the sun. "Gone bad" could mean a number of different things, from a soldier refusing his medications, to falling out of bed. Or in Cosmo's case, catching the S2 bus to the White House.

Cosmo lay back in the pillows and didn't make eye 'contact. "Fuck them. I said I wanted to do some fuckin' sightseeing."

Nursing might have been irritated, but I thought Cosmo's stunt to catch a public bus down 16th Street took real courage. And, because, like many of my coworkers, my knee-jerk reaction to anything remotely uncomfortable is humor, I thought it was drop-dead funny.

With an involuntary smirk on my face, I tried to imagine what Cosmo might have looked like to the surprised bus passengers when their bus pulled up to the bus stop. I knew the passengers on the 16th Street Line — it was the yuppie express. Every eight minutes another bus full of swollen, self-important egos left the law offices and accounting firms of downtown D.C. Even though Walter Reed was processing almost all of the American casualties out of Afghanistan and Iraq, most of Washington, D.C., had never seen a recently wounded veteran. The wounded and injured, the recently disabled, hung out behind the gates of Walter Reed, waiting to get better. Waiting to return to their former lives in small-town mid-America somewhere. I'm sure no one on that bus even remembered there was a war going on, until they came face-to-face with Cosmo.

The hilarity of it vibrated through me like electricity. I could see it so clearly: Cosmo in a hospital-issue wheelchair with his bandaged amputation, back brace, elbow splint, and leg encased in a long steel frame, waiting patiently at the bus stop. The bus passengers, recently released from the fluorescent confines of their important downtown office, eager to beat city traffic and get home.

I frequently catch the bus downtown. I know what it's like. You need to pay quickly and get to a seat, before the bus driver hits the gas and sends you sprawling headfirst into another passenger's lap. I asked Cosmo whether anyone helped him get on the bus. Cosmo rolled his eyes in exaggerated annoyance.

"Fuck no. Some fuck asked me for a fucking cigarette. Then the fucking bus showed up. Everyone looked at me and just went, 'Fuck.' "

# PSYCH WARD

Walter Reed's tree-lined campus opened on May 1, 1909, when Walter Reed General Hospital admitted its first ten patients. Instead of being named for a famous general, Walter Reed was named after a young army doctor, Major Walter Reed, who discovered the cause of yellow fever. During the Spanish American War, more Americans died of yellow fever than were killed in actual combat. In the century that followed, the hospital emulated the young researcher, becoming a world-renowned institution of research, training, education, and, of course, medical care. In the years I was there, Walter Reed through necessity became the world leader in the care of the poly-traumatic combat amputee.

At its hundred-year anniversary, Walter Reed Army Medical Center was a busy twenty-first-century facility with seventy-four buildings dispersed over 113 acres of fruit tree–speckled hills. It was bustling with modern soldiers, doctors, and newly wounded veterans, yet it still maintained a historic look. The original rose-red brick buildings, built in a distinct Colonial Georgian style with the door centered in the middle, cornice molding, and rectangular multipane windows, were still in use as administrative buildings, barracks, and educational centers.

The original hospital, Building One, had an elegant circular driveway overlooking a rose garden and sparkling blue fountain. Inside the main lobby were stone tile floors, elaborate wood molding, high ceilings, and comfortable leather furniture. The stone stairs sagged in the middle from a hundred years of footsteps.

In the front sitting room of Building One, a framed photograph of Vice President Nixon visiting a gaunt President Eisenhower, when Eisenhower was a patient at Walter Reed, hung above the mantel. And down the halls were photographs of every consecutive U.S. president from President Warren G. Harding, our twenty-ninth president, to President Obama visiting the soldiers at Walter Reed. But judging by the pictures, no president seemed to have come more frequently than Eisenhower, who visited the troops convalescing at Walter Reed as a World War II general, and then many times later as president, including several stints as a patient himself.

Shortly before winning his second term, Eisenhower had emergency abdominal surgery at Walter Reed. The surgeon who operated on President Eisenhower was Major General Leonard Heaton. In 1977, a new hospital was built behind Building One. Building Two, named Heaton Pavilion for Eisenhower's surgeon, would become the modern-day Walter Reed Hospital, the crown jewel of army medicine. Its top floor had a private ward with enhanced security, bulletproof windows, and secure phone lines. This ward, the Eisenhower Executive Nursing Suite, was reserved for the president, vice president, high-ranking military officials, foreign dignitaries, and medal of honor recipients. But before this suite was built, Eisenhower himself spent the last year of his life at Walter Reed in a room in the original hospital overlooking the main entrance, rose garden, and fountain.

Connected to Building One by an underground tunnel, Building Two was a squat cement building shaped like an upside-down wedding cake. The large second tier, floors three through seven, sat on top of a smaller first tier. The veranda running around the perimeter was exactly one-quarter of a mile and sheltered from rain by the larger second tier. No matter what time of day or night you happen to be entering Building Two, there was always someone running around the veranda. Usually these were groups of soldiers, but at 0640 it was most likely civilian staff in a solitary sprint to work.

No matter how bad you might appear after living through an explosion that killed your battle buddies, blew off your legs, and opened you up like a can of tuna, inside the glass walls of our clinic it was all smiles and jokes and the occasional cheer. In fact, it was not unusual for a therapist or an entire room of therapists to stand up and applaud a patient the first time they came down to the MATC by themselves.

"Look at you!" my coworkers would say. "You are doing great!"

The tour groups saw it all without sound. And from inside the Fishbowl, we saw them back, the looks on their faces reflecting something we didn't consciously experience. They were seeing the devastating toll of war for the first time: young men and women walking stiffly on metal legs, or pushing their wheelchairs with the stumps of their amputated arms. Some of the patients had steel rods holding their broken pelvis together, or abdominal wounds still dressed in heavy gauze. The spectators stared. They couldn't help it.

My coworkers and I were always outwardly happy. The MATC was our entire world. It was where we ate breakfast, lunch, and sometimes dinner. It was where we met up on the weekends to catch up on paperwork and go on bike rides. And during the week, between 0700 and 1600, it was where we treated a hundred to a hundred fifty new amputees.

We never talked about the staggering injuries we saw. Why? To us, it had faded into the background of day-to-day normalcy. We were cheerful because we were living our lives inside the crowded theater that was the amputee clinic, where we played the role of therapist and the soldier played the role of patient and we entered stage left and exited stage right.

It would be another five years before I heard the phrase "compassion fatigue." While our patients distracted themselves through their long, sleepless nights by playing violent video games, my coworkers and I were in our homes outside the hospital gates, not answering our phones, and keeping those niggling thoughts at bay by watching mindless television, zooming in on anything that caught our funny bone. The dumber the better.

Physical therapy had appealed to me because the hours were good and because it was a career that would spare me the heart-wrenching details of some of the other medical professions, notably death and terminal illness. It was a job that, at the end of the day, I could leave behind at the office. But that's not how it turned out at Walter Reed. Even when I had physically left the clinic, back at home, sitting on the couch in front of my TV, I couldn't keep my thoughts from flickering back to work. No one was dying in our clinic. But everyone was struggling with how to live with devastating and permanent injuries.

Most of the patients in the amputee clinic were young men in their very early twenties. They were usually from somewhere in middle America, and Walter Reed was their very first time in a city. They were mostly soldiers and marines — almost always infantry (ground soldiers). We frequently also saw combat engineers, helicopter pilots, and MPs caught short on a convoy. Once we had a finance officer — a mortar had randomly hit his personal trailer on the FOB (forward operating base). We had some women soldiers. They lost their limbs just like the men. But very rarely did a sailor or airman land in our clinic, unless they were a Navy SEAL or in the EOD (explosive ordinance detail).

The soldiers and marines who ended up in the amputee clinic were almost always enlisted, meaning they did not have the college degree required to be an officer. We also had a scattering of young officers, usually lieutenants right out of college, and every now and then a captain. But it was rare to get a high-ranking officer — a major or a colonel — unless they were really in the wrong place at the wrong time.

We had Coalition soldiers — Russians, Romanians, Georgians, and Armenians. (The "Coalition of the Willing" was a term George W. Bush used to describe countries who supported the 2003 invasion of Iraq.) And a scattering of international AP journalists; they got blown up, too. Unlike the American soldiers, these were older men and women, in their thirties, forties, and fifties. We called them our "foreign exchange" patients.

One of the foreign journalists was so influenced by American culture that Darcy started calling him "Hollywood." The other patients wore boardshorts and T-shirts with humorous amputee sayings on them like, "I Had a Blast in Afghanistan" and "Marine — Some Assembly Required" to their PT appointment, but Hollywood wore designer jeans, tight black V-neck shirts, and sunglasses.

One day Hollywood gave Darcy a nickname back. He called her "Yogurt." Darcy scowled so he told her that in Spain, where he was from, "yogurt" is a high compliment. But Darcy was initially not so sure she should believe him, because she had just taught him the word "booger," since he had one hanging out of his nose.

"Hey! Hey! Bat in the cave!" Darcy had said to him, pointing at her nose.

"Bat in the cave? What is this?"

"You know, booger."

"What is this? Booger? Booger? I do not understand."

When Darcy explained, he laughed. "Bat in the cave!"

Of course we wanted to know what the equivalent term was in Spain. But Hollywood refused to tell us. In Spain, they must have their mind on higher things.

From then on, Darcy looked for good pieces of American slang to teach Hollywood. These almost always involved bodily functions, since there is a lot of that happening in the amputee clinic.

She taught him "puke" for vomit, after one of us ran a plastic basin over to a soldier heaving in the corner.

And "crop dusting" for fart after Cosmo rolled mischievously past a group of young marines sitting on the therapy mats, who shortly afterward started yelling and cursing. "Disgusting! You are disgusting, man! How can you stand yourself?"

I laughed when I saw the commotion Cosmo was creating on the far side of the room. But then I caught sight of a tour group in the window, their faces revealing that they were trying to process all the injuries, and felt briefly self-conscious. I heard Cosmo yell, "Fire in the hole!" and saw Darcy lean over and translate this to Hollywood: "Fart." I laughed again, in spite of myself, before walking away from the window to check on Kai.

Most of our patients were missing their legs. One false step walking on a trail in the Afghan mountains, and an IED planted by the Taliban will take off your legs. But Kai had been riding in the back of an armored vehicle in Iraq when it hit an IED. Kai's left arm was ripped away close to the shoulder, and he couldn't see out of his left eye. His squad leader, a gentle man with an easygoing manner and a love of goofy jokes, took shrapnel to the head. But worst of all, Kai's best friend, who had been sitting beside him, died instantly.

Kai had terrible phantom pain at exactly 1100 every morning, coinciding with the time he was blown up. As 1100 approached, Kai would get edgy. He'd bite his nails and avoid eye contact, all while keeping his eye on the clock. But otherwise, he was quiet and polite.

Kai was from the Philippines. Joining the U.S. Army had put Kai on a fast track to U.S. citizenship. And, after losing an arm, an eye, and his best friend in Iraq, Kai had gone on to become an American citizen. Kai took a cab by himself to the Department of Immigration and, without fanfare or celebration, went through the citizenship ceremony alone.

Most soldiers had a family member with them during their stay at Walter Reed. The military is very smart about this. To ensure that the soldiers have someone there for them one hundred percent of the time, they sign up a family member, spouse, or friend of the soldier to be the paid nonmedical attendant (NMA). The NMA gets a salary and, in addition to providing companionship, is expected to assist the soldier to and from appointments, help with meals, manage medications, and assist with activities of daily living. They are considered an integral part of the care team.

But Kai's family lived on a distant island on the other side of the world, and so the quiet and brooding Kai was at Walter Reed alone. Even though he didn't need long-term physical therapy, I kept him on my schedule after he was discharged from the hospital just to make sure someone kept track of him until his army discharge papers came through.

In the meantime, he was living at the Mologne House, a luxury hotel on Post that, during peacetime, had been used to board generals and colonels staying at Walter Reed for routine medical exams and joint replacement surgeries. Now its rooms were occupied by young soldiers and marines who didn't need to be in the hospital but still needed months or sometimes years of rehab in the Fishbowl.

Kai celebrated his first week out of the hospital by going on a ten-day chocolate binge. Chocolate for breakfast, lunch, dinner, and snacks in between. I discovered it

44

only because Kai became more and more listless during his PT sessions.

"Did you eat breakfast?" I demanded one morning.

"Yes."

"What?"

"Chocolate milk."

"What else?"

"A Hershey bar."

"A Hershey bar? That's not breakfast. What'd you have for dinner last night?"

"Chocolate."

"Lunch?"

"Chocolate."

"What about breakfast yesterday?"

"Chocolate."

Kai defended his choice in food with a shrug. "I never got to eat chocolate in Iraq."

I sent Kai to see his doctor about his poor dietary choices, and she had him admitted to the Psych Ward.

I felt guilty for getting Kai stuck in the Psych Ward, so as an apology, I brought him Hershey bars every day and signed him out for physical therapy. But instead of going to the Fishbowl, we would sneak outside for a walk.

It was springtime, and Walter Reed was especially beautiful at that time of year. Kai and I would leave the building through a

45

side door and cut across the wide, green hospital lawn. The puffy pink cherry trees dotting the campus were at the peak of their bloom, while at their base, tulips with waxy red and yellow heads bowed gracefully in the breeze.

We would walk past the brick Old Red Cross Building, the original headquarters of the Red Cross "Gray Ladies," and Delano Hall, an administrative building with tall marble columns, built after World War I as a dormitory for army nurses. Kai and I would walk through fields of knobby crab apple trees weighed down with hard green apples and head over to Building One, with its sweeping white steps and high-pillared entrance looking as dramatic and beautiful as I imagine it did when it was originally unveiled a hundred years before.

The hundred-year anniversary was on my mind. There were signs all over the hospital promoting the upcoming centennial celebration, which was going to feature local barbecue, performances by the Army Band, and the parachuted arrival of the Army Parachute Team on the front lawn. Even the National Museum of Health and Medicine was in on the celebration, providing antique military outfits for the medical staff to wear on the day of the centennial.

46

There in the rose garden across from Building One, I would examine the thorny buds of new roses as Kai talked. During World War I, the Red Cross Gray Ladies used to host picnics and dances for the injured soldiers in the rose garden. Eleanor Roosevelt and Mrs. Calvin Coolidge had both attended Red Cross events there. But these days, Kai seemed to be the only soldier regularly spending time there.

Sharing a bag of Hershey's chocolate miniatures and surrounded by flowers, Kai would tell me joyfully about his new eighteen-month-old niece or remember funny stories from high school. I had to remind myself that, like most soldiers — and unlike me — Kai was only one year removed from high school.

We talked about movies and he recommended one of his favorites. One night, I popped the movie eagerly into my DVD player when I got home from work, looking forward to something upbeat and humorous — the type of movie I thought Kai would recommend. Even the name had sounded funny to me: *The Boy in the Striped Pajamas,* and I had laughed a little in anticipation. Instead it had turned out to be a movie about a young child dying in a concentration camp.

47

The next day, sitting in the rose garden, I was still slightly burned by the memory of the movie. "That wasn't a funny movie at all," I muttered to Kai, giving him a hard time. And Kai leaned in and laughed, "I *never* told you it was a *funny* movie." And then he added, "The first thing I saw after we hit that IED was my friend's head sitting on the floor of the vehicle. That wasn't funny then either."

"Are you joking?"

"No. His head was still alive. His eyes were looking all around."

I could smell the chocolate on Kai's breath, intermingled with the sweet scent of roses. Looking at Kai's sweet face, with his round cheeks still imbued with the vestiges of childhood chubbiness, my mouth went dry and a wave of horror rose up inside of me. For a few seconds I couldn't say anything. Then I asked, "Do you think he knew what had happened to him?"

"He knew. He seemed confused at first. Then he saw his body sitting in the seat next to me and he got this crazy look on his face. He looked over at me and we just looked at each other for a long time and then he died."

I thought about how gentle Kai was — lover of chocolate and babies and men who made him laugh.

"He was lucky he could look at you before he died, Kai."

Kai got out of the Psych Ward quickly and started eating a normal diet. His nerves and PTSD seemed to be under control, but mine sure were increasing. The casualties overseas were ramping up. My co-workers and I were all feeling the pressure. My rushed lunches of greasy cafeteria slop were not much healthier than pounding a few Hershey bars.

Around this time, we also welcomed the arrival of our first surviving quadruple amputee. In another era, this would have shocked the staff, to see a patient who was missing all four of his limbs. But after seven years of war, we were as enthusiastic as usual, standing up and clapping as he was pushed into the clinic.

I was on the far end of the clinic with Kai. Since getting out of Psych, Kai seemed happy and upbeat. He had a black-and-yellow carbon-fiber prosthetic arm in the colors of his favorite football team — the Steelers. And he had a new handpainted artificial eye, which looked like the real thing. But this morning, the day of the hundred-year anniversary, something seemed to take Kai by surprise. While he stood in the doorway of the clinic, looking

49

apprehensive, I automatically checked the clock: 0955. It wasn't the time.

I walked quickly over to him. "Is it starting? Are you in pain?" Kai shook his head and pointed across the clinic to a new guy walking with a walker. The guy was lurching along in the stilted way badly brain-damaged people tend to do.

"That was my team leader," Kai said.

He hadn't seen him since the explosion, when they, the two survivors, were pulled out of their vehicle and placed on separate stretchers. Kai came here to Walter Reed, and his team leader initially went to a brain rehabilitation facility in Richmond, Virginia. Now he was wobbling past us unsteadily, with a dented head and his physical therapist in tow. He gave no indication of recognizing Kai.

Tears spilled over Kai's bottom right eyelid, and I dragged him over to the other side of the clinic. Just then the door swung open, and the new amputee, the one who had lost all four of his limbs, was pushed into the clinic. My coworkers leapt to their feet with a cheer and began to clap. The new soldier smiled and held what was left of his arm aloft in a greeting.

That's when Kai really started to cry.

Outside the windows of the Fishbowl, attendees were gathering for the celebration. A drum and bugle corps marched by, and the crowd was staring up at the sky, trying to catch the first glimpse of the army's skydiving team. One of the members of the parachute team was a Walter Reed "alum" who had lost one leg at the thigh and the other leg below the knee. While all sorts of pandemonium was taking place in our clinic, he was circling ten thousand feet above us, getting ready to jump out of a plane.

In the hospital lobby, soldiers dressed in World War I uniforms were slicing up an extra-large sheet cake with a picture of the original hospital on it. All over Walter Reed, clinical staff were in costume. Doctors and nurses went about their business as usual while dressed in medical and military uniforms from distant eras, covering every decade Walter Reed had experienced in its hundred years of continuous operation. There were phlebotomists from the '70s, surgeons in tunics and tapered wool lace-up pants over knee-high wool socks from World War I, and nurses in Korean War uniforms. The hospital had the festive and fun feeling of a costume party.

But inside the glassed-in clinic, none of us was in costume. Two staff members lifted our new quadruple amputee out of his wheelchair and placed him on a therapy mat. Kai stopped crying. My coworkers moved quickly from patient to patient while another tour group assembled in front of the windows. On the front lawn of the hospital, a cannon fired and a marching band began to play as the first of the parachutists gently landed.

# SICK CALL

Each morning, work started at 0700. Which meant you were expected to present for duty at 0645. Except for the enlisted, who had to be there at 0615. That's fifteen minutes before 0645 to please the colonel and an extra fifteen minutes to please the staff sergeant, who had gotten there at 0545 to beat the first sergeant in. But since parking is an issue and traffic is always unpredictable, it wasn't unusual for many of my coworkers to arrive at 0430.

I was one of the few outliers. I had my commute timed to the exact minute, so I could rocket into the clinic just seconds before the minute hand hit 0645. My drive in was pure adrenaline, with every cell in my body on high alert anticipating anything that could screw up my arrival time: a badly placed red light, a school bus, a missed turn.

To avoid the inconvenient possibility of a car search by the armed guards at the front gate, I'd leave my car on the street outside of Walter Reed and rush across base with a half-dozen other highly vexed coworkers at 0640. My coworkers and I could see one another out of our peripheral vision, but there was no time to stop and chat, or even wait up for one another. At this time in the morning, it was every man for himself. The lucky ones would scoot in the door with under a minute to spare, ducking past the colonel who was standing in the hallway under the clock, glaring at the minute hand.

Unlike most jobs that start off slowly with a cup of coffee and leisurely checking your email, work at Walter Reed began with a bang.

Mondays and Thursdays were sick call, where at 0645 the physical therapy waiting room was filled with soldiers with run-of-the-mill musculoskeletal injuries. Many of these sports injuries occurred just a few buildings away, at the new Karen J. Wagner Sports Center, where roly-poly military personnel with desk jobs routinely sprained their ankles on the shiny basketball courts or tweaked their hamstrings in the cardio theater spin classes.

The Wagner Sports Center, responsible for many of our sick call visits, was a modern 35,000-square-foot glass-and-brick building located conveniently, a short ten-minute walk away. Lieutenant Colonel Karen Wagner was a medical officer who died at her desk at the Pentagon at 9:37 a.m. on September 11, 2001, when American Airlines Flight 77 slammed into its west side.

The Wagner Sports Center opened in her honor on September 11, 2003. It had two full basketball courts (Lt. Col. Wagner had played college basketball), a cardio theater, an aerobics and weight room, and three racquetball courts. In addition to sports, Lt. Col. Wagner had been a fan of cooking and baking. On her memorial website, her long-standing handyman wrote a moving tribute in broken English about how she had made him a cake and once took him to Red Lobster and bought him two lobsters. Lt. Col. Wagner seemed like someone I could relate to: At least once a week, one of my coworkers would spontaneously show up with a platter of food: cupcakes, bagels, or a Crock-Pot full of homemade meatballs. In the thick-skinned PT department, the way we showed affection was to ply you with food, too.

While the patients checked in with the receptionist, the staff would check in with the colonel and get their number. The numbers were, supposedly, given out in random order. But come late, and don't be surprised if you got slapped with number one for a couple sick calls in a row.

If you had number one, you saw the first sick call patient. Number two saw the second patient on the list, and so on and so forth. If, however, you were lucky and pulled a high number, like eighteen, chances were pretty good that you wouldn't have to see a sick call patient at all. Which meant you could spend the hour in the corral in the back of the room with the rest of your coworkers, watching the lower-number therapists work, and talking about them.

The gossip in the corral of high-number PTs was ruthless, and the unlucky PTs on the floor knew better than to make eye contact with anyone in the waiting pool — lest they bring attention to themselves.

One morning, all eyes were on the new lieutenant, who had been in the limelight lately after being consulted last minute to gait-train an elderly general on the cardiac floor.

The lieutenant thought she had scored an easy patient and had dashed off to the cardiac floor with her "winning" consult. But the problem wasn't that the general had bad balance or weak legs. He couldn't walk because, due to fluid retention from his heart surgery, his scrotum had swollen to the size of a cantaloupe.

To say that the lieutenant was caught off guard is putting it mildly. Still, the general couldn't get discharged until physical therapy had gotten him up and walking. Unsure of how exactly to proceed, the young lieutenant used a towel to make a "scrotal sling" and taught this elderly gentleman how to safely use a walker in his hospital suite while she walked next to him holding the towel. While her patient was eternally grateful for her tact and under-standing, once Nursing let the word out about the testicular sling, the lieutenant was front-page department news. She got a standing ovation at least once a day for the rest of the week.

The lieutenant laughed and shrugged it off. "Hey, you would have done the same thing." Because if there's anything you need to be a physical therapist, it's a sense of humor.

Unless you happened to be the colonel. At staff happy hours and potlucks, the colonel was relaxed and fun to be around. But on duty, she had absolutely no sense of humor. If the colonel heard any of the jokes coming out of the corral in the back of the room, the joker would get a long, silent stare.

In the clinic, the colonel's favorite expression was, "It's good for the corps." As if the world was divided up into what was good for the corps and what was bad for the corps.

The colonel certainly would not hesitate to classify all the joking and teasing that went on in the back of the room as being "bad for the corps." Even though the rest of the corps was tilting their heads back and roaring with laughter.

The colonel had the unenviable task of running a busy wartime physical therapy department. Her stress level was so high that even standing still, she seemed to quiver like a rocket about to launch. But she was our umbrella. Spread out underneath her were the four different physical therapy sections, each managed by either a civilian or military section chief: inpatient, outpatient, traumatic brain injury, and my section, the amputee section. The inpatient section, under the direction of an army major I quietly referred to as "Major Crazy," treated all the hospitalized patients, with the exception of those with amputations. These included complex pelvic fractures, limb salvage injuries, gunshot wounds, and the like. The inpatient clinic was on the fifth floor of the hospital, just down the hall from Ward 54, the Psych Ward, where every now and then an alarm would ring and a pajama'd Psych patient would be seen sprinting down the hallway.

Sharing the fifth-floor clinic with the inpatient team was the traumatic brain injury section, the TBI team, under the reins of a young captain. They handled the complex neurological rehabilitation of the brain-injured soldiers, many of whom had a portion of their skull removed. They were easily identifiable by the soft green helmets they wore to protect their damaged heads.

On the third floor of the hospital, the outpatient section had the difficult task of juggling the continued rehabilitation of complex combat casualties, discharged to them from the inpatient team, and basic run-of-the-mill Karen J. Wagner sports injuries — rotator cuff tears, low back pain, and the like. The outpatient section was under the firm control of a civilian physical therapist, who, when she wasn't sorting through difficult consults and managing a staff of complex characters, *really* liked to live. She quietly traveled all over the world on her yearly vacations.

Off the third floor of the hospital, a special

annex called the Military Advanced Training Center, or MATC, was my section, the amputee section. We had, at one time, also been housed on the third floor of the hospital. But we had gotten too crowded, and in September 2007, four years before Walter Reed closed, the MATC was built and connected to the hospital by an elevated walkway. The amputee section was run by Maj. Tavner, an army-trained physical therapist. Maj. Tavner was young for such a senior rank. But she was smart, soft-spoken, and a hard, hard worker. The amputee section straddled both the inpatient and outpatient rehab world. Because of our specialized amputee rehabilitation protocol, we began treating our patients as new hospital admissions and then continued to follow them, after they were discharged from the hospital, through their entire outpatient course of rehabilitation.

As I watched the colonel eyeball the ruckus in the back of the room one morning, I wondered with some guilt if I was one of those things that was bad for the corps. A civilian. This was my fourth job. I was eight years out of physical therapy school and still hadn't gotten my feet on the ground.

My military counterparts also moved around frequently. But for them, it was a way to enhance their career. Walter Reed was the army's flagship orthopedic hospital. Military physical therapists were sent to Walter Reed to gain experience in treating poly-trauma combat injuries, just as they might later be sent to Brooke Army Medical Center in San Antonio to learn how to treat burn patients.

But I hadn't been sent to Walter Reed for career enhancement. And my real motivation — convenience — didn't apply anymore, either. A bad three-day rainstorm had filled my basement apartment with water like a swimming pool, and I had ended up buying a cheap condominium in a dicey neighborhood seven miles away. I hated being at work so early, especially now that I couldn't just stumble across the street.

I had wanted to go to journalism school, but writing jobs were hard to find, so I had detoured into physical therapy school instead. I thought physical therapy would be an easy job that would let me write on the side. But instead, I was leaving my house at 0600 and I wasn't getting any writing done in the evenings because I was so wiped out from work. Waiting for my number to come up at sick call, I felt my lack of career direction hang all over me like an ugly poncho.

A chorus of laughter interrupted my

thoughts and I glanced across the clinic. In the back of the room, far away from the colonel, two of my coworkers, both captains, were busy entertaining the rest of the staff with their usual comedy routine where, in exaggerated military politeness, they repeatedly referred to each other as "Captain."

This simple skit was a fan favorite, and my coworkers tilted their heads back and roared with pleasure the minute they heard the first exaggerated refrain of:

"Hello, Captain."

"Good morning, Captain."

"Good morning to you, Captain."

"Thank you, Captain."

"My pleasure, Captain."

"Oh, Captain?"

"Yes, Captain?"

"Would you happen to have a pen, Captain?"

"Certainly, Captain."

"Thank you so much, Captain."

"Oh, my pleasure, Captain."

The one person who did not find the captains' comedy routine funny in any way was the colonel. She gave them a stern glance, but then was distracted by the clock. She turned her back to the captains and studied the clock. It was approaching the magic hour of 0745, the end of sick call.

She waited until the precise moment the second hand hit the twelve and then turned and gave us the signal to leave. No one waited for her to change her mind. In a clattering of feet, the forty of us split up and disappeared into our respective clinics: inpatient, outpatient, TBI, and amputee.

Before heading into the MATC to see my morning patients, my first order of business was to detour into the DFAC (dining facility) for breakfast and a morning blessing.

While the ER between medevac flights was a shuffling, yawning time warp, Walter Reed's dining facility was where all the action took place. It had all the energy and excitement you'd expect to find in a busy emergency department. You'd think the cafeteria of a military hospital would be organized with military precision. But the DFAC seemed purposely designed to keep you walking in a spiral: coffee and cream on one counter and sugar completely across the room. The grits were with the oatmeal, but the butter was clear across the cafeteria, stashed in a bowl at the bottom of the soda fridge.

The reason I ate oatmeal every morning was purely for the economy of it — because the brown sugar was nearby in a bowl.

With everyone making multiple trips back and forth across the room, the cafeteria appeared more crowded than it actually was. The only person not walking madly around was the ever-present new employee, who'd stand in the center of the room by the specialty bar, sadly clutching a bowl of scrambled eggs and asking anyone who would stop where they can find some salt. The salt wasn't located logically with the rest of the condiments, but behind the cash register on a table with little packets of relish.

There were usually four or five cashiers working the breakfast crowd, but everyone who'd worked at Walter Reed for a while lined up behind "the Cafeteria Lady." This white-haired African-American woman was easily the most beloved person in the entire hospital. She called everyone "baby" and "sweetie," greeting her regulars like we were long-lost family. It wasn't unusual to see staff members, after they'd paid for their cereal or bagel, lean over and kiss her on the cheek before heading off to work in the OR or cast room.

I always made sure to get in the Cafeteria Lady's line, where I got called "baby." I used to detour into her line because she was fast. But after I'd been at Walter Reed a couple of years, I got into her line, no matter how long it was, to get blessed. "Baby has oatmeal," she'd say automatically before recognizing me as one of her one hundred regulars. "Hey, sweetie! Good to see you! How are you doing today?"

I always asked the Cafeteria Lady how she was doing, too. I just didn't call her baby.

"I am blessed, baby, blessed. Thank you for asking, sweetie. Now you have a blessed day!"

Like everyone who has preceded me, I'd beam. "You too."

"Bless you, baby," she'd answer, and then turn to the next person, "Baby has two eggs."

It was my morning benediction. And, after having received it, I could head into the cramped chaos of the MATC to start my day.

# LEAVING WARD 57

Given how tedious and dull the hospital could be, I always expected hospital inpatients to be happy to see us. But they frequently had the opposite reaction. Patients cringed as soon as the door swung open to reveal, ta da! Physical therapy! Cosmo was no exception. Even though I consistently came to his room on Ward 57 at the same time every morning, and wouldn't expect to find him anywhere else, he always announced in a tone of pure indignation, "I am in the fucking bed!"

Hospital rooms are small and crowded with families, baskets of candy, celebrity visitors, and stuffed animals. Once a soldier's pain is under control, it's a lot simpler to take him down to the MATC. There, on the firmer therapy mats, it's easier to learn how to sit, roll, and scoot out of bed into a wheelchair than on the soft, slippery hospital mattresses. And there is more space to do

66

fun things like hopping and spinning on crutches, if you have an intact leg, or pop wheelies in your wheelchair if you don't.

Plus there's the camaraderie. Instead of listening to your family talking in soft whispers about your amputations, you could witness Cosmo teasing another soldier by rudely calling him "Ugly Stump" right to his face.

In the MATC, amputations were frequently commented on, displayed, and made fun of. The owner of the ugly stump that day ruefully rubbed his amputated thigh with a self-conscious grin at Cosmo's comment while the soldiers around him guffawed. His amputation was covered with discolored skin grafts pieced together to cover the end of his femur like a badly sewn patchwork quilt.

"Don't listen to him," I interjected while glaring at Cosmo.

"It's okay. I know it's ugly," he announced with tentative pride.

"That's right," Cosmo crowed as the marines and soldiers around him laughed in anticipation. "That's the ugliest stump in here. It looks like my grandma's bag."

Getting the patients out of their quiet hospital room and down to this crass sandbox is physical therapy goal number one.

The camaraderie, no matter how pointed, makes everyone feel better. It was the barrack mentality they'd have if they were back with their platoons in Iraq or Afghanistan.

The therapy tables in the MATC were big enough for two people, so the patients shared them, two per mat. In a civilian hospital this might be uncomfortable, but in an army hospital it was a good kind of familiar. Except instead of sharing a MRAP or Stryker vehicle, they were sharing a therapy mat. New patients arrived daily, usually in a disheveled state of bewilderment, transported to the MATC by their physical therapist and occupational therapist in a reclined cardiac chair, a rollable hospital chair that could be elevated and flattened out like a stretcher, with their wound VACs hanging off the armrests, feeding tube dangling out of their nose, and their IV pole pulled haphazardly behind them. We brought them down as soon as they could verbalize agreement — and transported all their hospital equipment with us. They needed to be with their battle buddies and they needed to see the MATC.

The therapy mats were in the center of the room, and were almost always filled with their peers — patients who were also still hospitalized. Hospital inpatients were easily identified by what Darcy referred to (in an exaggerated French accent) as their "accoutrement": wound VACs, IV poles, catheter bags. Balancing in a seated position, new inpatients practiced batting light balls to their therapists, or sliding over into their wheelchairs while their overprotective therapist hovered nervously, ready to catch them if they toppled over. But as they recovered from the initial shock of their injuries, they quickly progressed to sitting on wobble boards while this same, previously overprotective therapist pitched twenty-pound medicine balls at their heads.

And as soon as they could tolerate it, they did numerous body weight exercises, pushing their stumps into a padded bolster to lift themselves repeatedly off the bed, frequently with a weighted sandbag draped across their trunk for added resistance. They did good old familiar push-ups, except this time they balanced precariously on their new amputations — or to make it harder, just one stump on top of a padded bolster. They did stump lifts in all four directions while we provided manual resistance and loud cries of: "Again! Ten more! Lift me up!"

Beside the mat tables were two parallel bars — the next stop on their road to recovery. On the parallel bars, soldiers tried out their prosthetic legs for the first time. They did balance drills, balancing on their stiltlike metal legs — progressing from the level ground to wobble boards once again. They walked forward, backward, sideways. They walked against the resistance of elastic therapy bands tied around their waist and then their legs. They stepped over plastic cones and caught heavy leather medicine balls. They practiced stepping up and down on sturdy curb-sized boxes. And then they quickly graduated outward, to the track.

Around the periphery of the PT gym was the rubberized track. There, outpatients practiced agility drills, weaving through a floor ladder or zigzagging on shiny metal legs around cones. Some of them were suspended from a harness to a zip-line in the ceiling to catch them, should they fall. Meanwhile, running endless laps around the periphery of the room on carbon-fiber blade legs were "older" patients with earphones crammed into their ears. They dodged new walkers who were also on the track taking their first off-balanced steps outside the parallel bars as their physical therapist tottered beside them ready to yank them back upright by a belt wrapped around their waist should they stumble.

On the edges of the room were treadmills, elliptical machines, spin bikes, weight benches, jump ropes, kettlebells. Everything was in use. Soldiers pedaled the pedals right off the spin bikes. The elliptical machine developed a terrible screech. Walls were covered with errant dents from overly enthusiastic kettlebell swinging. And the jump ropes were always going missing. Because we weren't training soldiers how to walk again — they didn't want to walk, they wanted to *run.*

Walking from patient to patient to patient, and identifiable by our pastel-colored shirts, were the therapists, walking endless spiraling loops through the room. We never stopped walking. We saw two to three patients at a time all day long. Out of curiosity, I wore a pedometer at work for a week. I averaged just over five miles a day. No wonder at the end of the day, I just flopped down on the couch in front of the TV. While my friends downtown were typing on their computers at their quiet office jobs, my coworkers and I were racing around, climbing over mat tables, lifting soldiers out of wheelchairs, stretching patients out, carrying heavy wound VACs, and catching marines before they hit the floor.

New patients usually spent their first day in the MATC sitting on a mat in the center of the room, just watching the revolving display in front of them. Here, without even having to explain to them how their rehab would progress, or what was possible, they could see it for themselves. They could fast forward to the finish line. Which was why it was so important to get a patient down to the MATC as soon as possible. We needed to light that fire.

A patient's desire to get out of bed and come down to the MATC had very little to do with injury level. We could have a patient who was missing four limbs and very eager to get as strong and as mobile as possible, while in the room next door to him there could be a soldier with a single, below-knee amputation, who was adamant that he shouldn't be getting out of bed so early.

Some patients were so broken physically, and sometimes emotionally, that they needed five people to lift them out of bed into a cardiac chair. We'd pull on yellow gowns and blue gloves. We would be full of optimism, but the patient was always scared to death. He'd cross his arms across his chest, squeeze his eyes shut, and count aloud to three, and on three, we'd lift quickly and carefully — just like we promised — into the safety of the reclined cardiac chair.

Other patients were just reluctant. Their injuries might be relatively minor, or incredibly severe. Whatever their reason, they'd dig their heels in and refuse to come down to the MATC. After several refusals, we would send Elijah in to "talk" to them.

Elijah was deeply religious, gentle, and kind. If you had any kind of problem, Elijah was the one everyone on staff sought out. You didn't even have to find Elijah. He'd find you and, with a hand on your shoulder, guide you off to a quiet corner. "Can we talk?" he'd say.

Elijah listened thoughtfully and didn't judge. "Don't change a single thing about yourself," he'd say, and you'd instantly feel better. "You are perfect, just the way you are."

But when we sent Elijah in to see a patient, we weren't exactly sending him in to talk. Elijah was a former professional football player. He might have been the kindest man in the hospital, but he was also the biggest man in the hospital. He was exactly the same size as a hospital door. When Elijah stood in the doorway, the room darkened.

From the door frame, Elijah's voice was a low, dark rumble.

"Son, I am from physical therapy."

Elijah would then pause, like a preacher. The silence would have a dramatic effect on his congregation of one, who would quickly gather the bedsheets protectively around himself.

But Elijah was only choosing his words carefully.

"I am here. I am *here,* to ask *you,* Son, to *ask you* to *please* let me *help you* out of this bed. Son, it is the *only* thing I am asking you. I am *here* to help *you.*"

For a patient who didn't require assistance out of bed, but was stubbornly refusing treatment, just seeing Elijah wedged in the doorframe was all it took.

"I'm getting up!" he'd say, pulling his hospital gown around his legs and scooting over into the wheelchair.

"I am getting up!" he'd snap again, in a sudden rage at the humiliation of it all.

Other patients would just relax at the sheer size of Elijah.

"Okay," they'd whisper, hidden deep in the pillows.

For difficult cases, Elijah would wave the rest of the team in after his sermon, and five of us would help lift the patient out of bed and onto the reclined cardiac chair. But as far as the patient was concerned, Elijah was doing the lifting all by himself.

Elijah was modest and didn't understand the power of persuasion he had.

"He wasn't difficult at all," he'd confide to you later. "Are you sure this is the one everyone had a problem with?"

Some patients didn't require cajoling or assistance or Elijah to get out of bed. One patient got up and used his wound care supplies to tape his hospital door shut. Another patient moved into a hotel downtown and had to be physically brought back to the hospital by military police.

While the nurses were not pleased, for Elijah there was only one time a patient "went bad." Private, churchgoing Elijah happened to walk in on a patient passionately reuniting with his girlfriend while snuggled deep in the confines of his hospital bed.

Elijah stood next to the bed slightly surprised, but announcing anyway, "I am from physical therapy."

On getting no response, Elijah boomed out, *"I am in here!"*

*"It is time for physical therapy!"* Elijah shouted before running out of the room and returning with two male nurses who, under Elijah's command, separated the pair. *"We are going to physical therapy!"*

The soldier was tossed into a wheelchair and whisked down the hall to the physical therapy clinic.

I happened to be walking down the hallway when a tidal wave of physical therapists poured out of the inpatient physical therapy clinic. They collapsed in the hallway in various forms of exaggerated agony, clutching their sides and pirouetting around on tiptoe, trying to contain their laughter.

I was shocked when I heard what Elijah had done. He and I shared the same birthday. Every year I'd surprise him with a birthday card. I admired him on so many levels, and since we shared the same zodiac sign, I liked to think that in some ways we might be similar.

But we couldn't be more different. While Elijah is confident, I am uncertain. Elijah is a thinker, while I can't make a decision until I am totally backed into a corner. And in spite of being barely half his size, I am an impatient hothead.

I peeked inside the clinic, where I could see Elijah matter-of-factly handing his honeymooning patient a pair of dumbbells as though nothing out of the ordinary had just happened.

I had to admit, this was certainly not something I would have done. If I had walked in on a patient having sex, I would have immediately shut the door and quickly walked away. I would have been embarrassed and wouldn't have gone back. But then, I am not Elijah.

In spite of the intermittent chaos Cosmo created down in the physical therapy gym, when I'd come up to his hospital room to get him, Cosmo would generally do what I asked him to do. He had started coming down to the MATC almost immediately after his transfer to Ward 57. Pain didn't stop Cosmo. Nothing fazed Cosmo. He would scoot up in the bed, "Fuck!" and carefully roll left, "Fuck!" and right, "Fuck!" without twisting so I could snap his back brace on. Grimacing in pain, he'd help me lift his fractured leg up, "Oh, fuck!" so I could untangle his wound VAC, "For fuck's sake!" and IV lines, "Jesus Fucking Christ!" Once he was fully untangled, I'd hold his leg by the ex-fix, and he would slide carefully across the bed and into a wheelchair, "thank-fucking-God!" while I carried his broken leg across.

While Cosmo almost placidly let me put the back brace on — he wasn't allowed to sit up or get out of bed without his back brace — the second I turned my back, he'd be out of the clinic and in the smoking shelter having a cigarette. The brace would be off again and hanging on the back of his wheelchair. If it wasn't hanging off his chair, you could bet it was in his lap.

What really took the cake were the days Cosmo would wheel himself down to the PT clinic while his mother walked behind him *carrying* his back brace. She would glance over at me with hooded eyes, and sensing danger, I'd turn bright red. I was definitely no Elijah!

Cosmo's mom, with her beaklike nose and stiff hive of hair, reminded me of a hornet. Her angry personality was only magnified by her fondness for wearing tight, brightly colored pants and shirts that made her look like a poisonous fish. The only time she ever talked to me was to complain about other staff members. Our conversations were frequently peppered with the veiled threat, "I talked to my congressman yesterday." I tried not to set her off. Luckily, she usually ignored me, except to make small, jablike remarks.

Every day she called me a different name, and it never was Adele.

"Pain and Torture just showed up."

"Oh, look, it's Attila the Hun."

"Genghis Khan is here."

"It's Bloody Mary."

At first I laughed off her comments. But as the name calling continued, day after day, I stopped finding it funny. That was how she really viewed me. Even though she never answered me, I continued to politely say in response "Hello" and "Good morning!" and "How was your weekend?" But on the inside I seethed. I was a professional, not some thug who just happened to wander in off the street.

Cosmo's mom never stuck around for his therapy. As soon as I arrived, she left. Usually to go to the post office, where she picked up package after package of gifts that were mailed to her for Cosmo from her hometown. One day I asked her what they were getting in the mail, and she showed me a box full of sweatbands. She said she had requested these specifically for the "boys in the MATC." But then she never distributed them.

After a couple of weeks, thanks to his smoking habit, Cosmo didn't need physical therapy to get him out of bed anymore. With some assistance from the nurses or his mother, he'd scramble impatiently into his wheelchair and push himself outside to smoke. He had lost all of his lines and tubes.

The only piece of medical equipment still getting in his way was the back brace. He was now supposedly bringing himself to physical therapy. Except he never came on time.

As the end of the day approached, my phone calls to Ward 57 became more and more frequent. "Is he on his way?" I'd ask. "He just left," they'd always say. Except he was never on his way to PT. He'd go get a haircut at the third-floor barbershop, a new pack of smokes at the hospital PX, a Coke at the DFAC, or take a trip to the courtyard to sit outside in the sun.

Like the colonel, I am obsessed with time. Which might be why, in spite of everything, Walter Reed was such a good fit for me. My time thing began the minute I woke up in the morning: 0500. I monitored what time the morning paper arrived, I waited for it to hit the sidewalk outside my window while I lay in bed anticipating my alarm going off.

I once bought a digital watch with four alarms. The four alarms rang throughout the morning, alerting me as to what time to wake up, when to take the dog on a walk, when to get in the shower, and what time exactly to head out the door to work.

My time thing is completely due to my father, who used to wake me up when I was a teenager at 0600 every morning, even in the summers. If I didn't get immediately out of bed and he had to knock on my door a second time, I'd be instantly grounded. Similarly, if I was even one minute late for my curfew, I was grounded. My dad would be waiting for me in the kitchen, standing directly underneath the clock.

Growing up in my parents' house, I had all sorts of rules, usually made up on the spot by my father. Break a rule and you heard his high-decibel voice telling you that you were *grounded*.

"Grounded" could mean a number of things. It could mean mandatory labor, like leaf raking. It could mean a loss of car privileges, or a monetary fine of ten dollars — due immediately to my father. It could mean a loss of phone privileges or a loss of rights out of the house.

Other families used their refrigerator to post family pictures or postcards. Our refrigerator was used exclusively by my father, the warden, to post rules.

Reading our refrigerator was similar to reading a police blotter. It was a good way to find out about crimes committed by other family members. Like, for example, my younger sister, Nicki.

"NICKI. BEFORE LEAVING THE HOUSE YOU
MUST LEAVE A NOTE STATING:

1. SPECIFICALLY <u>WHERE</u> YOU ARE GO-
   ING — "TO PLAY B-BALL" IS NOT
   ACCEPTABLE.
2. WHAT <u>TIME</u> YOU WILL BE HOME.
3. IF MOM OR I ARE NOT HOME TO
   GIVE YOU PERMISION YOU <u>MUST</u> BE
   HOME BY 5:00 PM.
4. FAILURE TO FOLLOW THE ABOVE
   RULES WILL RESULT IN A 1-DAY
   <u>GROUNDING</u> (AT LEAST)."

Under no circumstance were you allowed to
remove a note.

"NOTES MUST BE LEFT POSTED — OR YOU
WILL BE GROUNDED."

Crimes were noted, and sentence dates
spelled out for all to see.

"ADELE HAS LOST PHONE PRIVILIGES FOR
ONE WEEK. TO END AT 9:00 PM ON 13
NOVEMBER."

Thanks to my father, I am still on high alert
for any kind of infractions I might uncon-
sciously incur— most notably, being late.

So I am constantly striving for speed. I have my morning routine perfected for optimum efficiency, from the way I towel off after a rushed shower, to the way I feed the dog while simultaneously making coffee. I know where all the speed cameras are on my way to work, slowing my tiny, nimble, gas-efficient car down for one precise second to avoid a ticket and then zipping back up to my normal frenetic pace. On a bicycle I am so reckless I've been hit four times, usually while trying to speed through an intersection. In the crowded DFAC, I am a star, having the menu memorized before I walk in and knowing which cashiers on duty are the fastest.

My time thing is well known by my patients, as I am constantly monitoring their arrival time and announcing whether they are early (good) or late (bad). But Cosmo never came on time. This is by far the biggest button you can push with me, and he was constantly pushing it.

One afternoon I watched Cosmo and his mom come down the hallway toward the clinic (late — bad!) and then, incredulously, detour outside to the smoking shelter off the hospital veranda. This was something I certainly would never have done — especially if I had been accompanied by my father.

I waited impatiently in the clinic for them to come back from the smoking shelter. Meanwhile, the clock was ticking closer and closer to 1600, closing time. Finally, I gave up and walked outside.

The smoking shelter wasn't exactly off limits to staff, but it had that feel. It was almost always filled with patients. Judging by the constant low-grade commotion coming from inside, commotion that died down the second a staff member walked by, it was obvious that the number one topic of conversation in there was the staff.

As usual, the smoking shelter became instantly quiet the second I approached. I thought, if I were Elijah, I wouldn't be intimidated. I would just walk on in. But I wasn't Elijah. I hesitated briefly outside the smoking shelter, trying to decide if I really should go in there after Cosmo. There were a few other patients besides Cosmo, staring at me sullenly when I broke code and walked in. Through the haze of smoke I could see Cosmo lighting up another cigarette. His back brace was off and hanging from the back of his wheelchair. His mom was gone, probably heading over to the post office to pick up another package of sweat-bands.

I wasn't going to overlook Cosmo breaking his spinal precautions while skipping out on physical therapy and smoking a cigarette to boot.

"You have to wear this!" I chirped before breaking out into an unfortunate coughing fit.

Cosmo shrugged, and my voice went up a few octaves as I squeaked out a meek threat. "Do you want to have emergency spinal surgery?"

Cosmo watched me with a cool smirk on his face before taking a drag on his cigarette and announcing, "My back feels fuckin' fine."

I took a step back. Cosmo seemed to be an expert at pushing people's buttons. I couldn't imagine how he'd handled the army, since he clearly was used to dodging and ducking all rules. Except he hadn't been in the army very long — less than a year, culminating in a terrible injury.

The only good thing about Cosmo's situation was that, even though he harbored some obvious disdain for authority, the army would fold him under its wing. It would call him brother and hero and take care of him for the rest of his life. Cosmo

85

didn't know it at the time, but the army would keep him outfitted in top-of-the-line prosthetics and make sure he had the best wheelchair; it would pay to have his car and home modified to accommodate his disabilities, and he would get enough money in medical retirement pay that he would probably never have to work again.

Cosmo didn't know any of that when he joined the army.

"Did you ever think you might get hurt when you joined?" I asked Cosmo, abruptly changing the topic.

"Shit, I wasn't scared."

"What made you decide to sign up?"

"I was watching TV and just decided to go down to the recruiter's office."

Cosmo didn't seem to have any regrets. He shrugged this decision off like he blew everything else off. It had seemed like a good idea at the time.

# WE ARE ON A CRUISE

Each Tuesday morning, there was a 0700 staff meeting of the entire physical therapy staff. All four of the hospital's PT clinics: inpatient, outpatient, amputee, and traumatic brain injury — about forty physical therapists — assembled for a big, sleepy powwow. The agenda was always the same. You could go to a morning meeting in August and it would be identical to one in December. The only thing that changed were the birthday, deployment, and wedding announcements.

The colonel always started with the most dreaded part of the meeting: the reading of the patient comment cards. These were employee kudos supposedly written by patients and dropped in the box next to the front desk receptionist. Week after week, the same person was featured — the front desk receptionist, who, after dozens of comment card kudos, left for a better-paying administration job in the government.

The colonel would read the first comment card aloud in a stern tone, "Darcy is a great PT," and then pause and wait for a scattering of applause, before flipping over the next card. "The front desk receptionist helped me schedule my appointments." More soft claps. The colonel would glare around the room at therapists who had already started to nod off, and then pick up the next card. *If only disgruntled comment cards were read aloud,* I frequently wished to myself. That would really liven the meeting up. Instead, I'd sit in my usual place and clap appropriately whenever yet another person received a 5 out of 5 for customer service.

After the reading of the comment cards, each clinic section chief was given a chance to speak, and then the staff sergeant and the department NCOIC (noncommissioned officer in charge). The infection control officer, a young captain who had been assigned this dull job, would speak about the latest hand-washing survey. And then the fire and safety officer would weigh in. It was a long, slow roll call.

Then came the safety briefings, during which the army liked to spend time beating us over the head with advice on common-sense issues. They almost always had a holiday theme. Thanksgiving's safety briefing, for example, usually involved what not to do when deep-frying a turkey. According to the fire and safety officer, you should never deep-fry a turkey in your living room, under a low-hanging roof, or in a garage without ventilation.

In the summers, safety briefings would focus on the use of sunscreen and the avoidance of tick bites. During the New Year's drinking-and-driving briefing, the staff got key chain Breathalyzers.

After the safety briefing was read aloud, the NCOIC would circulate a piece of paper for everyone to sign. The room would briefly erupt into small tornados of chaos as everyone tried to sign off quickly so the meeting could conclude. Getting through the safety briefing was of utmost importance, because safety briefings were ripe for Major Crazy to start his usual safety skirmish.

Maj. Crazy was the only one who ever really listened to the safety briefing. Knowing the immediate exit to retreat to during a fire alarm was not enough for Maj. Crazy. He'd interrupt and want to know what we should do if an entire wing of the hospital was on fire. Or if a 250-passenger airplane had just taken out half the building. Maj. Crazy's questioning was frequently prefaced by his favorite phrase, "As a combat veteran . . ."

While Maj. Crazy was busy reminding everyone that we were in a war zone, in the back of the room a few therapists would bounce up and down on physioballs and impatiently check their watches. Once, I spied one of the new lieutenants surreptitiously doing curls with small barbells, keeping the barbells close to her side where she thought no one could see.

I watched, totally entertained, as after a few minutes of barbell curls the lieutenant started slowly bending and straightening each knee rhythmically under the table. After thirty repetitions, she moved on to small, practically imperceptible crunches while balancing on a rolling stool. She leaned back slightly, held it, and then curled back up.

Beside me, completely unaware or uninterested in the lieutenant's gymnastics or Maj. Crazy's morning safety skirmish, was usually my friend Jasmine, who would spend the time updating the calendar on her smartphone.

Most people sat by section. All the amputee therapists sat together by the supply closet. The outpatient therapists took over the back of the room. The TBI therapists sat around a large mat table. I was the only one who'd break rank and sit with the inpatient team on the far end of the room beside the treadmills.

I'd sit with the inpatient PTs because Jasmine worked in inpatient and I had known her for twelve years. We were classmates in PT school, and then later, colleagues. Since Jasmine had come back into my daily existence, I'd spent every Tuesday morning sitting beside her as she updated her calendar and I ate my watery cafeteria oatmeal.

I read once that you are most likely to establish long-term friendships with people who live in close proximity to you. While Jasmine and I had very little in common, we became friends because we had adjoining cadavers in our physical therapy school's anatomy lab. Except to say hello and goodbye, Jasmine and I didn't talk to each other during the morning meeting, but I count Jasmine as one of my oldest and most beloved friends.

In her high heels, manicured nails, and salon-styled hair, Jasmine stood out in the cadaver lab. She referred frequently to a black leather planner, where the dates of our exams and assignments were carefully written in tight, neat cursive swirls and highlighted in yellow marker. This was before smartphones and military staff meetings.

Compared to Jasmine, I was a total disaster. I wore the same green sweatshirt to school every day for an entire year, had hair that resembled a lion's mane, and wrote exam dates on small scraps of paper.

I used to tease Jasmine about her obsession with her planner, until the day I missed our biomechanics midterm. While the rest of my classmates were in the lecture hall sharpening their pencils, I was around the corner in the cadaver lab, wondering where everyone was. Not one of my sixty-seven other classmates was in there. Later, on my way to the vending machine, I happened to pass the lecture hall, where I was stunned to see my classmates writing furiously.

Two people noticed me sneak into the room and sheepishly pick up an exam: the professor and Jasmine. Jasmine gave me a withering glance that instantly rooted me to the floor. And the next day she had a special gift for me — a black leather date book. When I opened it up, all of our exams and assignments were labeled and underlined in Jasmine's exquisite Victorian handwriting.

Once a week, Jasmine would do a surprise inspection of my date book. I was required to have it on my person at all times, and on request, I'd immediately turn it over to her. She'd frown slightly while flipping through before she'd update the assignments and exam dates herself. She would review the bulleted reminders with me before quizzing me on important upcoming events.

Jasmine was all business. The entire encounter took about five minutes, and then, like a passport control officer, she would snap the little book shut and hand it back to me.

And then we were together again. During the Tuesday meetings, I struggled to look like I was paying attention, while beside me, Jasmine would, as always, be perfectly composed as she updated her calendar. In the front of the room, the fire and safety officer would drone on, probably reminding everyone where the fire extinguisher was. I'd feel a shift in the people around me, everyone suddenly becoming alert. The morning meeting was concluding.

I'd say goodbye to Jasmine and rush to the MATC. I was glad that Jasmine was still in the trenches with me. The wards were getting more and more full but our staff didn't increase. Instead, everyone, the colonel, the therapists in all the different sections — inpatient, outpatient, amputee, TBI — just rolled up their sleeves and poured on the elbow grease. Comment cards or not, we were going through an intense experience that no one outside of Walter Reed could even begin to understand.

The ten of us in the Fishbowl did our paperwork while squeezed into a small workspace four feet deep on the far end of the clinic. We shared two desks, six computers, and one printer. There was one phone. Above the desks were four shelves, which had been divvied up among the ten of us. Each of us was allotted a precious twelve inches of space for our personal items, personal items that were frequently pulled down on the agitated head of the person sitting at the computer underneath the shelf. Standing on tiptoe, your behind would be an inch away from that person's eyeball, breaking all kinds of polite societal personal space laws.

The tight quarters by the workstations gave our clinic an *Apollo 13* flight capsule feel. Except instead of three astronauts strapped into seats and hurtling through the Earth's atmosphere, there were ten of us vibrating around one another like Mexican jumping beans.

The administration deliberately did not

give us enough computers, because they wanted the therapists out on the floor of the clinic, to give the tour groups something to look at. But at the end of the day, every computer was taken and the therapists who didn't get a computer, instead of being out on display on the floor of the clinic, lurked behind your shoulder trying to intimidate you into typing your notes faster. Your bladder might be about to burst, but give up your computer and there was no way you were leaving work by 1700 — even though our shift officially ended at 1600.

At 1610, the therapists who managed to get on a computer first (and who probably worked through lunch) victoriously gathered their things together and left. They lingered by the door, waiting to see if any of the rest of us were in any way ready to leave. Their smug looks would prompt my coworker Jim to suggest that they "Take the rest of the day off!" Which is also what he said when I grumbled about leaving at 1630.

Jim is a tall man who would be best described in a medical chart as being "well nourished." Even when he is obviously making fun of you, Jim is always polite. He combines good manners with spotless grooming. Pleasant and cleanly shaven with a haircut that was never too long or too short, Jim wore polo shirts in cheerful colors — orange, blue, yellow, coral. His shoes were neatly tied and matched his belt. And it went without saying that Jim never took the rest of the day off — because he seemed to almost always be in the clinic until 1700.

Answering the phone was like picking up a live grenade, leaving you praying under your breath that you wouldn't be required to take a message. Taking a message would send off a desperate scramble to find a pen, a piece of paper (maybe), and a place to leave this message for the person to find. There were little sticky notes everywhere, from weeks earlier, still patiently waiting for their intended recipient to find them, read them, and discard them. And it was with frequent dismay that you yourself would discover an important message left for you on a sticky note that had fallen to the floor days earlier.

Having such chaos for a shared workspace did not help people like me who are already disorganized to begin with. Every few weeks, one of my coworkers would have a breakdown and go on a cleaning rampage. Sgt. Hernandez was the most ruthless of the bunch, sweeping everything off the shared desk into a trash bag.

I longed for a desk of my own. A place to

keep a notepad and pen. A place I could plan my day out. A way I could finally become organized.

Because of the cramped conditions, my coworkers and I became huge germophobes. It wasn't unusual to get off a computer to see another coworker spray the keyboard down with disinfectant, as if you were some sort of louse-encrusted pig. There were pump bottles of hand sanitizer sitting on every available surface, and my military coworkers carried their own bottle of military-issued hand cleaner in a camouflaged bottle. If you couldn't fit hand cleaner in your pocket, the small packets of alcohol pads were a quick substitute and handy for many sorts of social hazards, like elevator buttons.

We compulsively washed our hands in between every patient, after we answered the phone, touched a questionable surface, and many times for no reason at all. Touching your face at work was our definition of risky behavior and would start off a spree of hand washing that could last several minutes. We were obsessed with people who touched their nose, and were on high alert for these social deviants and never, ever got behind them in line at the cafeteria salad bar.

In spite of all our hand washing, our clinic was a ship of contagion as the staff members caught illness after illness from the dozens of patients and visitors and small children passing through our clinic on an hourly basis.

You might get over a bad head cold one week just to get laid low with a fast-moving stomach flu. I'd leave a few Rolaids on a coworker's clipboard, only to eat them myself an hour later.

The countertop in the staff area was covered in a variety of cold, flu, and antidiarrhea medications, and it was not unusual for a bottle of DayQuil to be passed around with small Dixie cups during the morning meeting like a bottle of Jim Beam. The staff members, the ones who were huddled up in fleece jackets and sniffling like they were about to explode, would pour themselves a quick and thankful shot.

One year, our clinic was struck with the norovirus, a virus that causes prolonged gastrointestinal discomfort, and is commonly found on cruise ships because it spreads quickly in self-contained environments. The only one who didn't catch it was Jim. Whenever another staff member called out sick with GI symptoms, Jim would smile and cheerfully quip, "We are on a cruise!"

All clinical staff at Walter Reed were required to get the flu shot and the H1N1 shot, and for a couple weeks out of the year, Walter Reed turned the large classrooms on the second floor of the hospital into a makeshift health clinic so dozens of people could get vaccinated simultaneously.

The military was very efficient, and after they scanned your ID, checked off your name, and jammed a needle into your deltoid, you were sent to a holding pen in the back of the room to make sure you didn't go into anaphylactic shock. This holding pen was monitored by a mean staff sergeant standing underneath a big clock. Every ten minutes, she selected a few people out of the group to be dismissed. In the meantime, she paced up and down our line of chairs. She carried a bag of lollipops and randomly gave out a lollipop to a person here and a person there, but not to everyone.

The psychology of this I did not understand, but I knew that for those of us sitting in the pen without a lollipop, we were *dying* for a lollipop. I hated myself for it, and I hated the staff sergeant, but at the same time, I couldn't stop the soundtrack that was coursing through my head: "Pick me! Pick me!"

In addition to the flu shot, Walter Reed

monitored the viral load of its employees through routine blood tests to make sure you were current on tetanus, hepatitis, whooping cough, measles, and mumps vaccines. Which was how, in spite of being up to date on all my vaccinations, I found out I was deficient in antibodies against the measles and the mumps.

I was initially notified by email, which I ignored because I thought it was some sort of fluke. Then I received a phone call to report to employee health, immediately. I meant to go, but never got around to it.

A few hours later two burly men in white coats showed up in the clinic and escorted me quickly to employee health. They tried to engage me in small talk as we walked through the long hospital corridors, but I was too freaked out to say anything.

The medic in employee health was waiting for me. He had three vaccines already prepared — in case I put up a fight. Flanked by my two escorts, I wasn't going to fight anyone, and I was quickly and efficiently vaccinated against the measles, mumps, tetanus, and the flu.

My father had been an infectious disease officer in the Public Health Service, and my family had been sent to Bangladesh for three years during the height of the smallpox epidemic. While my dad worked in a field hospital, my mother volunteered on the smallpox eradication team, and they would go from village to village vaccinating people. Not everyone understood what they were trying to do and some would try to escape, which meant inevitably the vaccination team would have to corner them and forcibly vaccinate them.

*Sort of like what is happening to me right now,* I thought as the medic roughly plunged the first needle into my arm.

Now, several years later, I've been vaccinated against the measles and the mumps five times and I never produce antibodies. I fall into a rare category of people who, in spite of having had the vaccine, will never be immune to those diseases. This is a little piece of knowledge I would not know about myself if I hadn't worked for Walter Reed. I should be grateful, but mostly I am regretful. On a day-to-day level it only adds to my paranoia, and when a mumps outbreak occurred in the Northeast, I read about it online with barely contained hysteria.

"It's on its way!"

My coworkers tried to shush me and one got up and started washing her hands. They could do without the melodrama.

■ ■ ■ ■

I should have anticipated that Walter Reed existed in its own orbit when I received a 0600 phone call to come in for a job interview.

When the phone rang in my dark apartment, I sprang out of bed so suddenly I almost blacked out.

*Someone must have died,* I thought as I sprinted down the hallway in bare feet and picked up the phone with a pounding heart.

Instead, a voice that was all business surprised me.

"Is this Adele Levine?"

"Yes," I said, bracing myself for the worst.

"This is Colonel ＿＿＿＿＿at Walter Reed Army Medical Center."

The colonel rattled off her name in a manner that suggested she was used to people snapping to attention. Those people obviously weren't civilians at six in the morning.

"What?" I half shouted.

"This is Colonel —"

"I know that," I interrupted. "What time is it?"

"Six."

"You're calling me at six in·the morning?

102

I thought someone *died.*"

"I'm calling because you applied for a job here," the colonel said.

Up until that morning, I was very interested in working at Walter Reed, but standing in the dark hallway in rumpled pajamas and bare feet, I wasn't so sure.

"Are you interested or not?" the colonel snapped.

"I don't know," I replied testily. "Why are you calling me so early?"

"Because I wanted to make sure I'd reach you."

"Well, you got me."

"Are you coming in for an interview?"

"When?"

"How about today?"

"Of course it would be today," I said sarcastically. But if the colonel heard it, she forgave me, and I felt instantly bad. "Okay," I said quietly. "Okay, I'll be there."

My coworkers laugh every time they hear this story, because the colonel's brisk attitude frequently rubs people the wrong way. But I like her bluntness, and I like the colonel. You always know what she is thinking. She's brief, to the point, and all business. And she's loyal. When one of the captains got sick and had to be hospitalized, there were two chairs in her hospital room — one for her mother and one for the colonel.

And to the colonel I will always be grateful because she gave me a job that ended up changing my life.

I graduated from a local PT school, thirty miles away from Walter Reed, in May 2001. Four months later, September 11 happened and our world changed forever. But no one knew it at the time. We were finishing the last of our classes and looking forward to graduation.

A couple weeks before graduation, the financial aid counselor came into the lecture hall to give us our final student loan packages. Before she passed them out, she asked my classmates how many of us had a five-year plan. I had no idea what she meant by this, but a handful of my classmates raised their hands. And five years out of PT school, all those people who had raised their hands were on their way to becoming very successful. They owned their own businesses, they were well respected. Then the counselor asked us to raise our hands if we had a three-year plan and, finally, how many of us had jobs lined up for after graduation. I am pretty sure I was the only person in that room who didn't raise a hand after any of the questions she asked. I didn't have a job, I didn't have a plan.

I didn't go to physical therapy school looking to specialize in amputee rehabilitation. Neither did most of my coworkers. And none of us could have dreamed up a glass-walled clinic where celebrities gaped at us through the windows, instead of the other way around. I didn't know what kind of job I wanted. But I, probably more than anyone else, was particularly dead-set against "buttonholing" myself into any sort of specialty. I didn't want to narrow my job prospects by becoming specialized. After all, I had ended up in PT school after a string of poor-paying, dead-end jobs and several soul-searching rounds of unemployment.

To pay for the two and a half years of pre-med course work I had to pass before applying to PT school, I worked a slew of menial and depressing jobs. Like dishwashing, a job I was sad to see I showed remarkable prowess for. In the end, the only thing I hoped to get out of PT school was a gig that didn't involve standing at an industrial sink in a waterproof apron.

I passed my final exams, graduated, and had no idea what to do next. I had a work-study job at the university gym that paid me fifty dollars a week, and I figured I could survive on that for a few weeks until I found a real job. What I didn't plan on was that as soon as I graduated, my work-study job would end. Because of course, work-study jobs are for students and I was no longer a student.

Luckily I quickly found a job at a small outpatient clinic associated with the University of Maryland Medical Center. But they didn't have an opening for me until July — six weeks away. Once I paid off my rent and my bills, I had sixteen dollars left. My parents lived thirty miles away but I didn't want to call them and admit my latest fiasco involving lack of planning, so I figured I would just make it work. I had a bunch of beer left over from my graduation party, a big jar of peanut butter, and a jumbo box of Fla-Vor-Ice popsicles in the freezer. I lived off of peanut butter sandwiches, popsicles, and beer for almost a month. It was terrible. I lived close to a Chinese takeout, and the smell of Chinese food wafting down the sidewalk would literally stop me in my tracks and make me salivate like a dog.

To make matters worse, as the days ticked by, my attic efficiency apartment began to get hotter and hotter. Walking up the four flights of stairs was like approaching the surface of the sun. Each floor got noticeably warmer, until you reached the door to my 300-square-foot apartment, where heat oozed from the floor, walls, and ceiling. It must have been at least 120 degrees in there. I had moved into the apartment in the middle of winter and had no idea that when the summer came I would literally be cooked alive.

It was so hot at night I couldn't sleep. I would get up again and again, to take a cold shower, or pack another ziplock bag of ice to hug to my chest. When morning came, after yet another miserable, sleepless night that I frequently spent in front of the open window, I flew down the stairs and got out of my apartment as quickly as I could. Except I had nowhere to go. I walked aimlessly about. Baltimore was blazing hot. Everywhere I went was hot, hot, hot.

Four weeks into my personal hell, I broke down and walked downtown to the clinic I was supposed to start working at and begged them to let me start working sooner. By this point my core body temperature was probably consistently 115 degrees. I just needed to be somewhere with air-conditioning. If my new boss was alarmed by my maniacal state, she suppressed it. But she said she would see what she could do.

Outside I ran into a former classmate of mine. She was working at the hospital, and was clearly taken aback by my scorched appearance. On seeing a familiar face, I completely broke down into a tearful confession of my lack of financial planning and the human oven I was forced to reside in.

It took me over an hour to walk home. When I got inside, the phone rang. It was my classmate. She had a used window air conditioner I could have. If there is such a thing as manna from heaven, this was it. In the air-conditioning, I had my first good night's sleep in several weeks. The next morning, I was practically a new person. I checked my mailbox — in the mail was a graduation bonus check from my old work-study job, and a scrawled note from my former boss congratulating me on my new *career*. This was another lifeline, if there ever was one. I couldn't believe it. I cashed it and went straight to that Chinese restaurant. I bought a half-dozen take-out entrees and ran up the four flights of stairs to my apartment. I spread a sheet out on the floor like a big tablecloth and sat there surrounded by take-out containers of Chinese food. It was the best meal I'd ever had in my life.

You think I would have learned my lesson

about not having a plan during those six extreme weeks. That I wouldn't spend six years at Walter Reed trying to decide if I should stay or if I should go. At Walter Reed, I became just like the colonel, calling people at six in the morning. Because I forgot that, even though I'd been up for an hour already, the rest of the world was still very much asleep.

"Hey, I'm in line. Whatchu having?"

"Huh? What?"

"I'm at *Starbucks.* What do you want?"

"What time is it?"

I snapped to attention, and looked at the screen of my cell phone. Dana. Oh no. Instead of calling Darcy, I'd accidentally dialed the number listed alphabetically right before hers — Dana. My friend Dana was a night owl who slept in a bedroom outfitted with blackout curtains to block the morning sun. Who knew the last time Dana had woken up before 1100?

"Dana," I said in my best colonel voice, "it's Adele. I accidentally called you. Go back to sleep. You will forget I called."

Dana didn't take my suggestion as casually as I'd offered it. She slammed the phone down so hard in the cradle I almost burst an eardrum.

I felt guilty, but only for about five minutes, since I was frequently awakened by people calling me at 2130 (9:30 p.m.). And in six years, I'd never left for work without the stars still being out. I might have gone in early, but I unfairly also got out late. I got home, with the rest of D.C., at 1730 or 1800.

While I would have liked to start dating someone, it was impossible considering that after work I rarely left my living room. The only people I saw regularly outside of work were my parents, because they lived close by and, unlike me, kept food in their refrigerator. My father had taken to disapprovingly calling me the "Ghost Eater" because I would sneak over, eat the leftovers in the fridge, and then disappear back to my apartment just in time to walk the dog and go to bed.

There were no happy hours in my world. I stopped swim team when they changed practice from 1900 to 2030, to 1930 to 2100. It was doable before, when I could get changed into my pajamas in the pool locker room and go home and get straight into bed. But I couldn't still be in the pool swimming intervals with the swim team during my bedtime.

My evening activities now consisted of me flopped on my couch reading the morning paper that I never had time to read in the morning. I didn't answer the phone because I'd spent all day in a chaotic one-hundred-person environment.

Across town, I know my coworkers all did the same thing. In fact, we frequently sent out feelers via text message.

"Whatchu doin?"

"Couch. You?"

"Couch."

I read the paper because it made me feel like I was at least accomplishing something, but I was frequently interrupted by text messages from my coworkers, alerting me to the latest reality show they were getting ready to watch. *"Project Runway* — five minutes!"

When it came to television, I shared my coworkers' passion for reality TV only when it came to the trashiest of shows. Shows like *Hoarders,* about people so dirty they live inside homes packed from floor to ceiling with garbage and dead cats. And *Rock of Love,* a dating show between a washed-up metal rocker and a group of single women culled from trailer parks and strip bars.

With the morning's *Washington Post,* I liked to think I had my mind on higher matters. But really, I didn't. I was all about the crime section of the paper. I skipped the movie reviews, world affairs, and went right to local muggings, carjackings, and killings.

# THREE-RING CIRCUS

Things happened so quickly in the Fishbowl that if you left, even for five minutes, it was very possible that you would return to find your coworker lying on a table in the back of the room with a bag of ice on her head and life in the clinic going on as usual.

I approached Capt. Dumont cautiously.

"What's going on?"

Capt. Dumont didn't stop staring at the ceiling to answer me. "I got hit in the head with a medicine ball."

"What?"

"I got hit in the *fucking* head with the medicine ball."

"How?"

"How the hell would I know? I was talking on the phone, minding my own business, and someone fucking pitched the ten-pound medicine ball at my head."

It was hard not to burst into laughter. Capt. Dumont was a hyper personality in the amputee section. Next to Maj. Tavner, she was second in charge and a total workhorse. They were like opposite bookends. Tall, blond Maj. Tavner with her relaxed Midwestern manner and easy laugh. While across the room was Capt. Dumont, with dark hair and eyes that noticed everything. While Capt. Dumont tried to project a feeling of calm, it was hard for her to not reveal an undercurrent of hard-charging energy.

Capt. Dumont worked practically around the clock. She ate her lunch — peanut butter and jelly sandwiches — between patients, standing up in the back of the room, ready to run out onto the clinic floor the second a patient on new wobbly legs fell over. Except to go running at lunch, Capt. Dumont never took a break. I had never seen her thumb through a *People* magazine or even duck out to use the staff restroom. She was the very last person I ever expected to find under a bag of ice in the corner.

"Go ahead and laugh. For all you know I could be dead in the morning."

Coming across an injured coworker stuffed casually in a corner, like Capt. Dumont had been, would be a rare experience at, for example, a law office; it was just a typical day in the MATC.

The physical therapy gym was a raucous

place, a crowded, sun-filled room of people. Between the patients, family members, the therapy dog, and the physical therapists, there were usually a couple of nurses, the wandering physician or surgical resident, higher-level military officers, celebrity USO visitors, Red Cross volunteers cleaning down the equipment, chaplains counseling patients, and the ever-present media.

In the chaos of the amputee clinic, a captain felled by a ten-pound medicine ball quickly fades into the background. Even I soon turned my attention elsewhere.

I was eagerly anticipating the arrival of fifty clowns. While we had a frequent parade of celebrities, sports figures, and politicians through the clinic, we had never had one clown, let alone fifty of them.

I usually didn't pay attention during those rare moments when we were notified, via email or gossip, which celebrities or heads of state were going to visit that week. As a result, I had been completely surprised to meet Vice President Richard Cheney, and another time, Hamid Karzai. But the announcement of visiting clowns had pricked my attention.

The thought of fifty clowns squeezing into our already cramped clinic was so distracting that I had discussed it throughout the morning with whoever would listen. Most of the people in the clinic, coworkers and patients, tuned me out. Celebrity visitors, clowns included, were hardly anything new.

Yet the idea of a mass of clowns, fifty clowns, did eventually drum up some interest as we tried to imagine how it would be possible for so many clowns to squeeze into the clinic, even though squeezing into small places is a clown specialty.

The clowns were supposed to arrive at 1000, but no clowns showed up. By 1200, the only clown in the clinic seemed to be me, after a full five hours of clown talk.

At 1330, five clowns arrived. This was an egregious dyslexic number error on my part. How I could have mistaken five for fifty was incredible, but I was just relieved to see the clowns in the clinic.

The clowns were not funny, but thanks to five and a half hours of anticipation by one semi-obsessed physical therapist, they were given an enthusiastic reception.

When the clowns arrived in the afternoon, the clinic was packed with the usual players: patients, therapists, chaplains, doctors, nurses, Red Cross volunteers. About forty people. Soon everyone was wearing balloon hats, but still going about business as usual, unwrapping bandages, walking with

116

crutches, and throwing medicine balls back and forth across the room.

Cosmo had decided to surprise me by coming that day in full uniform. He'd cut the pant legs and pinned them to fit over his ex-fix and to accommodate his missing leg. In his desert fatigues, Cosmo dutifully went through his standard mat routine while I stood in the back of the room scanning the clinic for him and fuming, "Where is he?"

Cosmo's progression from inpatient to outpatient had taken the normal course. He was slowly weaned off his nerve blocks and then his IV pain meds. He lost his wound VACs, his urinary catheter, his drains, and his IV antibiotics. He no longer needed assistance to turn onto his side, scoot from the bed into his wheelchair, or get to the bathroom. He could get dressed, bath, shave, eat, do all essential "activities of daily living," and so he was discharged from the hospital to the Mologne House, where our patients were boarded once they were discharged from the hospital.

While I had been distracted looking for the appearance of dozens of clowns, I failed to notice the one directly in front of me.

Finally, in frustration, Cosmo sat up and cast a long, pointed look in my direction. It was like seeing a ghost materialize before my startled eyes.

"Cosmo?"

"Fuck! I've been waiting for you to notice me," he said accusingly, and I felt a painful stab of guilt.

Because most of our patients were young men with short hair in their late teens and early twenties, my coworkers and I frequently described our patients by injury, the same way they had been initially presented to us on the new patient list. A triple. A double AK. A double BK. A quadruple. An AK/BK. Even the patients did it. Sometimes they even came up with their own crude variations, like the time I overhead one of the hip disartics (a hip disarticulation was a leg amputated right at the groin) refer to another hip disartic as an "articulator."

We weren't trying to be callous, although this way of identifying people had started to creep its way outside the clinic for me. Whenever I saw a person I couldn't place, I quickly looked at their legs — as if that would help me identify them.

Cosmo was "an AK with an ex-fix." Except when his AK and his ex-fix were covered up under long fatigue pants, and then I apparently had no idea who he was.

118

Just then, the door to the clinic opened, and a yellow lab trotted enthusiastically into the clinic. Cheers and whistles went up around the room. Walter was back! Walter was our clinic's service dog. He had been assigned to Walter Reed after failing out of blind dog school and spending an additional year and a half getting rerouted through service dog school. Walter ignored his passionate welcome and got right to work sniffing the garbage can.

In spite of thousands of dollars spent on his training, Walter was not exactly what I would call well behaved. In his prim service dog vest, Walter was aloof and conniving, frequently sneaking out of the clinic and trying to make it down to the cafeteria without getting busted by the colonel.

Off duty, he was a sweet, playful dog. But stuck in the clinic, his actions were entirely self-serving. Walter worked the room like a drug addict, trolling the clinic for baked goods. Whenever possible, he would try to leave his duty station (physical therapy), where he was usually caught with his head buried in the trash can outside the occupational therapy kitchen. If it was possible for a dog to look embarrassed, Walter looked downright mortified as he was led, head hanging in shame, back into the clinic.

The only person who wasn't a fan of Walter was the colonel. The colonel saw right through Walter's tricks and sacked him on a semi-monthly basis for inappropriate behavior, which, depending on the colonel's mood, could range from tennis ball chasing to sleeping in a corner. His most notorious sacking happened after the colonel discovered a large pile of dog poop in her office. (The dislike between the colonel and Walter seemed to be entirely mutual.) Yet Walter always returned to Walter Reed with great fanfare, bursting into the Fishbowl to an enthusiastic round of cheers.

The staff was always happy to have Walter back, but not nearly as happy as the inpatients who lay like sardines on the mat tables. Still attached to portable wound VACs and IV poles and in a lot of pain, they distracted themselves by trying to lure Walter over their way.

The patients weren't allowed to feed Walter but they were allowed to invite him onto their mat table for a nap. Which, when there were no cookies to be had, was something Walter could really get into. If someone was having a bad day, Walter would jump onto his mat table and flop down beside him. Snuggled up with his head resting on an injured soldier's chest, Walter was at his very best. The patient would wrap his arms around Walter, and Walter would stretch out and squeeze his eyes shut at the pure luxury of it.

A week after the unfunny clowns came to Walter Reed, a woman and her husband walked into the clinic pushing a baby carriage. Inside the carriage wasn't a baby, but eight pug puppies, each one the size of a fluffy tennis ball.

They lived nearby and decided to bring in the puppies to cheer the soldiers up. The puppies were strictly contraband and the couple knew it as they sneaked them past the armed front gate guards. But the staff turned a blind eye. The puppies stayed for the rest of the afternoon. They scampered around the clinic, yipping excitedly as they climbed over prosthetic feet and chased errant physioballs to the amusement of everyone in the room. Tired puppies curled up on the mats, rolled over, and nipped at their own tails, before walking across a new hospitalized inpatient with their tiny paws searching for a good place, like an armpit or underneath a chin, to take a nap. The soldiers and marines in the parallel bars would stop walking for a moment to carefully bend down and pick up a puppy, holding on to the rail with one hand while clutching a small puppy to their chest with the other. And in the back of the clinic, an explosive ordinance detail (EOD) soldier missing an arm laughed in surprise when the puppy he was holding close to his neck with his one good arm enthusiastically started licking his gunpowder-pocked face.

Work went on as usual. I stood by the phone trying to page one of the ortho docs while watching one of my patients pulling on his prosthetic legs in the parallel bars. Behind him, a small puppy was chasing his tail.

Two floors above us, Ward 57 was an entirely different experience. Ward 57 was clean and medicinal. It exuded a feeling of quiet and calm. Bedpans, shots of morphine, and milk shakes were dispensed with military precision. The nurses manning the nursing station on Ward 57 were absolutely no-nonsense. And you better have a staff ID clipped to your collar or security quickly escorted you out of there.

Meanwhile, down in the boisterous amputee clinic, we were awash in puppies, candy, pizza, and Girl Scout cookies. Unlike Ward 57, we were a nonstop party. We celebrated everything — birthdays, promotions, even the anniversary of the terrible day that brought you to Walter Reed, a day we referred to in a celebratory tone as your "Alive Day." Local grandmas came in and out of our clinic bringing homemade cookies and fudge, because nothing soothes phantom limb pain better than a homemade brownie. Rock stars, professional baseball teams, and the patient's favorite type of visitor — cheerleaders — were frequently escorted around the glass perimeter.

Most people enjoyed the circuslike atmosphere inside the physical therapy clinic, with the exception of one man — the marine liaison, a squat, flat-nosed man who resembled, at a distance, a fire hydrant. Worried that the army was babying his marines, he frequently surveyed the chaos in the physical therapy clinic with a frown. Cheerleaders? Cookies?

After he witnessed yet another cookie/local grandmother incident, a meeting was scheduled. The marines versus the army. Everyone silently resenting the other. The marines didn't say much. They didn't have to. Maj. Tavner and Capt. Dumont were too busy being defensive. They swore up and down that they had no control over the visitors, but that they would try and stanch the flood of cookies and brownies.

For a week or so, food in the clinic was

banned. But then it started trickling back in, cookies still warm from the oven. A few of the soldiers, learning how to totter around occupational therapy's kitchen on prosthetic legs, spent an afternoon baking brownies. One of the surgeons came back from his deployment and we welcomed him home with a huge ice cream social in the amputee clinic. And suddenly we were right back where we started.

Whenever we saw the marine liaison walking sternly down the hallway, we automatically panicked. He hadn't busted our clinic yet, but our immediate reaction was guilt. Guilt for spoiling the soldiers and marines. Guilt for feeding them cookies and too much love. Guilt for sneaking in puppies and scantily-clad cheerleaders.

Our visitors were usually arranged in advance by the public affairs office, but one day a local woman showed up unannounced, pulling a large harp into our clinic on a hand trolley. She lived in the area and that morning made a spontaneous decision to do something to cheer up the wounded soldiers. Without a word to the staff, she casually set up her harp in the middle of the clinic and, amid the chaos of medicine balls whizzing past her ear and patients tottering about on unsteady prosthetic legs, serenaded us with beautiful classical music.

My coworkers and I walked endless loops around the clinic, picking up a medicine ball here, delivering a bottle of water there, giving one patient a set of exercises to do while monitoring another patient climbing up onto the treadmill, all while the harp music seeped into the room. I leaned against the parallel bars and relaxed for a few minutes, allowing myself the luxury of listening to the harpist. Combined with the smell of freshly baked chocolate chip cookies, I felt like I was wrapped up in warm fleece blanket.

No one noticed the marine liaison walking down the hallway. When his face appeared on the other side of the glass, the trancelike feeling in the room shattered. No one moved. We held our breath in animated suspension, waiting for him to see the harp, but he was business as usual, surveying his marines through the glass walls and ticking them off in his roll book.

The harpist continued to play, swaying back and forth, unaware of the drama unraveling in the room all around her. Which was exactly when the marine liaison noticed her.

Staring at the animated harpist through the glass window with complete disbelief, he seemed to silently implode.

To be caught by the marine liaison with a harpist in the clinic was horribly embarrassing. We waited for him to erupt into the room and start yanking marines out, but instead his eyes narrowed and he spun on his heel and marched quickly away.

The harpist kept playing and the marines went back to walking in the parallel bars and lifting weights. The next circus act, I was sure, was right around the corner.

# STANDING

At noon, above the din of the physical therapy clinic, Jim would always announce that it was time for our lunch break with an exuberant, "Shall we dine?" He'd say this several times and then wash his hands, looking around to see if any of the volunteers or patients were interested in accompanying him to the "café." The café was what Jim called the hospital DFAC.

Jim was such a fan of the DFAC that he personally introduced himself to the dour major managing it. I saw him do it and almost dropped my cafeteria tray when I thought for a split second that Jim might actually go so far as to kiss her hand. Luckily she was flattered by Jim's gracious introduction, which was why Darcy and I were able to convince her later to use Jim as one of the main line servers during the DFAC's Cinco de Mayo festival. It was a joke, but Jim was all for it. We dressed Jim up in a big sombrero and colorful poncho and sent him down to the cafeteria. If the servers were surprised to have Jim working with them, they weren't nearly as surprised as one of Jim's former patients, who, after Jim passed him a serving 'of enchiladas, commented wryly, "So, they have you working here now?"

Jim was our resident foodie, but he wasn't a snob about it. He loved food because, to him, food was a way of connecting with people. And there was no better place to get to know interesting people than in the hospital DFAC.

Once a badly brain-injured patient accidentally wandered into the Fishbowl. He was in the wrong wing of the hospital, and when Darcy and I looked his appointment list up, his appointment in the traumatic brain injury clinic wasn't for another couple of hours. We could have escorted him to the TBI clinic and left him in the waiting room. But instead we brought him over to Jim. Tall, winterized Jim in his cheerful orange shirt. He stared down at this young, disheveled soldier who was wearing big black sunglasses and squinting up at him in the quiet, light-sensitive way of someone who has really had their marbles rocked. Jim shook his hand. "Shall we dine?"

Jim loped off to the DFAC with a few of the new patients in tow, while Darcy and I sat at a table in the clinic, waiting for our latest copy of *People* magazine.

You would think that as medical professionals we would spend our lunch break reading journal articles and medical textbooks, but really, short of the online cafeteria menu, we didn't read anything aloud with greater gusto than *People* magazine. When the newest *People* arrived, it was carefully squirreled away by the staff and put in a safe place — usually under a computer keyboard — until lunchtime. Lunchtime sent everyone scurrying to the cafeteria and back with greater urgency than usual, because no one wanted to miss out on the group reading of *People* magazine.

The group reading was led by Emma, a willow-thin, shy physical therapist who was transformed by the power of *People* magazine into an aggressive and opinionated commentator. So much so that we referred to Emma as *ET,* in honor of her favorite celebrity gossip show: *Entertainment Tonight.* (Or as we called it, Emma Tonight.)

Emma would start on page one, the celebrity sightings, and slowly flip through the magazine, page by page, while the rest of the staff huddled behind her. "Oh my gosh!

Demi Moore isn't wearing her wedding ring!"

The group reading of *People* magazine was one of my very favorite parts of the week. I tuned everything out and settled into the warm glow that was my coworkers and a crisp new issue of *People*. Which is why I didn't immediately notice the shout that came careening through the open doorway of our clinic one afternoon.

*"It's time!"*

The shout came quickly again. *"It's effin' time!"*

I turned and looked cautiously over my shoulder and saw Cosmo in his wheelchair in the doorway of the clinic. He was tipped back and balanced in a perfect wheelie. His back brace, as usual, was hanging off the back of his wheelchair like an old sweater.

I jumped up and ran toward the phone. I knew exactly what he was talking about. "I'll page the doctor," I yelled.

Receiving a prosthetic leg is something that happens a few weeks after your final surgery, after your stitches are removed. The orthopedic doctors are pretty strict about the time line, and most patients are told in advance that their stitches can come out three weeks after their amputation has been sutured shut. The sooner you get your

130

stitches out, the sooner you'll get your prosthetic leg, so getting stitches out is a much-anticipated step toward learning how to walk again.

Cosmo could have made an appointment and had his orthopedic surgeon or physician's assistant remove his stitches, but that might have taken an extra day or two. So he detoured into the physical therapy clinic instead. He must have known I would drop anything to pull his stitches out, because nudging and pulling out the perfect stitch is a task on the level of squeezing row after row of perfect blackhead pimples, or picking off sheets of sunburned skin. Disgusting, but extremely gratifying.

But mostly, Cosmo knew I was eager to progress his rehab program and could barely wait to get him up on a prosthetic leg and in the parallel bars, even if it meant sacrificing my lunch hour to pull out his stitches.

The doctor quickly returned my page and I rushed back across the clinic toward Cosmo, rubbing my hands together in anticipation.

"He's okay with it. Now lie back."

Cosmo lay back on the mat table, sighing once in satisfaction. He was, for once, perfectly behaved. No cussing. No snide comments. I sprayed his stump down with disinfectant. I might as well have been spraying a windshield with Windex; I am always heavy on the disinfectant spray. This was followed quickly with an aggressive rubdown with a four-by-four-inch gauze pad.

"Hey, hey! Heavy hands! Heavy hands!" Cosmo yelped.

"Ooops. Sorry," I muttered, leaning forward to stare closely at the first stitch.

To remove a stitch, you grab the knotted end with tweezers and pull the stitch away from the skin until the loop at the bottom of the knot is revealed. Then, with a special hooked scissor, you snip the stitch and gently pull it out of the skin with the tweezers.

I pulled the stitches out quickly, moving from left to right. If there was any blood, I'd dab it with a gauze pad before continuing. When all the stitches were out, I ran a line of adhesive down either side of Cosmo's puckered incision line and stretched steri-strips — thin, translucent tape — across the incision line to help hold it together. Steri-strips aren't usually required, but I liked adding them just for the flare. Cosmo and I both paused to admire the masterpiece.

Cosmo even gave me a compliment: "Fuckin' awesome!"

"Thanks," I said, breaking into a grin. "Okay, go show your prosthetist and make an appointment." In a couple of days, Cosmo would start walking.

Our soldiers and marines, having experienced the highest amount of pain possible — having a limb or two broken into bits or torn from their body — seem immune to normal pain. They can calmly tolerate the type of discomfort that would have the rest of us cringing in apprehension. Like having your heavy-handed physical therapist pulling your stitches out.

Every couple years, the Joint Commission on Accreditation of Health Care Organizations (JCAHO) did an inspection of Walter Reed. Their latest focus was pain management, so we were required to ask our patients what their pain level was at every treatment. JCAHO wanted specifics: a number on a scale from 0 to 10, a description, and a location.

This elicited an almost immediate look of irritation from our patients.

"It's a zero."

I wouldn't press them, and dutifully recorded their pain level as zero in the chart, even though they could have multiple fractures and amputations and chunks of missing muscle and bone.

Stitches? They knew what real pain was, and it wasn't this.

Sometimes I did some part-time evening work for my friend Maria, who owned her own physical therapy clinic in Chevy Chase, an affluent D.C. suburb. She treated only the very wealthy. I liked working in her clinic because it was a surreal experience. There, I could quietly ultrasound a VIP's sprained ankle and listen with a professionally blank face as she described her pain as being, "A ten out of ten."

The day after doing one evening of work in Maria's clinic, I was back at our clinic, drinking a cup of coffee and watching Emma dig stitches out of a soldier's freshly amputated stump. Emma's eyes were wide open in concentration, seemingly oblivious to anything but the immediate task at hand. She stacked each stitch carefully, one on top of the other, on a square two-by-two-inch gauze pad. From a distance it looked like she was organizing a pile of small black spiders.

Emma stopped for a moment, pushed her glasses up the bridge of her nose with the back of her wrist, and asked earnestly. "Did you watch *The Bachelor* last night? You

134

didn't? Oh my gosh, let me tell you about it."

While Emma talked about the latest reality show breakup, she carefully picked all the dead skin and scabs off of her patient's stump before applying a solid glob of moisturizing cream to the end.

The day after Cosmo's stitches were pulled out, a plaster cast of his stump was made in the prosthetic office. A plastic socket matching the contours of Cosmo's stump was made in-house from the cast and attached to a prosthetic leg. Twenty-four hours after getting casted, Cosmo tried his new leg in the prosthetic department.

Not everyone is able to stand up unassisted the first time. Some patients might need two or three staff members to help pull them up and support them upright. And the ones who can't tolerate a full upright position, the soldiers with bad pelvic fractures, are strapped onto a tilt table. On the table, the prosthetic leg is slipped on, and then the table is slowly tilted vertically to a manageable angle.

Regardless of how the patients try on their new legs, it's always a time of celebration. Their families bring in cameras and take pictures. Even the physical therapist, who until that day has been seen as an unwelcome tormentor, is pulled into the picture. Posing next to his or her patient with side-by-side smiles, the table is tilted up, and a soldier stands again for the first time.

Cosmo held his breath and slowly slid his fractured leg off his wheelchair's leg rest and onto the floor. Grabbing the parallel bars, he pulled himself upright. Once he was standing with his weight resting on his new prosthetic leg, I was surprised to discover that Cosmo was almost a full head taller than me.

We posed for a quick picture. I was happy for Cosmo. Getting a leg — that was a big step.

But Cosmo didn't look happy or excited. He just looked like he was in pain. He held his breath and looked up at the ceiling. Finally, after a short twenty seconds, he collapsed back in his wheelchair. "My leg is fucking throbbing." In the short time Cosmo had been upright, his intact leg had turned a motley purple color.

# THE TEMPLE OF JIM

Sergeant Chen, one of the occupational therapy techs, called from the flight line. She was on the runway at Fort Hood, Texas, with the rest of her company, waiting for the plane that would take them to Iraq. Since Chen had left for Fort Hood to train up for her deployment, we heard from her a lot.

The phone would ring in the clinic and whoever answered it would suddenly grimace and hold the phone away from their ear as Sgt. Chen's signature *"Yoooooo!"* came blaring through the receiver.

Sgt. Chen would laugh for a long time and then suddenly get serious. "What's up, son?" she'd say. Chen called everyone "son," regardless if you were male or female. Then, if the person didn't recognize her, she'd shout out her signature tagline, *"It's* Chen!" Usually Sgt. Chen would have to shout this two or three times until we realized who it was, because Sgt. Chen didn't like to enunciate.

We liked to tease Chen that she should come with her own translator. But since Chen had been in Texas for a month, we'd all gotten used to understanding her phone voice.

Sgt. Chen had been a joyous presence in our clinic, poking fun at everyone, patient and therapist alike, regardless of rank. *"Hey, man!"* Sgt. Chen had shouted loudly one day at a soldier who was wheeling out of the clinic. *"You* left your *vagina* on the mat!" And then Chen had slapped her thigh and brayed loudly at her own joke. (The "vagina" in question was a piece of putty Sgt. Chen had crafted to fill the indentation this patient had on the end of his amputation. Sgt. Chen and the patient both thought it helped keep his skin from pulling apart further inside his prosthetic socket.)

If Sgt. Chen was scared to be getting deployed, she didn't show it. But she sure called frequently.

The Fort Hood shootings happened during Sgt. Chen's first week there. A disgruntled army psychologist, who had been previously stationed at Walter Reed, opened fire in a pavilion full of fellow soldiers.

Those of us at Walter Reed heard about it

first, and it consumed our collective consciousness. Before it was announced on the news, it spread through the hospital by word of mouth and staff email. In between patients, everyone was glued to CNN — or hunkered down trying to reach Sgt. Chen on her cell phone. Thankfully we got through to her and she was okay.

One afternoon, shortly after the Fort Hood shootings, a loud boom reverberated through the building. Everyone, patient and therapist alike, cringed and sucked in their collective breath. The boom seemed to come from the direction of occupational therapy — and everyone's face turned toward the OT clinic. We remained silent and unmoving for what seemed like several minutes but was probably only a few seconds. An entire room of people, fifty-something individuals, frozen in time.

I knew it was probably nothing. But at the same time, the Fort Hood shootings gave me a feeling we could be next. My patients, who had all survived ambushes, looked as hypervigilant as I felt, and on either side of me my coworkers looked equally terrified.

OT must have known we were freaking out, and a shout came down the hallway, "It's okay! Everything is okay."

Everyone remained cemented in place,

and an occupational therapist cautiously poked his head into the room. "We dropped a heavy box," he explained to the roomful of suspicious eyes. "Just a box," he said and backed out the door.

I realized in that moment what a singular group we were. A group that was hunkered down and getting through the wars in a way no one else in the country was.

My strategy for coping with all the intensity: visit the Temple of Jim. Sit next to Jim and I would be healed.

Each evening as everyone got their coats on to leave, Jim started his third shift of patients, the ones who had slept through their therapy appointments because they couldn't sleep at night. They showed up around 1500 or 1600. Some still wore their pajamas, rolling their wheelchairs with groggy urgency down the hallway to the physical therapy gym, trying to scoot in under the 1600 hour — which was when we were supposed to be closed.

But Jim never turned anyone away. He lived in Virginia and his commute was terrible. He chalked up his third shift as a way to miss the worst of the traffic.

The 1600 hour was really the best hour to be a patient. The clinic was yawningly quiet, briefly tidy, and calm. Jim had finished his notes and, since his home computer had died, was almost always checking his personal email. This involved a dramatic reading of his email to everyone in the room, especially his junk mail.

"Viagra! Can you imagine? Who would send this to me?"

Jim's email ritual almost always spiraled into an Internet search for a new restaurant, recipe, or iris bulb for his garden. The patients, the ones who had been up all night with nightmares, gathered around Jim and listened to him discuss his plans for his new garden. They helped him shop for flower bulbs and respond to emails. But their favorite activity of the day was selecting a restaurant.

They'd comb through the online reviews of restaurants close to Walter Reed. In between food reviews, the patients took turns stretching or doing some light walking in the parallel bars.

Finally at 1730, Jim would round up all the stragglers, and they'd head out for dinner at a restaurant they'd picked out together. Jim was a total foodie, and they sure weren't going to be eating at Golden Corral. When Jim's patients left Walter Reed, there were two things you could guarantee: They would be walking on prosthetic legs, and they would never eat at a chain restaurant again.

After a few months in the Temple of Jim, Jim's patients, now well-nourished and happy, weren't scooting in the door with such desperation anymore. They even started to come when they were supposed to, in the morning. But at 1600 they'd show up again and gather around Jim's desk. "Where are we going tonight, Jim?"

On cue, Jim would look up from his computer. "There's a new tandoori restaurant I'd like to check out. Oh wait, listen to this, it's from my friend Barb at the Kennedy Center: *'Dear Jim . . .'* "

Jim's patients were, as a whole, completely mesmerized by him. He was an exotic creature whom, under normal circumstances, they never would have met: a middle-aged man who loved theater and lived alone. A man who preferred baking cakes over football and stunned everyone when it was revealed that he was a retired army lieutenant colonel.

Their first impression of Jim, whom they met on their second day in the hospital, was that he was the only person who didn't seem to notice their injuries. Instead, he entertained them with running monologues about his life.

"So last night I tried a new pound cake recipe. Do you like pound cake? This one was a pepper pound cake. Can you believe it? Pepper. And let me tell you, it was incredible!"

Jim's new patients watched him with bewildered curiosity. Was it the drugs, or was a guy reciting a cake recipe to them while they were full of bullet holes?

At least once a week he would bring in a new pound cake and everyone was pressed into sampling it. His cakes were incredible. Dense and delicate at the same time, hearty pieces that dissolved in your mouth like the finest French pastries. He would wait until everyone in the clinic had finished his or her slice of cake before revealing the secret ingredient, which could be anything from 7UP to guava paste.

In addition to the usual clinic cake, Jim baked a special cake for each of the patients on their birthday. This favor went out to all the patients, not just the ones on his roster. They made a point of stopping by his desk the day before their birthday to put their order in. Even Cosmo, clearly influenced by Jim, requested a coconut cake with lime frosting.

He was a man of many interests besides cake and kept very few secrets. "Oooh. Did

you hear that?" Jim announced one afternoon as he walked past me and Cosmo in
clinic. We looked up and he repeated himself, "That noise?"

He started bending and straightening his
knee in front of Cosmo's face, a cacophony
of snaps and pops erupting from his joint.
Cosmo, sitting in his wheelchair, bundled
up in his clamshell back brace, looked
alarmed.

"What do you think?" Jim asked.

Cosmo squinted up at him. "That sounds
like it hurts."

Jim beamed and, newly invigorated,
limped purposefully away. Across the room
I could hear him heatedly discussing his
knee pain with another soldier. Jim's knee
pain was the top conversation item for the
rest of the week, promoted mostly by Jim.

By the next week, Jim was more concerned
about whether he should plant a redbud tree
in his garden. Would it look right? What
color? Was the nursery's sale price reason-
able? He solicited opinions from everyone,
even the Red Cross lady pushing her patient
goody cart of candy, movies, leather wallet
kits, and model cars. All comments were
welcome. The nursery usually offered good
deals, and it was on Jim's way home from
work. But the best thing about the nursery

where Jim might or might not purchase his redbud was that it was a long, long way from Iraq, Afghanistan, and Fort Hood.

# WALKING

In order to comfortably wear a prosthetic limb, patients protect their stumps with a thick, socklike silicone liner. Cosmo liked to crudely suggest to any patient learning to roll the liner over their stump for the first time to "roll it on like a condom!"

The liner provides some padding and protects the patient's skin from the abrasion of the hard plastic socket, but mostly it functions to suction the prosthetic socket onto the wearer's stump. In a well-fitting socket, pressure is distributed equally around the end of the patient's leg so that the patient's weight bears through the snug fit of the socket and not on the end of their stump. Most amputations are not designed to be end bearing. If the socket does not fit tightly, the patient will "bottom out," bearing weight on the end of their amputation — which is painful and damaging to the remaining tissue.

Amputations are delicate orthopedic surgeries. No longer is the skin and tissue just sutured around the freshly cut bone to create a flabby, wobbly bag. The surgeons at Walter Reed carefully dissect out the remaining muscle, anchoring select muscles down to bone, and then layer and stitch the other muscles around the residual limb to form a protective soft-tissue envelope. Because of the proximity of leg to bomb, lower-extremity amputations are more common than upper-extremity amputations at Walter Reed. But if the explosion is bad enough, especially with everyone on foot patrols in Afghanistan, arms are also frequently lost.

Cosmo was an above-knee, or transfemoral, amputee — his leg was amputated at the midshaft of his femur (thigh bone). In the beginning, Cosmo started learning to walk on a stump that was still very swollen from surgery. Just like a badly sprained ankle can remain swollen for weeks, stumps can stay swollen for six months or more. To accommodate for fluctuations in girth, patients add cotton ply socks on top of their silicone liners to maintain the snug fit of their socket.

New prosthetic users are regularly questioned if they are "pistoning" in the socket, or "bottoming out." These are all situations in which the socket is too loose for the patient and he or she needs to stop, sit down, pull the leg off, and add another one-ply sock on top of their liner. But if they are "not touching bottom," they need to stop and take a sock off. If they have too many ply socks on and aren't getting all the way into the socket, they are walking on a pocket of air that can cause a hickey or blisters to form on the bottom of their stump.

Even with a perfectly fitting socket, most amputees, even years after amputation, change girth during the day and need to take their prosthesis off and add or subtract one or two socks. In a new amputee, this can happen as frequently as every five to fifteen minutes.

It's one of the most frustrating aspects of amputation for new amputees, who are under the impression that they can just put their new leg on like a shoe and walk around without a problem for the rest of the day. Instead they are constantly taking their leg on and off and messing with different ply socks. And if you are a bilateral amputee and missing both legs, you are doing this twice as much.

To avoid the financial costs of recasting new amputees every few weeks to accommodate for initial girth changes, amputees on the civilian side may wait up to a year after their amputation before getting fitted for a leg. But at Walter Reed, without insurance restrictions, we got our patients up and walking as soon as they were physically able. This prevents a lot of secondary decline in function and overuse injuries of the intact side. Subsequently, they may go through six or seven temporary sockets as their stump shrinks to a permanent size.

As they get further away from their amputation date and their residual limb loses most of its initial puffiness, their subsequent sockets get smaller and tighter. Six months later, most patients reach a stable size and the temporary plastic socket is replaced with a lighter, nonadjustable, carbon-fiber socket. They've reached an elite group. A group that can now feel free to tease newer amputees about the "big bucket you're putting your ugly stump in."

But socket fit wasn't what was slowing Cosmo down. His problem was his "intact" side, the leg he still had. While theoretically he could walk on it — the external fixator held the broken bones in place — it was just too painful. In a dependent position (standing up), the blood would rush down his leg making the calf and foot turn an angry eggplant color, and orange-yellow fluid would leak out of the pin sites.

The nerve damage had caused his toes to curl and his calf to atrophy. Because he had lost large chunks of muscle from the front and back of his thigh, he had difficulty controlling what little motion he had left in his knee. Instead, what was left of his thigh muscles was spontaneously converting to bone. Abnormal bone growth, or heterotopic ossification, such as this was casually known around the clinic, by staff and patient alike, as "HO," with each letter being pronounced separately. The bomb blast mysteriously denatured the muscle and bone cells, making muscle convert to bone, and bone grow out of control.

Cosmo's HO made his thigh appear bumpy as new shards pressed up underneath his skin. It wasn't growing through the skin yet, but if it did, he would have to have surgery. The problem was if his surgeon removed the HO before the bone had matured, it would just grow right back. So right now we were stuck watching it grow.

Contrary to what my parents or friends might have thought I did inside the walls of Walter Reed, I wasn't "teaching" anyone "how to walk" again. Why? We all know how to walk. A newborn baby, if you hold it upright and support its trunk, will make automatic stepping motions. We all come preprogrammed. I wasn't following anyone around the MATC saying anything ridiculous like, "And now you swing your leg forward — that's right! Past your other leg. There you go! Now land on the heel of your foot. Good! Good!"

Walking is largely dependent on joint control. Are you strong enough to control the motion of your stump inside the socket? Can you balance on your nubs and propel yourself forward on heavy prosthetic legs? Which is why, after patients learned how to take short wobbly steps in the parallel bars, we really crammed the strength training in. The stronger you were, the better you would be able to control the sometimes unpredictable motion of your prosthetic leg against the ground.

Sure, there were tricks to walking with a prosthetic leg. Tricks to go up stairs and down hills. Tricks to pop over a curb, walk backward, squat, and kneel. There were computerized knees, all of which functioned differently. There were "new technology" knees with motors in them that would supposedly propel you upstairs, but actually just bucked you around like a rodeo horse. There were mechanical knees that kept the knee locked out until you put weight on the toe of the foot. There were prosthetic ankles that rotated. Feet with built-in shocks and springs. Carbon-fiber feet with a split toe were designed by the manufacturer to accommodate for uneven ground surfaces — but were requested by the patients because the split toe enabled them to wear flip-flops. But first, before all of that, you had to be strong.

We usually started the patients out with squats in their prosthetic legs on the leg press machine, box step-ups in the parallel bars, and later on, modified lunges around the clinic using a rolling walker for stability — and then later on with nothing. We had our patients do push-ups, not to look pretty on the beach, but to practice balancing on the tips of their new prosthetic toes. Balancing in a push-up position on the tips of two prosthetic legs was good, but just for a beginner. We quickly pushed our patients to progress to one-legged push-ups balanced on one prosthetic leg, and when they got stronger, to do the same drill while gripping a wobbly rocker board. Because the better they could control their prosthetic leg, the better they would walk.

The patients practiced negotiating curbs and stairs on their wobbly stainless-steel legs by stepping up and over increasingly higher boxes inside the clinic. We made this harder and more interesting later by having them step up on unstable surfaces, like the mini-trampoline or inverted BOSU balls. To work on walking speed and power, patients walked forward and sideways on various inclines on the treadmill. For added intensity, they'd tow their therapist around the clinic with resistant bands tied around their waist and later around their prosthetic legs. They walked on uneven surfaces in the clinic, on squishy foam mats, inflatable balance discs, and in the grass outside, before facing the steep grassy hill behind the clinic.

But Cosmo wasn't doing any of this. New leg or not, he couldn't walk on it because of the incredible pain in the "intact" side. His shattered bones had a low-grade infection and weren't healing together. When he tried to take controlled hops in the parallel bars on his prosthetic leg, the pain in his infected, broken leg was practically unbearable. Cosmo stopped wearing his prosthetic leg. It stayed in the back corner of our leg closet, covered in a neat layer of dust. For Cosmo it was less torturous to just stay in his wheelchair. In the meantime, we waited for the infection to get better and his remaining leg to heal.

# SPORTS MEDICINE

In spite of our obsessive germ precautions, my coworkers were completely reckless when it came to sports, and every August were consistently laid low with Army Ten Miler–itis. The "Army Ten Miler" is a local running race we encourage our patients to do — either on a hand-crank cycle, a recumbent bicycle that you propel with your arms, or in a walk/run fashion. For the patients, it's all about recovery, but for the staff, it's a crash course in distance running. Having goofed off all spring, we do exactly what we, as fitness professionals, advise others not to do: go from minimal training to zealous overtraining in two weeks' time.

With just two months to train for a ten-mile race, we were cramming it all in. By the third or fourth week, some staff members had been peer-pressured into training routines that could include running six miles each way to and from work (Sgt. Hernandez), or a random fifteen-mile high noon "test run" (me). This is overtraining in its finest form, and by the time September hits, we are all injured.

Most people would take a couple weeks off, but we just consulted one another and found tricky ways to keep on running. Before the patients came into the clinic, there was almost always a staff member sprawled out on a treatment table in agony.

The patients may be running with prosthetic arms and legs, but limping beside them were an army of medical staff held together with athletic tape, heel lifts, and knee braces. We were supposed to be there to encourage the patients, but it could sometimes be the other way around.

Ignoring all of our self-inflicted injuries, my coworkers started discussing the possibility of signing up for a twenty-mile race the weekend before the Army Ten Miler, because it was no longer about wounded warriors, but about punishment and finishing any way you can. I listened to my coworkers discuss this fascinating idea, as some of them reeled in doubters with earnest suggestions such as, "You can walk a minute every mile," and "I'm sure there's a Metro stop along the way."

The possibility of doing a twenty-mile run

with just two weeks' notice sent me into a spiral of self-doubt, and I started to question not just my knee pain — which I was sure would require surgery — but what I suspected was a complete breakdown in my overall body metabolism. Instead of filling out the online twenty-mile race registration under the guidance of my misery-seeking coworkers, I left work early for a doctor's appointment.

My problem? Not overtraining, but over-sweating. I was sweating so much on my training runs that I had to leave my running clothes in the bathtub when I was finished. No one I consulted at work was taking me seriously, which was why I had to step it up a notch and see my doctor.

Thankfully, he took me seriously and asked me a series of questions about my "hyperhydrosis." It wasn't my face or my hands, but my whole body. Not at night, but rather, during the day. Not all day, usually at noon, specifically around mile five or six.

I was starting to feel slightly silly, but the good doctor took me seriously. He took my temperature: 98.6. And my blood pressure: 116 over 64. My heart rate: a steady 52.

We discussed the possibility of me running in the early morning or late evening, when it wasn't so hot out, and he sent me off to get my blood work done. Later I returned to work, where — was it my imagination or did my coworkers seem unusually amused? — I felt a spasm of irritation. It lasted only for a second before I joined the fray collecting in the back of the room. There, surrounded by patients with badly fractured legs and missing limbs, was a coworker seized with a sudden cramp in his right calf.

If we thought we were taking exercise to new levels, we had nothing on the staff dietician. Capt. Jones was a competitive bodybuilder and drove a jeep with a license plate that boldly proclaimed "FIT." She spent hours and hours in the gym and was so defined that as soon as she approached the weight bench, the men, even Elijah, would shamefully leave the weight room and get on a stair climber or elliptical machine instead.

Our clinic was on Capt. Jones's way to the gym, which led Capt. Jones to drop in several times a day under the guise of nutrition counseling. The amputee clinic, with its ongoing stream of homemade cookies from local church ladies and cakes by Jim, was her perfect nightmare.

Capt. Jones was intimidating in manner as

well as physique and had an alarming habit of sneaking up on you. As a result, whenever anyone brought up Capt. Jones in a conversation, they first checked over their shoulder, and even then would just mouth her name.

For a nutrition counselor, Capt. Jones seemed to do very little actual counseling, but her presence in the building was usually enough. The minute Capt. Jones appeared in the clinic, patients and staff everywhere dropped their cookies. Capt. Jones would pop in, do a quiet survey, and then sneak back out.

One morning Capt. Jones surprised us by slipping in during our lunch hour. We were huddled around a computer looking at our latest favorite website, ThisIsWhyYoureFat .com — a site featuring disgusting food creations designed to immediately sabotage your cardiovascular system. It was so outrageous it became an immediate staff favorite. Whenever anyone had a free minute, they'd dial up the site and read the latest submission aloud with relish: "Deep-Fried Spam Wontons!"

Our love affair with this particular website ended at exactly 1209 the day we discovered Capt. Jones in our huddle. Unlike us, she wasn't enraptured by the cholesterol-laden image on the computer screen. Instead, she was horrified. Horrified to the point where she was unable to move. We immediately clicked the site closed, but the damage had been done. It probably would have been better for us to have been caught red-handed with one donut than to be seen reading with genuine appreciation about a deep-fried bacon-wrapped glazed donut.

One of my extra duties was to manage the department in-service calendar. Our weekly in-services were a form of required continuing medical education and usually consisted of medical lectures on topics pertaining to physical therapy. Every Friday morning we had a department in-service, and I was the poor soul tasked to arrange it. If I couldn't find a speaker for a particular Friday, I ended up presenting an in-service. The drama of having to come up with a forty-five-minute presentation with sometimes only minutes to spare was incentive enough to keep the in-service calendar booked weeks in advance.

With that huge guillotine hanging over my head, everyone was a possible in-service candidate to me, even Capt. Jones.

For a person of few words, Capt. Jones was passionate about public speaking. But in spite of her enthusiasm she had relatively

159

little to say. She tried, unsuccessfully, to launch a series of nutrition seminars at the hospital, where there was a noticeable lack of attendance by physical therapy, probably because we were back in our clinic enjoying yet another piece of cake.

While Capt. Jones was on a constant campaign to get us to eat healthfully, there was Jim, her nemesis, and he was just as passionately doing the opposite. They were the devil and angel. On one shoulder was Capt. Jones telling you not to eat that piece of cake, while on the other shoulder Jim was handing it to you.

Besides his homemade cakes, Jim brought in all sorts of culinary treats for the clinic to sample. Under Jim's tutelage, we enjoyed Garrett's cheese popcorn from Chicago, homemade caramel sugars from a specialty store in Maryland, chocolate-covered bacon from California, and Korean noodle dishes he transported from his favorite Korean restaurant, heated up in the occupational therapy kitchen and then distributed in Styrofoam cups to patient and therapist alike.

Capt. Jones must have known what was happening in the PT clinic because she wangled me into setting up four 60-minute nutrition in-services for the physical therapy department. The first and second in-service

I eagerly set up, but by the time Capt. Jones was giving her third and fourth in-service to our department, I was a little more reluctant. Capt. Jones was a dull, dull public speaker. But she peppered her talks with strange gestures, something my coworkers in their boredom had instantly picked up on. After a Capt. Jones lecture, my coworkers spent the rest of the week imitating her whenever I was around. "Just a little fat," they would say, and then they would pretend to pluck an apple off a tree — Capt. Jones's peculiar gesture for fat.

Which was when Capt. Jones decided to do a bodybuilding in-service. This in-service was posted on the staff calendar and was surprisingly highly anticipated. Not because Capt. Jones had miraculously become an interesting public speaker, but because a rumor was stampeding through the department that this was the in-service where Capt. Jones would reveal her secret diet and exercise plan.

The in-service day arrived and the entire department was assembled in the clinic, anxiously awaiting Capt. Jones and her diet and exercise secrets. Capt. Jones did not disappoint, and halfway through her talk, she passed out what seemed to be her personal eating and workout regimen.

She might as well have been handing out gilded copies of the Holy Grail. The rush to get a handout practically resulted in a riot. Luckily there were enough to go around. Everyone settled down and immediately tuned out Capt. Jones as they quickly scanned the printout for information on how they could look like her.

Her exercise plan seemed simple and straightforward. So simple, in fact, it looked like a novice gym routine from the Internet. Which was exactly what it was, I found out later when I dared asked Capt. Jones. "Oh, that's not my plan," she said, scoffing at the very idea. "Mine's much more intense."

The diet plan revealed no great secrets, either. Just the usual well-balanced meal of carbohydrates, proteins, and a small amount of fat.

Capt. Jones remained as unapproachable as ever. But I had a strange experience. I ran into Capt. Jones in the hospital PX (shop), standing in line and loaded down with an armload of potato chip bags and chocolate peanut butter cups. I sneaked up on her. Her face looked pinched and thin. I imagine she had just finished starving herself for a bodybuilding competition.

"Yes," she admitted morosely when she discovered me in line behind her, "I occasionally eat junk food." I waited for her to make her strange plucking gesture. But she didn't. Instead I ran down the hall to my clinic to alert my coworkers. We were free to resume our bad habits.

# TORMENTOR

One morning I got to work to find my coworker Melody waiting, smiling and cheery, with a message for me. Even though Melody is in her early sixties, her skin is smooth and unlined and she doesn't have a single gray hair. Her cheeks are rosy, her body is strong and solid, and she looks like someone who should be standing sturdily on top of a high mountaintop.

Next to Melody, I looked positively pasty. I tumbled into the new century straight out of Generation X, hung over and disappointed. While the color of my skin had taken on a pale yellow cast from so many hours under fluorescent lighting, Melody's cheeks had a healthy alpine glow.

I could tell that Melody had been waiting for me to show up so she could pass along this fun little message because she knew it was exactly the sort of thing that, at 0630, would make me completely nuts.

"Are you seeing Stanz?"

"Yeah."

"His doctor wants him out of bed immediately."

"Which doctor? *Trauma?*"

"You guessed it."

"What's wrong with them? Do those people ever sleep? It is six fucking thirty in the morning!"

Melody laughed and I bolted out of the clinic and ran up four flights of stairs to the ICU, grumbling in irritation.

Melody's patients call her "the Destroyer." Her patients leave the clinic drenched in sweat. Rather than being offended, Melody takes this name as a high compliment and looks pleased anytime it is used.

In the amputee clinic we worked very closely with the doctors in physical medicine and the doctors in orthopedics. Most of the injuries we saw in the amputee section were orthopedic injuries: injuries to bone, muscle, and joint. After the orthopedic surgeons had completed all the surgeries they needed to do, they stepped off the case, and the physical medicine doctors took over the patient's hospital management. The ortho docs and the physical medicine and rehabilitation docs knew all of us and referred to us by our first names, and never

165

called anyone the Destroyer.

But since a blast sometimes opens up bellies, displaces skin, and destroys vessels, the trauma surgeon was also frequently involved. The trauma doctors weren't as familiar with us as orthopedics and PM&R, but they must have heard about the Destroyer, because they were suddenly paging physical therapy about fifteen times a day.

As far as Trauma was concerned, we were thugs for hire. Used to blood and guts and spilled intestines, once they've finished suturing a patient's abdomen shut, they didn't see any reason why they should still be in bed. They frequently consulted us from the intensive care unit, demanding we get the patient out of bed and into a bedside chair. They might have just pushed the patient back from the OR a few hours earlier, but regardless, they wanted us to get upstairs immediately and get this patient moving.

Because in Trauma's world, it is all about what will kill you. And bedrest can certainly kill you. Without movement, blood clots can quickly form in your legs and travel to your lungs; from there it is a short slip into your heart and all of Trauma's hard work is wasted. Lying in bed without coughing or deep breathing can cause pneumonia to develop. If you are immune compromised from other infections or blood loss, pneumonia can kill you. Lying in bed can cause bed sores to form. In a comatose or insensate patient, the skin can break down all the way to the bone: the perfect route for infection to enter your bloodstream and kill you.

If the phone rings in the PT clinic at 0700, we know who it is. It's Trauma. They've been speed-dialing physical therapy since 0600, waiting for someone to show up and answer it. No matter who is calling from the Trauma team, they all sound like they've just done fifteen espresso shots. Everything is urgent. Life or death. "Physical Therapy? It's Trauma! ICU bed four needs to get in a bedside chair, immediately!"

It is almost always a logistics nightmare. The lines and tubes in the ICU aren't long enough. Then there is the question of the ventilator. And the large external fixators. Not to mention the pelvic fractures, which are held in place with a large and cumbersome frame. And then there are the patients themselves. Regarding us with nervous eyes like we are some sort of monster, they will say, "I don't think I should be getting out of bed," as they watch us size up the length of their chest tube.

Still huffing and puffing from my sprint

up the stairs, I exploded into the ICU and ran over to room four. The bed was empty.

I ran back down to the MATC. Melody was still the only person in the PT clinic.

"That was quick," she said, barely looking up from her notes.

"Yeah. Stanz was in the OR. Ortho was doing a washout."

"That shouldn't have stopped you," Melody said, smiling across at me.

"You're right," I grumbled. "I should have busted into the OR with a wheelchair. Trauma's orders!"

Unlike the trauma docs, the orthopedic docs had much better communication with physical therapy. They wouldn't have sent me barreling up the stairs at 0700 to get a patient who had already been scheduled for surgery.

Nearing retirement, Melody had the contented look of someone who had led a gentle life. Her kids were grown and her life was in order, which is why Melody spent her weekends at her lake house "floating."

Melody usually omits the alarming detail that her vacation house is next to an active nuclear power plant. The lake that Melody floats on is the cooling reservoir of the power plant, and the current tumbling out of the power plant rushes toward her on her serene float so strongly that Melody hangs on to a rope tied to the dock to keep from getting blown across the lake. Having seen Melody in this man-made lake just reaffirms for me that Melody has nerves of steel. Something that Melody's patients have known for quite a while.

One of Melody's patients would come back to visit frequently. She liked to tell the story of the first time Melody came into her room. Both of her legs were amputated, and her arms were badly damaged. Melody, she said, looked at her lying in the bed and asked, "What can you move?"

"My wrist."

"Okay. Lift it up ten times."

I'm sure it was more complicated than that. But I laughed every time I heard this story, after first glancing over at Melody. She always looked delighted.

This is exactly the type of poignant rehab story that Trauma is looking for. They know what the Destroyer learned a long time ago — lying in bed doesn't rehabilitate anyone.

Getting Cosmo from his wheelchair to the mat table in the physical therapy clinic was a labor-intensive and painful process. Cosmo would pull his wheelchair up sideways next to the mat table while I lowered it, bringing it to the same height as the seat of his chair. Then Cosmo and I would wrestle his armrest off so he could start to slide himself over, while I followed behind, carrying his shattered leg across. The problem was that I was never quite able to keep up with Cosmo because his leg was so heavy. So in the process of moving over to the mat I would inevitably jerk his leg.

"Fuck," he'd say, and I'd inhale sharply, "Oh! Sorry!"

We would start with the easy stuff — strengthening exercises for his left leg, the amputated side. His amputation never gave him any problems. He would do four-way planks balanced on his stump, and dozens of sit-ups and push-ups while I arranged towel-covered bolsters to support his shattered right leg. Inevitably I'd clumsily bang into his leg and Cosmo would suck his breath in and freeze. I'd begin to apologize, but Cosmo would just squeeze his eyes shut.

I would stretch out his hip on the amputated side, and then Cosmo and I would tackle the problem that was his right leg. Life sure would be a lot easier for Cosmo if he had had the strength to move it. Holding the cage with two hands and standing on a stool to get some leverage, I'd help Cosmo lift his shattered leg up and down. It was swollen and heavy. Red-orange fluid would frequently run in rivulets down his thigh and calf.

Cosmo's knee was starting to fuse together with scar tissue, which needed to be manually broken up. He was a big man. Next to him I felt like a little circus monkey. Climbing on his mat table and grabbing the steel frames encasing his tibia and thigh with both of my hands, I'd lift his leg up and quickly kick a large padded bolster underneath it before my back gave out. With the bolster positioned underneath his knee, I'd kneel in front of him, slide my hands in between the spokes of the ex-fix to grab his tibia just below his knee. Leaning forward, I'd put my weight through my hands to bend his knee. I could get it to about forty-five degrees, and then I'd hit an invisible barrier. Keeping Cosmo's knee at that end point, I'd oscillate up and down like a jackhammer, trying to break through the scar tissue that was keeping his knee from bending. Sweat would roll down my back and I'd feel the muscles in my shoulders and chest tighten up.

I watched Cosmo's eyes while I mobilized his knee, because he would never admit it was painful. Instead, if I pushed too hard his eyes would tear up.

171

When Cosmo's eyes filled with tears, I would hate myself and I would hate my job. What was I doing? What kind of thug had I become?

Still Cosmo was Cosmo. He was going to go home for a couple of weeks on convalescent leave and wanted to know if he could go out on his all-terrain vehicle. "Do you really think that's a good idea?" I asked him. Cosmo stared at me coldly. "Well, wait and fucking see." He said it snidely, feeling around his wheelchair for his packet of cigarettes before pushing himself out of the clinic in a huff.

Cosmo was my last patient that day. After he left, I joined my coworkers in the back of the room to do my notes. It bothered me that Cosmo wanted to bounce around on his ATV when he had enough trouble just getting out of his wheelchair. "He's going to screw his leg up," I muttered to my coworkers, who were busy grumbling about the crazy stuff their patients had done that day, too. "Oh yeah, Tommy took his legs home with him. You've seen him walking. Crazy, right? He is so *not* safe. I told his wife. Do they ever listen to me? No." And then we complained about how we were still at work. Darcy started laughing and said, "If I ever get out of work on time, CNN better do a breaking news story about it."

It was moments like this that drove my Tums addiction. Which was why I stopped at the supermarket on my way home. I was in the antacid section looking at the new chewy cherry Rolaids when someone tapped me on the shoulder. Tracy. We had gone out a few times and then she had started dating someone else.

I had been secretly devastated.

I certainly hadn't planned on running into her while surrounded by tubes of rectal ointments.

While Tracy was filling me in on the latest details of her summer, my heart was revving up and down like a race car engine.

What I really wanted to do was tell Tracy how much I liked her. And how my job was wrecking my stomach lining. And how lonely my life was outside of work, where I isolated myself in quiet conflict-free activities like writing and swimming. But instead I headed off in the direction of the cereal aisle and stepped on an egg.

The fact that an egg was on the floor in the pharmacy section was surprising to me. But I barely had time to register it. My leg shot out from underneath me and I swooped across the aisle with an audible whoop.

It was no wonder Tracy was dating Jessica

instead of me. I was just a hook-up. But Jessica was the real deal.

Jessica had her act together. She wore suits to work and smiled frequently. She carried a BlackBerry and lived in a nice neighborhood. She'd never spent a day bending a guy's knee to the point where it made him cry.

I was nervous and wore beat-up running shoes. I had a beeper clipped to my belt so my boss could use it as a tracking device, and during the day, I stretched mangled legs destroyed by roadside bombs.

I never talked about my job and no one ever asked. Because, I guess, I was not a lawyer or upper-level management; I was just a good person stuck in the trenches of humanity.

I didn't turn around to see if Tracy had witnessed me slip and almost fall. Instead, I tripped out of the supermarket, shaking egg off my shoe, and walked down the block to the liquor store to pick up a six-pack of beer.

Back at home I took two Tums EX, popped open a beer, and began tediously writing, a hobby I had recently picked up again. *Perhaps,* I thought, *if I could add "published author" behind my name, my life would miraculously come together.* I would be a real person, and not a physical therapist with an antacid addiction.

I took a break from writing and went downstairs to get the mail. In my mailbox was a rejection letter for the book of short stories I had been trying to shop around. Even though I'd gotten dozens of rejection letters and should be used to it, this time my ego caved in like a crumpled-up paper bag.

Suddenly I couldn't stand to be inside my apartment one more second. Not sure exactly where I should go, I decided to drive over to Home Depot and buy the rug I'd been admiring online for weeks. If I could have mail-ordered it I would have, because only a root canal was more painful than going to Home Depot — an entire warehouse of people in the clutches of a home disaster.

But I lucked out because the guy in the rug department was nice and gave me a twenty percent off coupon that I could redeem at the service counter.

There were two people standing behind the service counter studiously examining their cuticles. No one seemed to notice me, even though I had a nine-foot carpet rolled up and towering precariously over me. I stood there patiently until one of them abruptly snapped, *"Lady, go to the cashier!"*

I went to the cashier.

There were only three people ahead of me and the guy in front was buying only a roll of duct tape. I felt lucky. But suddenly the guy at the front wanted to go back and get another roll of duct tape. The cashier let the guy go and the line watched, slack-jawed, as the guy disappeared into the back of the store.

We waited, all faces turned expectantly toward the end of the store like we were standing at the end of the marina awaiting our luxury ocean liner to crest the distant horizon. Except we weren't. We were in the Aspen Hill Home Depot in a bad part of town with shopping carts full of drywall and cans of paint.

After ten minutes, we saw the guy re-appear. We watched in amazement as he carefully shuffled back with his roll of duct tape and an armload of different-sized plywood boards. He staggered back to the front of the line, breathing heavily and perspiring, dropping his boards loudly in front of the cashier.

The cashier started to slowly scan each board as the tape guy perused the candy display.

I looked at my watch and realized it was almost nine thirty. My alarm was going to be ringing in seven and a half hours! And then I'd be back at work, neck deep in chaos. Why was I at this Home Depot? I should have been at home right now crawling into bed. I looked over my shoulder and was alarmed to see our line had grown to nine people.

Suddenly the cashier announced that it was time for his break and his line was now closed. After a few seconds of angry protests, my line scattered. Everyone ran into other lines except me. I couldn't move anywhere fast with my heavy rug. I dragged it past check-out lane after check-out lane, realizing I was number fifteen in every single line.

I went back to the service counter.

At the service counter, the cashiers alternated between ignoring me and looking at me with disgust. Suddenly one of them piped up, "Hey, lady! What are you doing here again? Are you stupid?"

*Am I stupid?* For a second all I could see was white. I *was* stupid. For trying so hard to pay for a rug that no one wanted to sell me. For the ten hours a day I spent working with patients who would never really get one hundred percent better. And for always losing the girl because I never have any self-confidence.

I hoisted the rug onto my shoulder and

looked at the guy behind the service counter. He had already started to ignore me again. And then I pulled a move one hundred percent inspired by Cosmo, who never gave a damn about what anyone else thought. I blasted past the service counter and right out of the store.

Stealing a nine-by-twelve-foot rug is not like stealing a pack of gum. It's blatantly obvious, like stealing a dishwasher.

But no one said anything to me.

*"Hello!"* I wanted to shout. *"Look at me! I'm stealing a rug."*

But I was as invisible as ever.

I stalked out to the parking lot, past the fleet of spotless SUVs to my Ford hatchback. I opened the hatchback and roughly shoved the rug in. Even though I pushed the rug all the way up to the windshield, half of it stuck out behind my car.

I left it that way and drove home.

I didn't drive slowly, I drove fast, zooming past the other cars as I talked excitedly into my cell phone to my friend Melissa who worked in a nursing home and was not used to getting these sorts of phone calls.

I spoke in point-by-point descriptions, like a police blotter.

"Leaving the parking lot."

"Turning on Georgia Avenue."

178

And then, "What do you think I should do?"

Melissa, who up to this point had been listening quietly, screamed, "What do you mean what do *I* think *you* should do? *You've* already done it, if *you* ask *me*!"

I had gone to Home Depot in an attempt to straighten up my life. But somewhere between the flooring department and the parking lot I had turned into a criminal on the run.

The next morning I was back in the amputee clinic. Cosmo slid out of his wheelchair and onto the therapy mat while I carefully carried his leg across.

*"Fuck!"*

"Sorry!"

While Cosmo struggled through the first set of painful mat exercises, I sat on a rolling stool beside him. I was exhausted from my late night. In the window, a tour group was examining us with wide eyes. I'm sure they thought I was some sort of devil. I thought guiltily about the rug, still rolled up along the back wall of my living room. I was the devil.

"Cosmo," I said after a long silence, "if you want to try going out on your all-terrain vehicle, I'm fine with it."

Cosmo grinned. "Fuck, yeah!"

"Just don't go stealing any rugs," I joked. Cosmo looked at me curiously for a second, and then quickly scooted out of the clinic before I could change my mind.

# It's Not Me, It's You

One day when working with my patient Sam, an above-knee amputee, I noticed he was swinging his prosthetic leg in a half circle at the knee joint when he walked. "That's an alignment issue," I said. "You need to go see Pat."

Sam's prosthetist, Pat, is an anxious round man with pink skin and thinning gray hair. He's a nice guy, a dedicated prosthetist, but he has no sense of humor — a trait that Sam instantly picked up on. "That dude is so fucking serious!" he'd tell me. And then in the next breath, describe what "Big Sexy" was wearing. "Big Sexy" was what Sam called Pat. Pat despised this nickname and around Sam would become immediately sour as he anticipated Sam's next stunt, including such memorable events as when he showed up for a prosthetic fitting appointment without any underwear on.

Sam was fascinated with Pat. He constantly commented on what Pat was doing, wearing, thinking, usually with the lead-in "Big Sexy." Pat, on hearing his hated nickname, would just scowl and snap, "Don't call me that."

Pat sent Sam right back to me. "He says to tell you it's operator error," Sam reported. Meaning, it's the physical therapist's fault, not the prosthetist's.

There were seven full-time prosthetists at Walter Reed. They were responsible for fitting the patient with an artificial limb (prosthesis). They customized the prosthesis to the patient, and aligned the joints in the artificial limb to match the patient's available range of motion, balance ability, and strength. On the other end of the building, the physical therapist taught new amputees how to use the prosthetic limb, worked on increasing their strength to be able to move a heavy prosthesis, and did numerous balance and agility drills to build confidence and the skills needed to negotiate uneven terrain, curbs, and hills. Together we got the soldier walking again. But it didn't necessarily feel like a team effort. It felt like a civil war. We might work out in the gym with the prosthetists during lunch, but as soon as we were back on the clock, we went right back to the status quo — which was to immediately disagree with the other's recommendation. The only thing we ever agreed on was that the other one was to blame.

Sam's interactions with Pat usually took place in front of an audience of at least eight other amputees, all of whom were clamoring for Pat's attention. The prosthetics department was always busy. It was the local diner, the corner bar, the barbershop. It was the place to be and be seen. The place to hang out, shoot the shit, get the gossip, and complain about your physical therapist. While you were hanging around, maybe you could coax Big Sexy into padding your socket a little here, filing it down there, and maybe order you that cool new prosthetic foot you just saw another guy bounding down the hallway in. When the prosthetists left the clinic to get a little reprieve, they were always easy to spot — and corner — in their white Santa's helper aprons covered in a haze of casting plaster. They also left a handy trail of Hansel and Gretel dusty white footprints behind them.

Because of the constant commotion in the waiting room, the prosthetic department never answered their phone. Which meant in addition to patients, physical therapists were also squeezed into the melee. The noise of the phone ringing and ringing just faded into the background, as everyone shouted over one another, vying for the prosthetist's attention.

When the commotion got to be too much to handle, usually after a short, overwhelming two-minute appearance, the prosthetist would escape back into his locked laboratory. There was a combination lock on the door to the lab, a combination that had to be changed weekly as more and more patients and physical therapists figured out the four-digit combination and skirted past the mob in the waiting room to walk right in.

Behind the locked door was a world that could have been Santa's workshop. A half-dozen work benches lined one wall. Prosthetic legs were everywhere. And a big oven in the corner, used to heat up the plastic for the sockets, kept the room toasty warm. Sockets and legs were assembled onsite, usually with a lightning-fast twelve-hour turnaround.

Sometimes the prosthetists would try to avoid the chaos of the prosthetic clinic by seeing a patient in the amputee clinic instead. The amputee clinic had a black rubber floor, which meant there was inevitably an explosion after a prosthetist walked halfway across our freshly mopped floor, inadvertently leaving a trail of messy white footprints.

*"Aarrgh. Stop right there!"*

But in spite of them tracking up our floors, we were always ecstatic to see a prosthetist in the clinic because all of us, patients and therapists alike, needed just a few minutes of their time. The prosthetists, when properly buttered up, were magicians. They could clean up our patients' gait deviations with just a few clicks of an Allen wrench. They reminded me of my bike mechanic who could, with a few seemingly minor adjustments, get my bicycle shifting smoothly.

Often, when Big Sexy walked through clinic, I would grab him. I always had a patient who needed some prosthetic adjustments, and these days it was Sam. Pat would sit on the floor, stick his Allen wrench in and out of Sam's prosthetic leg, and alternately tighten one screw and loosen another. By changing the angle of the prosthetic foot, Sam was miraculously able to roll over his toe in a way he couldn't before.

But, as usual, before reluctantly agreeing to any adjustments, Big Sexy first blamed Sam's gait deviations on "operator error," while I was just as stubbornly insisting it was an "alignment issue."

Both of us could agree on only one thing: *It's not me, it's you!*

When I couldn't get Big Sexy's attention to make an adjustment, I'd just try to do it myself. Like many of my PT cohorts in a busy amputee clinic, I knew enough prosthetic adjustments to be dangerous. The patient might have just had the pylons on his prosthetic legs extended five minutes earlier in the prosthetic clinic, making him taller (and more attractive to the ladies), only to have them immediately shortened in the physical therapy clinic. "What are you thinking? You look like you are on stilts!" We'd recommend Genium knees for a new patient because they were durable and could stand up to our strengthening drills, only to have the patient show up the next morning in power knees — heavy prosthetic legs that motored the patient around. We might send a patient down to see the prosthetist about plantar flexing the foot to get him landing on his heel better, only to have the patient sent back to us with a suggestion to strengthen his quads instead.

We PTs were partly to blame because we treated the prosthetic department like a walk-in clinic. "Just go see if he can see you now," we'd say. The prosthetists were much better sports at receiving the gift of a patient five minutes before they closed. If a prosthetist did the same thing to us, we had a complete meltdown. The patient would approach us apprehensively, seemingly fully aware this was going to happen, probably because his prosthetist briefed him before sending him in.

"She's going to have a meltdown. Just ignore it. Now, you need to work on landing on that heel. Strengthen your quads. Tell her it's operator error."

While we were constantly sparring with the prosthetists, we followed the orthopedic surgeons around like yogi mentors. We treated the same patients, frequently passing them back and forth. The orthopedic surgeon did the surgery, and later, the physical therapist did the rehab. We envied the surgeons for the luxury they had of only having to see an irritating patient for a short ten-minute consult. After that, the patient was in the OR already heavily sedated.

Physical therapy has a high burnout rate. The long hours of intense one-on-one time is emotionally fatiguing. And while we universally love our patients, there's always one rotten apple in the bunch who just breaks you down. Which might be why if you query most PTs, they'll tell you if they ever decided to change careers they'd become an orthopedic surgeon, or, if they're being really truthful, a dermatologist. "Can you imagine? Getting *paid* to pop pimples?"

Once a week I was sent over to the orthopedic surgery department to help cover Dr. C's sports medicine clinic. For the patients who weren't surgical candidates, I would start them on their initial physical therapy exercises. And for the ones who were going to have surgery, I would explain what their upcoming rehab would consist of.

Dr. C is a tall, thin man with a pleasant manner. He listens carefully to the patients, spending much more time with them than any of the other orthopedic surgeons do. The patients talk for a long time, but Dr. C doesn't. His explanations are to the point and make absolutely no sense.

"Well, sir, I would say you've got cowboy knees."

"What?"

"I could drive a truck in between your knees. Now, we could talk about surgery, but you've got to tell me if the pain is bad enough to talk joint replacement."

To the patients who want surgery but are not good surgical candidates, he uses a farm analogy.

"Ma'am, I would say the horse is out of the barn."

"Excuse me?"

"The horse has left the barn."

"Does this mean you're going to operate on me?"

"Well, that would be like poking a skunk. I know it hurts, but you've got to think of it as fleas and ticks. Annoying, but not a show stopper."

Dr. C doesn't reserve his colloquialisms for just his patients. On hearing that two of his residents were dating each other, he sniffed it off as "picking low-hanging fruit" and advised, "I wouldn't throw myself on that grenade."

Once a day, Dr. C encountered a difficult patient. A difficult patient in Dr. C's world is a patient who doesn't seem to get his farm analogies. This patient is usually a quiet patient, seemingly devoid of personality who, instead of nodding at Dr. C's skunk and horse analogies, just fixes Dr. C with a blank, empty stare. When this happened, Dr. C would be quick to lose his cool.

*"Team meeting!"* he'd announce, pointing to the X-ray room.

No one was allowed to skip these special team meetings, not even the physical therapist.

189

"Oh no. You're coming in here, too. Now shut that door."

I shut the door behind me and Dr. C would look at all of us for a long time before he asked the question he always asks.

"Did anyone feel a vacuum in there?"

No one says anything.

"Did anyone feel a breeze?"

Dr. C would go around the room.

"Anna, did you feel a vacuum in there? No? John, did you feel a breeze?"

Everyone knew better than to say anything, and we held our breath waiting for the impending explosion.

*"Because he was sucking the life out of me! Sucking the life out of me!"*

We'd bite our lips and try not to laugh.

*"Anna!"*

"Sir?"

*"Did you find this patient to be difficult?"*

"I did, sir."

"How did this patient get on my schedule?" Dr. C would demand, before bellowing, *"Who put this patient on my schedule?"* and storming out of the room, as if to find the source.

The source was sitting down the hall, and Dr. C knew better than to actually storm into her office. Chris was Dr. C's secretary, but the rest of us referred to her as the Moat

190

Dragon. She knew about her nickname and did not care. She knew we were all afraid of her.

My first introduction to Chris had been at a CPR renewal course Chris taught for the orthopedics department. Every two years we needed to renew our CPR requirements. For me, a relatively new staff member, it was my sixth CPR renewal course since starting physical therapy school. I could only imagine how many times the more experienced staff members had sat through the familiar four-hour course — a course that, by the second time you take it, you can do in your sleep. We all poured into the lecture hall with our crossword puzzles and cups of coffee, braced for the endless mandatory videos broken up by taking parts of the multiple-choice exam.

Chris stood on the auditorium stage, monitoring that everyone was seated and quiet.

"Are the doors shut?" Chris yelled. "Make sure those doors are shut!"

Then Chris turned her attention to the crowd of orthopedic residents, surgeons, physician assistants, occupational therapists, and physical therapists squeezed into the auditorium.

"Okay, listen up. *Listen up!* You all just

passed. *Did you hear me? You passed.* If you have a problem with this, come down and *see me.*"

Everyone sat upright in their chairs, but no one moved.

"Did you hear me? You all just passed. *Now get out of here.* And if anything that happened in this room gets out, you will sit down with me for a full four-hour review session."

Stunned, no one moved. But only for a second. In a clattering of feet, everyone jumped up and ran out of the auditorium.

Chris would overhear Dr. C's temper tantrums and yell down the hall, *"I put him on your schedule. Is there a problem?"*

And with that, Dr. C was always silenced.

But everyone loved Dr. C, especially Chris. You couldn't help but like him, and I found his colloquialisms to be useful analogies applied not just to clinical scenarios, but to life in general. No class in physical therapy school prepared me to counsel a patient dealing with a life-changing injury. But luckily there was Dr. C, who provided the words, the script, and the self-help.

When the injuries were ramping up, Dr. C's phrases became a way to tread lightly: "Don't poke a skunk!" and a suitable way to comfort a patient: "The horse hasn't left the barn yet."

If they were having bad phantom pain: "Think of it as fleas and ticks. Annoying but not a show stopper."

After a couple hours with a difficult and noncompliant patient, I sometimes felt a buzzing in my ear. Was my job sucking the life out of me? How *did* this person get on my schedule?

# RUNNING

On my bike ride to work one morning, I came across a duck sitting in the middle of the bike path. I slowed down and waited to see if he'd fly away, and when he didn't, I got concerned. Concerned I would have to do something and I was already late for work.

I felt bad for the duck, but mostly I felt bad for myself. Why did I have to be the one to find him? My morning routine didn't need any additional wrenches thrown in. From outside appearance, he seemed okay. No ruffled feathers or dirt under his beak. But he wasn't moving.

I laid my bike down and walked up to the duck, thinking I'd put him in my messenger bag and bring him to work with me and let Capt. Dumont deal with him. Capt. Dumont is a big animal lover. She has four dogs and a cat, and anytime anyone goes out of town, they drop their dog off at the captain's for the weekend.

As I was unbuckling my messenger bag, I could hear Melody in my other ear, annoyed. Despite looking like a wholesome Swiss miss, Melody is much more practical. She wouldn't have stopped. "Bring a duck to work? That's crazy. And then what? You think he wants to sit in a box behind the weight bench all day?"

Luckily the duck made up his mind and hopped quickly off the bike path. I followed behind him making clucking noises, as if that would entice him to trust me. He flapped his wings at me.

If the captain had been there, she would have just grabbed him quick, around the middle, before he had time to react. Capt. Dumont would have forcibly saved him.

I looked down the bike path and considered calling Capt. Dumont on my cell phone. She'd rescue the duck for sure. But it was 0615 and Capt. Dumont was hidden away in the hospital doing whatever it was she did every morning before the rest of us got to work. There were a few joggers in the distance. I figured one of them might eventually help the duck, and got back on my bike.

At work I mentioned to Melody that I was late because I stopped to try and catch an injured duck. She looked predictably annoyed and asked, "Why on earth would you do that?"

Later I saw Capt. Dumont and told her about the duck. She smiled and took a sip of her coffee and said exactly what I thought she'd say: "I would have caught him and brought him in here. I would have grabbed him quick, around the middle."

I hung my head a little bit. Of course Capt. Dumont would have saved the duck. If the hospital was on fire, Capt. Dumont would pull burning people out of the building until she caught on fire herself. Capt. Dumont is absolutely selfless.

That week, eight new triple amputees arrived. The week before, four.

These were challenge patients, rare patients, back in the days of Iraq, but now they were seemingly the norm. While we had seen complicated patients out of Iraq, in 2010 most of our patients were coming out of Afghanistan. At this point in the game, the insurgents were much more adept at building highly destructive bombs. And on the opposite end, our medics and surgeons had become much better at saving the lives of patients who would have easily died a few years earlier. With everyone on foot patrol and stepping on buried bombs, the injuries were many and extreme. Almost all our patients were at least a double amputee. If we saw a patient with just one missing limb, we stopped to take a second look and asked each other how that was possible.

Capt. Dumont always took the worst of the worst. She shielded us.

That week, one of her patients died in the ICU. His legs had been amputated just below the groin and his belly was splayed open. The infection was uncontrollable. It spread up his body. He remained fully conscious and aware of what was happening to him to the very end. His mother was there. And Capt. Dumont.

We only heard about it afterward, at a work happy hour. Capt. Dumont didn't go into details. The happy hour got quiet, each of us thinking about it in silence over matching mugs of cold beer. How was it possible that a soldier had dissolved into death and we had been so busy with our own patients that we never even knew about it?

And I'm sure we all hit on the same thought: If there was anyone you'd want with you at the very end, it would be Capt. Dumont.

Before going with patients to their death, Capt. Dumont had, during the days of Iraq, accompanied several soldiers' wives to the delivery room. While their husbands were drifting in and out of consciousness in a hospital bed at Walter Reed, their pregnant wives delivered their babies with Capt. Dumont at their side.

Because if you had a problem, Capt. Dumont would be there for you. It didn't matter what it was. Need a ride to the airport or an attachment for your lawn mower? Capt. Dumont would help you. Fell off your bike and hurt your arm? Capt. Dumont would answer her cell phone on the first ring and be there ten minutes later to pick you up, dust you off, and drive you home. I've never gotten arrested, but if it happened, I knew who my one phone call would go to.

For someone so giving, Capt. Dumont never revealed any personal details about herself — no one even knew her first name. From her pressed army camos, to her athletic build and short hair (common in a military setting), Capt. Dumont didn't have to work hard at not sticking out. Which was exactly the way she preferred it. Capt. Dumont liked nothing better than to blend right into the background.

The staff bulletin board was decorated with pictures of everyone on staff, but one person's photo was subtly missing: Capt. Dumont. Capt. Dumont never allowed photographs of herself to be taken. With one exception. In the back of the clinic, carefully concealed behind the mailboxes, where Capt. Dumont never went because she never checked her mail, an aging Polaroid was taped to the wall. It was a picture of the heavy metal band ZZ Top posing with Capt. Dumont.

Staring sternly at the camera and surrounded by the long-haired, long-bearded band members, some of whom had their arms draped over her shoulders, Capt. Dumont looked completely, wackily, out of place. Nonregulation pictures, signs, even calendars were not allowed on the walls. The army is totally militant about this. But this one photograph — because it was so brilliant — was the one exception.

Right before things got so heated up in Afghanistan and we weren't seeing so many new patients, the administration thought we should also start seeing retired amputees. Older patients. Each of us would get a retiree.

Each day, another one of my coworkers was introduced to their retiree, usually a gentle and active member of their community. Emma's patient was a short, spry woman in her sixties who worked full time, was all over Facebook, and as fate would have it, had a weekly subscription to *People* magazine. Jim got a diabetic patient who was constantly cheating on his diet. Learning how to walk on a prosthetic leg just enabled him to escape into the cafeteria and eat banana cream pie.

I waited to see who I was going to get.

One morning I came to work and at the far end of the room was a wheelchair with what appeared to be a pile of coats in it. Capt. Dumont pointed to the wheelchair. "Your retiree."

There was Mr. Jones, a pleasant elderly man in a hat and overcoat. He was eighty years old. He was so sunk down into his wheelchair, I couldn't tell where his coat stopped and he began. I asked him if he could scoot out of his wheelchair and onto one of the treatment tables and he lurched back and forth, trying to gather the momentum to stand up.

"Oh, hang on," I said, reaching for him. "Let me help you."

"No, no. I can do it. I can do it!"

He hadn't walked in over a year. His leg had been amputated below the knee and afterward he'd been sent to a nursing home, where he spent so much time in his wheelchair that he couldn't straighten his legs out anymore. Lying on his back on the therapy mat table, his knees and hips stayed bent at ninety-degree angles like he was still sitting in a chair.

I glanced over at my coworkers, who watched me with some amusement as I struggled to stretch Mr. Jones out. He couldn't stand up on his remaining leg because he couldn't get it straight. I could feel the first few trickles of sweat tickle down my ribcage as I worked on Mr. Jones's legs, and with a shiver of fear, I knew getting him to walk again was going to take a long, long time. Something that Capt. Dumont must have known when she assigned Mr. Jones to me.

The fast pace of the amputee clinic was perfect for me, but when it came to a slow-moving, gentle eighty-year-old veteran, I was totally out of my element. Or as Darcy would explain to Hollywood while pointing at me, I was "thrown under the bus."

I needed time to work independently with Mr. Jones before the room turned into a complete zoo, so I needed to sell him on the 0700 time slot. It was a rare patient who wanted to come in at that hour, but to my surprise, Mr. Jones snapped it up. He was Mr. Motivated, and eager to get out of that nursing home. Walking into work in the morning, I could see him in the back of the room, a lone figure on the recumbent bike, pedaling slowly with one leg.

I'd take my coat off and he'd slide off the bicycle and into his wheelchair. He would propel himself slowly over to the mat table, where I'd wait, clenching and unclenching my hands, eager to get going.

"How about I give you a hand?"

"I can do it. Just taking my time."

"I can help you."

"No. No. I'm getting there."

I'd eye the clock and get frantic; soon the room would be crammed to the gills with other injured soldiers and marines. If Mr. Jones didn't get on a mat table soon, I wouldn't have one-on-one time to spend with him. With each new medevac flight, one-on-one time was fast becoming a rare commodity in our clinic.

I timed him once. Twelve minutes! I took a breath in, trying to calm myself. A hard thing to do in our clinic, which was *Go! Go! Go!* all day long.

After I'd finish stretching Mr. Jones out, we'd head over to the parallel bars and practice standing up. I knew by then it would take Mr. Jones at least eight minutes to get to the parallel bars, but instead of being productive, I'd dash back and forth in the parallel bars, reserving our spot in case anyone in the clinic didn't realize I was trying to hurry my octogenarian in there. Not sure how to handle what I perceived as wasted time, I constantly fretted indecisively, *Should I log onto a computer and do some notes? Should I try and get him moving a little quicker?*

"You okay?" I'd yell across the room.

"I'm okay. Just taking my time."

"Okay. Just checking."

And then fifteen seconds later. "How's it going? How about a push? Should I give you a little push?"

"No, no. I'm getting there. I'm doing all right."

"Okay. If you say so."

I'd stand in the parallel bars, sweating and feeling the pulse beat in my neck. *Should I catch up on paperwork? Should I organize the wound care cart? What should I do?*

In the meantime the clinic would start to fill up with patients. My other patients would trickle in. Gradually Mr. Jones would make his way over to the parallel bars, and I'd exhale in relief. He was there.

As the casualties from Afghanistan increased, Capt. Dumont and Maj. Tavner started to argue about Mr. Jones. *I should discharge him. I should keep him. I should discharge him. I should keep him.* Since no one could come to an agreement, I kept Mr. Jones on my schedule.

During lunch, while the rest of the staff gathered around Emma for a group reading of *People* magazine, Capt. Dumont would go running.

For someone who was so private, Capt. Dumont was always suspiciously casting around for a lunchtime running partner. I'd watch her do it and couldn't figure out if she was asking us just to be polite, or if she really did want the company. One day I decided to find out. I changed into shorts and a T-shirt and joined Capt. Dumont outside, where she was nonchalantly doing some light stretches. When I came out, Capt. Dumont smiled. "Ready?" I nodded and Capt. Dumont blasted down the service road beside the hospital like she had been shot out of a cannon.

I sprinted after her, my feet drumming quickly across the asphalt. I couldn't imagine why on earth we were running so fast, but tried to maintain a good sprinting form as we rounded the corner and careened past the Old Red Cross Building and up the hill past the National Museum of Health and

Medicine. The Mologne House, where I caught a smudged glimpse of Cosmo sitting on the back deck smoking a cigarette, was just a colorful blur. We ran past the administration building and the plaque where the famous "Sniper Tree" had stood. Confederate soldiers, hiding in the branches of the tall tulip tree, had fired at the neighboring Union Fort Stevens back when Walter Reed had been a Confederate camp in the Civil War.

There's no way any of them would have been able to get a bead on Capt. Dumont, but I would have been an easy target.

We raced out of the 16th Street gate and headed south toward downtown Washington. I tried to engage Capt. Dumont in some small talk, hoping it would slow her down. But Capt. Dumont didn't take the bait. She answered with brisk, one-word answers and kept up her blistering tempo.

Across the street from Walter Reed, we detoured quickly into Rock Creek Park. There in the park we ran through autumn leaves and along the creek that, if you continue to follow it, empties out into the Potomac. It was so far removed from the fluorescent lights and craziness of the hospital, I half couldn't believe we were out there.

We ran along the creek for a couple miles before beginning our descent back to Walter Reed. This time we left the park and ran back through the neighborhoods surrounding Walter Reed. Walter Reed's 16th Street side backs up to gorgeous million-dollar homes, while its Georgia Avenue side backs up to a street full of liquor stores, panhandlers, and the occasional early morning prostitute.

A half mile from Walter Reed we passed Fort Stevens, the site of the only Civil War battle inside the District of Columbia. The conflict only lasted two days, but was notable for being the one time an American president came under direct combat fire. Abraham Lincoln and his wife, Mary, had ridden out for the day to watch the battle. In spite of Confederate sharpshooters firing at soldiers from Walter Reed's Sniper Tree, President Lincoln kept climbing around on the parapet of the fort in his trademark stovepipe hat. A young captain, Oliver Wendell Holmes, is credited with yelling at Lincoln to, "Get down, you damn fool!"

The Confederate troops suffered heavy losses and quickly retreated. Their commander later remarked, "We didn't take Washington, but we scared Lincoln like hell."

The forty-one Union soldiers who died defending Washington during the battle for Fort Stevens are buried at Battleground National Cemetery, a half mile away from Walter Reed. As Capt. Dumont and I ran past it in Walter Reed's hundred and first year, the tombstones were much weathered and the cemetery was listed as one of the most endangered historic sites in Washington, D.C., by the D.C. Preservation League.

We got back in time for a quick two-minute shower, and I headed back into our chaotic clinic with a bright red face and feeling slightly faint. I had never turned that kind of color before.

The clinic was packed as usual with staff members, patients, visitors, and a few wandering celebrities when I sat down behind one of the computers to get a jump-start on my notes. Capt. Dumont was standing near me, gazing out at the chaos and eating her afternoon grapefruit. She absentmindedly offered me a slice despite the fact that she had been habitually offering me a piece of her grapefruit every afternoon for the past four years and I had always said, "No, thank you."

Then she sat down at the computer next to me. I heard her tapping on the computer and then suddenly inhale in alarm. I glanced over at her computer screen. "8 U.S. Soldiers Killed in Afghanistan." Soldiers killed meant another medevac full of amputees was heading our way. For such a private person, Capt. Dumont surprised me with her outburst. But her patient had just died, and a new one was en route.

I felt Capt. Dumont tap me on the shoulder then, no doubt to offer me a slice of grapefruit. Without looking up, I said, "No, thank you."

I absentmindedly repeated, "No, thank you," when Capt. Dumont tapped me on the shoulder again, and said it again when I felt Capt. Dumont tapping me again. Suddenly Capt. Dumont clamped her hand down on my shoulder and gave me a vigorous shake. I turned to look at her. She had her hands around her neck in the universal sign of choking. When I didn't react, she pointed urgently at her throat. "Would you like a towel?" I asked, pulling a clean folded towel off the shelf.

Capt. Dumont quickly shook her head no and frantically made the sign for choking again and I paused, towel in the air, as it slowly dawned on me what was happening. For a second I panicked. Then I grabbed Capt. Dumont quick, right around the middle. With her back to me and my arms encircling her, I forcefully did the Heimlich. Nothing happened. I cursed and repeated it harder. Capt. Dumont slumped against me, and on the third try, the grapefruit wedge shot out of the captain's mouth and ricocheted off the wall.

We paused for a moment, Capt. Dumont with her hand on the wall, and me standing anxiously behind her.

"Thanks," Capt. Dumont said ruefully.

"No problem," I said, feeling suddenly awkward. Capt. Dumont was the one I constantly ran to for help — all day long. She was my superhero. Now, by some weird twist of the universe, we had momentarily flip-flopped. Not knowing what to do or say, I dropped back down in my computer chair and went right back to finishing my notes. Capt. Dumont lingered briefly, and then walked out onto the floor of the room. The chaos in the room continued all around us.

Staring rigidly at the computer screen, I felt little pricks of panic bubble out onto the surface of my skin. What if it hadn't worked? What if Capt. Dumont had died? I was astounded and slightly furious that in spite of being surrounded by fifty other people, no one had noticed me lifting Capt. Dumont off her feet as I gave her the Heimlich in the back of the room.

Capt. Dumont was grateful and brought it up to me later a few times, but I always brushed off her thanks. I didn't want to talk about it. I felt awkward and bashful. And I would get upset all over again just thinking about the day Capt. Dumont almost choked to death in the back of the Fishbowl.

Instead, I kept running with Capt. Dumont. It remained agonizing and torturous, and I always felt like I was on the verge of having a heart attack. During those moments when I felt like the big one was near, I consoled myself with the knowledge that if my heart exploded in Rock Creek Park, Capt. Dumont would save me.

And I ran with Capt. Dumont because it was something I could do. Something I wouldn't have been able to do as a Walter Reed amputee. With legs cut off high at the thighs and a belly splayed open.

I avoided reading any news about Afghanistan, and Capt. Dumont avoided eating grapefruit. Still, no one could come to a decision about Mr. Jones. Influenced by the other patients, Mr. Jones had started wearing beach shorts and T-shirts with slogans across his chest. He was walking sturdily around the clinic now with two canes, a metal prosthetic leg, and a pair of sporty black Reeboks. He would survey the young soldiers around him. He laughed at their jokes while simultaneously telling them to behave.

Every other day another medevac arrived. The new soldiers made their first appearance in the amputee clinic via cardiac chair, with lines and tubes and machines draped across them. They looked bewildered, scared, angry, sad. The other soldiers and marines reassured them. And from across the room, Capt. Dumont and I would watch as Mr. Jones got up and began to walk slowly and steadily toward them.

# WINTER IN JULY

"What's wrong with you?" King Cosmo interrupted his conversation with another soldier to ask, after he noticed me shivering uncontrollably in the corner. I was bundled up in multiple layers, but our clinic still felt like a walk-in freezer to me.

While I resembled an arctic explorer, in long underwear and a thick wool sweater, Cosmo, in his shorts and T-shirts, looked like he just stumbled off a tropical beach. He didn't think it was cold, and most of the other patients didn't either, because as amputees, they have less surface area and have a harder time cooling down.

It was so cold in there that it wasn't unusual to see a physical therapist wiping down mat tables with disinfectant spray in the morning while the puffball on the end of his ski hat bobbled above his head. While the patients chugged bottles of Gatorade and wiped the sweat off their faces with gym towels, ten feet away a group of physical therapists huddled around a portable plug-in heater we'd nicknamed "The Fire."

For several years we had lobbied for a coffeemaker. The frigid temperatures would at least be slightly bearable, we told the administrators, if we had access to hot coffee. But the administration didn't want us drinking beverages in the clinic, since we were on display to high-profile visitors through the glass walls.

But then Darcy got divorced and showed up at work with a hot water kettle. The kettle had been a wedding gift. While it was shocking that there was an actual contraband tea kettle in the clinic, it was more unsettling that Darcy was the one who brought it in. Darcy never rocked the boat. She was high-spirited, but always professional, and a hands-down fantastic physical therapist.

But we all enthusiastically agreed, after a few weeks of hot tea every morning, that Darcy's divorce was the best thing to ever happen to us. The kettle was amazing. Fill it with water and press a button, and in under a minute you had hot water. And when someone important came in, we could easily hide it away under the sink.

We branched out from Tetley to Earl Grey

and chamomile, hot chocolate, and instant chai. In the frigid arctic air, having a cup of something hot to drink was soothing. It made being at work at 0630 seem not so bad. After all, if I was at home, I'd probably be drinking a hot beverage, too.

The kettle was on first thing in the morning and then throughout the day. It was standard to announce to the entire clinic, in a singsong voice, "The kettle is on!" when you put some hot water on for your tenth cup of tea.

There was really only one problem with the kettle, and that was this: It was not a coffeemaker. Soon we began creating tea bags filled with coffee to dunk in our hot water. This was an elaborate and time-consuming project that lasted only two weeks, at which point Sgt. Hernandez made a unilateral decision and brought in a French press.

While Hernandez preferred coffee over tea, what really motivated him to bring in the French press were all the tea bags that were accumulating in the clinic. He hated clutter and attacked it in a slash-and-burn fashion, blindly sweeping everything into a large rubber trash can. If there weren't any important personal papers to throw out, he would go through the staff refrigerator ruthlessly tossing out lunches, including, once, a sandwich I had purchased only a few hours earlier.

Hernandez quickly converted the counter-top into a highly complicated barista station. This wasn't Nescafé he was brewing. Humming busily to himself, Hernandez filled the illicit kettle with water and turned it on. Then he got out the coffee beans, grinder, and French press — which he stored in a hospital-issue emesis basin under the sink. While Hernandez ground the coffee beans and filled the French press with coffee and hot water, coffee drinkers eager to get on Hernandez's good side scattered off to the DFAC to get creamers and sugar. Meanwhile, back in the MATC, the coffee grinds soaked, and Hernandez set out coffee stirrers and napkins he kept in a box under the sink. We pulled the contraband DFAC creamers and packets of sugar out of our pockets and took turns squeezing into the small space beside Hernandez to rinse our coffee cups out at the sink. And then finally, after a quick glance down the hallway for administrators, the coffee was dispensed.

It wasn't long before we were all addicts. Our cup in the morning turned into two cups, followed by a cup or two after lunch.

Hernandez's coffee was incredible, out-done only by his coffee snobbery. We started with Seattle's Best but after a few weeks moved on to Peet's and other gourmet brands at twelve dollars a pound. And what was a French press without a subscription to *Gourmet* magazine?

Food magazines began piling up around the clinic desk. In between writing notes early in the morning, we also thumbed through the latest issue of *Gourmet* or *Bon Appétit*.

Our patients might be reading *Tattoo* magazine and drinking Red Bull, but we had our minds on higher things. We were brewing coffee constantly. So much so that we broke the French press. A wail went out among the staff when we made the terrible discovery. By midafternoon that day, we were holding our heads together, convinced our skulls were going to split apart. Luckily, help arrived in the form of a small, four-cup coffeemaker, given to us by Cosmo. I was astounded by this gift for several reasons. The first being, of course, that it had come from Cosmo. But even more, I was flattered that he had noticed our coffee addiction at all. I always assumed patients saw us only as one-dimensional background figures. Paper dolls who fluttered around the physical therapy clinic with no interests, no personalities, no tangible qualities beyond the single-minded rehab of a roomful of combat amputees.

"It was on sale at the PX. Don't worry about it," Cosmo said with a shrug, tipping his wheelchair back and balancing in a perfect wheelie, then spinning on his wheels and zipping out of the clinic before he'd have to actually do physical therapy.

The coffeemaker was manna from heaven. Our secret was out, and this time we didn't bother hiding it. It was a gift, after all, and coffee was again brewing constantly.

Brewing coffee all the time wasn't good for the thin glass carafe, which quickly developed a crack. But we kept making coffee anyway, dumping the coffee from the cracked carafe immediately into a thermos before it had a chance to leak too much. The crack got worse and worse, and finally Sgt. Hernandez bought another French press.

But by then the novelty of having coffee in the clinic had worn off everyone except me. Fully addicted, I followed Hernandez around like a junkie hoping to score a free fix. He was the first person I looked for when I got to work, and again when I returned to the clinic after lunch. Nothing made me happier than to see him there, standing by the sink, grinding coffee beans. He'd turn around. "Quoffy?" he'd ask in his Brooklyn accent. "Sure!" I'd say, rushing over to rinse out my cup.

Sgt. Hernandez's coffee was unlike any I had had before. It was dark and mysterious, just like him. Hernandez, who frequently went back to Brooklyn to buy clothes and specialty food items, mystified me. My favorite sweater was one I had found abandoned on a sidewalk in Baltimore. It was a little dirty, but fit me perfectly. As far as food went, I was equally unoriginal and could live off of a box of cereal for a week.

But Hernandez's coffee was thick with personality and flavor — practically espresso. And in each steaming cup, I inhaled what I imagined was Hernandez's vibrant Brooklyn lifestyle. It was nothing like the cheap yellow can of Chock Full o' Nuts coffee I'd been drinking for years.

In the morning we'd toast each other with two hot, steaming cups.

After lunch, Hernandez would be working the coffee grinder again. The smell of freshly ground coffee was irresistible. I'd sneak off to the DFAC for some creamers.

"Coffee?" Hernandez would ask.

"Yes, thank you," I'd say.

Cups four and five were equally incredible. Life was good. I'd see the last of my afternoon patients, pound out my notes, and ride my bike home where, thanks to my highly caffeinated state, I stayed up late into the night doing household chores and laundry.

We experimented with different beans. Once I screwed up and brought in a bag of preground coffee. Hernandez turned his nose up at it, but we ended by drinking it anyway.

I learned which coffee Hernandez especially liked — strong espresso blends — and I made sure I bought beans.

And then one Monday I came to work, eagerly anticipating my morning cup of joe at Hernandez's coffeehouse, and Hernandez wasn't there. At first I thought he was off in the DFAC or just running late. But by 0730 I started asking, in a trembly voice, "Where's Hernandez? Where *is* he?"

The fact that Hernandez had left on vacation for an entire week without even warning me was more than a little upsetting. I'd been thrown under the bus! But if I was upset at Hernandez, I couldn't focus on it very long, because the pressure building up behind my eyeballs made thinking too long about any one thing unbearably painful.

I got out Hernandez's coffee grinder and tried to figure it out. I had just finished grinding the beans when I realized that Hernandez's French press was gone. I quickly checked Hernandez's locker. Unlike the rest of us, whose lockers were crammed with so much junk the hinges were starting to bend, Sgt. Hernandez's locker was a shrine. Beside his shaving kit and bottle of after-shave was a neat space for his toothbrush. A pair of iPod earphones were coiled up beside a bottle of vitamins, and surprisingly, on the top shelf of his locker was the spare bag of exercise bands that everyone had been looking for. Apparently Sgt. Hernandez had independently decided he should be the one to keep and distribute one measly band at a time, as if none of the rest of us could possibly be trusted with them.

Darcy, who was watching me poke around Hernandez's locker, reported with some amusement that she had seen Hernandez leaving work with his French press on Friday afternoon. Hernandez had taken his French press on vacation with him!

I settled into my misery. There was no time to run to the cafeteria for a cup of their watery coffee. Coffee that Hernandez frequently described as "bathtub water." The clinic was full of patients. I felt like I was under water. It wasn't just the pressure squeezing my skull; my comprehension and ability to think was gone. Everything slowed down. I was deep, deep under water, struggling to simply walk or talk.

I've heard of experienced marathon runners hitting "the wall." Of mountain climbers overcome with exhaustion left to die in the snow. With my caffeine habit suddenly kicked with no warning at all, I felt like I had joined their exclusive club.

In between patients, I sat on a rolling stool in the corner, squeezing my head with both of my hands. I'd had several cups of strong tea, courtesy of the kettle. But it didn't do a thing. I felt like someone had pinned me to the bottom of the deep end of the pool.

At lunchtime I gulped down some DFAC coffee. It was just like Hernandez described it. My pounding headache continued unabated.

That night when I got home, I crawled directly into bed and fell into an uncomfortable sleep.

The next morning I went straight to the DFAC, where I was shocked to see the coffee machines were all out of service! There had been a water main break. No coffee. No Coke. No iced tea. No water. Without tap water, even the kettle was out of service.

I spent my free time between patients on a stool clutching my head. If the day before had been rough, it was nothing compared to day two. Cosmo, I noticed, was taking full advantage of my weakened state to spend the entire morning holding court in the smoking shelter.

The next morning, I brought in a thermos with coffee. I was slowly starting to swim up from the bottom of the pool. It was Wednesday. Hernandez was coming back on Sunday. I could get coffee at Starbucks on the weekend, but it was nothing compared to Hernandez's exclusive blend. Five days to go. I exhaled in relief. But what if his flight was delayed? My chest tightened as I fretted about this quietly to myself.

On Monday morning I rode to work early. Walking apprehensively to the clinic, I was overjoyed to see Hernandez in the window, rinsing out the French press in the sink. The sun was rising. The air outside was a thick 80 degrees. But I knew that inside the clinic the temperatures were crisp and cold. I could already smell the coffee brewing. It was going to be a great day.

# GIRLFRIEND LAND

On reality TV, when things get bad, instead of venting privately, characters are invited to air their "private" thoughts to an offstage video camera. Which must be why when things got really crazy in the clinic, Emma would pull me off to the side and say dramatically, "I need to do an on-camera monologue!"

My favorite show is a spoof on reality shows, a cop show called *Reno 911!* This show, under the pretense of being a reality show, made fun of police shows, race, disability, and sexual orientation. It reminded me of our clinic, where, in order to handle the chaos and stress, we turned everything into an exaggerated joke.

In my new borderline condominium, Comedy Central played endless loops of *Reno 911!* right around the time I got home from work. I would carry my bicycle up the steps to my second-floor walk-up. The only furniture I had owned during the flood had been an aluminum-frame futon couch and a floor lamp. Damage to me had been minimal. But my friends were always after me to buy furniture. I was sleeping on an air mattress, which I had bought for twenty dollars, and that I liked because it was portable, and now, because of its ability to float.

My air mattress was a real date buzz kill.

If I was in a serious relationship, I told myself, I'd buy a bed.

But if it didn't work out, then I would have that constant reminder every time I climbed into my new bed.

Which was why I had decided it was just safer to stay with the air mattress.

I'd lean my bicycle against the wall of my sparse living room and walk immediately into the bathroom, where I'd aggressively scrub the imaginary smell of the hospital off my hands and arms with a big block of scented soap. I'd change clothes, wash my hands again, and then take the dog outside for a walk. After the walk I was back in my condo. I'd head straight for the fridge, grab a beer, drop down on my futon couch that still smelled slightly of mildew, and laugh my way through the first rerun of *Reno 911!*

My friend Vern had once compared my

dating style to that of a spider: "You leave your apartment every six months and drag some alcohol-poisoned victim back." I had bristled immediately at this harsh comparison, because I didn't do one-night stands. But most of what Vern said was true, I had a long history of short, casual relationships. I blamed it on my job schedule. "No one wants to get serious with someone who gets up at five."

While blaming Walter Reed for my lack of intimacy was convenient, the truth was that I hadn't been in a serious relationship in about twelve years. In spite of getting burned over and over again, I couldn't help myself from constantly going after my top hit: the Cold and Unavailable. But now, thanks to my work schedule, I wasn't even meeting the Cold and Unavailable. Instead, month after month passed with me just puttering around at home with the dog, watching *Reno 911!* and reading *The Washington Post.*

On *Reno 911!* the head police deputy, Lieutenant Jim Dangle, wears tiny uniform go-go shorts. The cameras highlight this as Lt. Dangle yells, "Freeze!" pointing a pistol at a criminal from a deep squat, as the viewfinder zooms in on his behind.

One morning in the clinic as a joke, for

patients and staff members who don't themselves watch *Reno 911!* I pretended I was Lt. Dangle, and dropped down into outrageous squats to pick up towels off the floor.

No one was surprised that I am a fan of *Reno 911!* but Maj. Tavner, who is smart, well-traveled, and a rising military star, surprised everyone by admitting to being a fan of the show, too. I was initially taken aback. Maj. Tavner, who kept her blond hair pinned up in a perfect bun and once talked me into reading a book about organic container gardening, seemed way too sophisticated to enjoy such lowbrow humor. But the same Maj. Tavner who was always calmly eloquent when addressing visiting generals and high-level political visitors would become visibly excited when trying to summarize an episode of *Reno 911!*

"Ha ha!" Maj. Tavner would laugh, interrupting herself and stumbling over her words while trying to describe the finer points of the latest episode for me. "Did you see it last night? Trudy started dating a serial killer on death row."

Even though I had seen the episode, I didn't answer Maj. Tavner. I was too distracted trying to imagine her lying on her couch in ripped jeans and a paint-splattered

T-shirt, drinking a beer with the remote on the floor. Was she like me? Did she push a bicycle through an apartment completely bare of furniture?

Maj. Tavner laughed to herself again, typing her notes and reliving last night's episode, while beside her I smelled my hands involuntarily. They smelled like hospital disinfectant.

While I might, as a joke, pretend to be "lithe like a cheetah," as Lt. Dangle describes himself in video monologues, Maj. Tavner was the real deal, and one day she proved it. Cosmo was sitting in a wheelchair just outside the parallel bars. Since the infection in Cosmo's leg had gotten worse, his life had turned into nonstop pain. His leg had been painful before, but now it was barely tolerable. His surgeons were going through all sorts of heroics to save it. Who can blame them for trying to prevent Cosmo from losing both of his legs? But with the nerve damage, destroyed knee, and the cage that held the shattered bones of his thigh and lower leg together, it was an infected, pus-filled appendage, hot and swollen and oozing fluids. Cosmo couldn't move it, let alone walk on it.

Cosmo would creep into the clinic in his wheelchair, with his leg resting on his wheelchair's elevating leg rest like a grotesque trophy on a shelf. His entire PT course lately seemed to consist of riding the arm bike, pedaling slowly and resolutely. I don't know if it was the infection or the nerve pain that occasionally made his eyes roll back in his head.

Which was why it was horrifying when a heavy mirror near him inexplicably rolled down the ramp at the end of the parallel bars and started to fall over on top of Cosmo, of all people.

I was rooted to the ground in disbelief and horror, as was everyone in the room. Except for Maj. Tavner. She sprang out of her chair with catlike agility, leaped over a stool, and caught the mirror right before it hammered Cosmo into the floor. Seeing her almost do a split in midair while leaping over a chair was jaw-dropping. All she needed was a pair of go-go shorts to complete the picture.

Just then, as if sent by divine intervention, the cast of *Reno 911!* came to pay a surprise visit to Walter Reed. I had no idea they were coming. When I saw them walking down the hallway at that precise moment wearing their too-tight police uniforms and bulletproof vests, Lt. Dangle in his trademark tiny shorts, I started to shake.

I'd seen Oprah, Michelle Obama, President George W. Bush, Kevin Bacon, Jon Stewart, and John Mayer, to name a few, but I had never had this kind of reaction to any kind of celebrity visitor before. I stood beside Cosmo with my hands at my sides, visibly trembling.

Cosmo asked me then if that was really the *Reno 911!* cast. I looked at him and whispered in reverent disbelief, "Are you a fan, too?" We both were. If I was surprised that Cosmo watched the show, Cosmo seemed even more surprised that we had something in common. He must have thought of me as a prison guard and not much more.

*Reno 911!* stayed for the entire afternoon, hamming it up for the clinic. Lt. Dangle, of course, was a hit. In his short shorts, he put his foot on the armrest of Cosmo's wheelchair and leaned in and asked him how he was doing. Cosmo tilted his head back and roared with laughter.

I don't know if the laughter cleared Cosmo's head a little. Lt. Dangle moved on to another patient and Cosmo and I watched him clowning around in the distance, dropping down into deep squats and practicing fake karate moves. We were both laughing at Lt. Dangle's antics when Cosmo quietly announced, "I'm done with this fucking pus-filled leg."

I looked at him in surprise.

"It's killing me. I fucking swear it."

I silently agreed with him. "Cosmo, you know, once it's gone, it's gone."

Cosmo pushed himself out of the clinic with a new vigor. One year after begging his surgeons to save his leg, he asked their permission to amputate it.

That afternoon when I got home from work, I took my dog, Howie, for a long walk, and then, because it was nice outside, went to the park by my apartment building and threw the tennis ball for Howie, his very favorite thing to do. I thought glumly that it was something Cosmo would love to do, but instead Cosmo was back at Walter Reed rolling in pain and watching *Reno 911!* It was a Friday and I was under no pressure to run inside and throw in a load of laundry or do any other last-minute work prep. In fact, I had absolutely nothing to do.

All of my friends had recently disappeared to a place I referred to as "Girlfriend Land." *If I wasn't constantly single,* I thought to myself while pitching the ball for Howie, *I'd probably have dinner plans or movie plans or something. GFL,* I thought, throwing the tennis ball in complete annoyance, *popula-*

*tion two.*

My cell phone buzzed and I picked it up. It was Maria, the therapist who sometimes hired me to do part-time work in her private practice. Maria and I had gone to PT school together — she had definitely raised her hand when the financial aid counselor asked who had a five-year plan. Maria was going out of town and wanted to know if I could see a few patients for her. We discussed days and times, and then out of the blue, I blurted out, "I don't suppose you'd want to set me up on another blind date?"

Maria had fixed me up on a blind date seven years earlier. A blind date I had completely mangled by showing up drunk with an even drunker friend, who managed, in the short time before Maria and my date arrived, to start a bar fight that ended with me getting a pitcher of beer dumped over my head and the two of us getting physically expelled out of the club by the bouncer.

While I continued to see Maria socially and, later, work for her, Maria and I had never discussed how I managed to so spectacularly blow her fix-up.

Maria initially didn't say anything, which made me nervous. Surely there had to be some sort of statute of limitations on poor behavior?

"I promise I won't show up drunk," I said.

Maria laughed. "Actually, I do have a someone in mind and I think she could appreciate your sense of humor."

The next Friday I met Maria's friend at a coffee shop around the corner from Walter Reed. Ashley was a tall, blond knockout, and a behavioral scientist. Which, according to my friends, was the only reason she was showing any interest in me. This observation was slightly better than the spider comment and I decided to take it in stride.

While I was suspicious of becoming a research subject for Ashley, in Ashley I discovered someone who completely understood me. On our second date she gave me a book, *Swimming to Antarctica.* I already owned a copy. It was not a mainstream type of book, but a book devoured by myself and the people I swam with. Ashley had somehow discovered it all on her own.

Ashley was smart, had her shit together, and I appreciated that she had a job — which, besides looks, had been my only real requirement. Be as cold and unavailable as you wanted, but if you were still living with your parents, I was not interested. The problem with Ashley, and there really was only one problem with Ashley, was that she

232

liked me way too much.

I called my friend Dana up to discuss the situation. "So let me get this straight," Dana said. "You are dating someone who is good looking, smart, nice, and has a professional job."

"That's right."

Dana continued, "And she's chasing you around?"

"Yes, that's it!" I said, pleased that Dana had so quickly gotten to the root of my dilemma.

Dana paused and her voice grew irritated. "You would rather be with someone, how should I put it, *reluctant*?"

I got sour. "Well, if you're going to put it that way."

So I kept going out with Ashley. Only because she was just so darn nice and because I was mad at Dana and still slightly afraid of what Maria would do if I screwed up again.

When I balked at getting more serious, Ashley did something that took me completely by surprise. She called me up on the phone. "I want to come over and give Howie a bath." This was something that no previous girlfriend, no friend, no relative, no one had ever asked to do. This wasn't something I even did.

"Howie doesn't need a bath. He is a self-cleaning dog."

This was true. Howie always groomed himself and he never smelled bad to me. In fact, I loved the way he smelled. His smell had never changed. One whiff of his paws brought me right back to the moment I had carried him up the steps of my fourth-floor walk-up in Baltimore as a tiny, abandoned five-week-old puppy.

But Ashley persisted. "He smells bad to me."

"I don't think cornering a sixty-pound pit bull in the bathroom is a good idea."

Still, Ashley couldn't be deterred. She showed up a half hour later, in shorts and a bikini top. Her hair was pulled back into a ponytail and she had a bucket of shampoos and conditioners.

"Just don't drag him into the bathroom," I said. "Let me handle that."

Ashley got Howie's bath prepared and then I coaxed Howie gently into the bathroom. I had a tennis ball and some treats to lure him into the bathtub. But one look at Ashley and Howie just meekly climbed in all by himself.

I went back out to the living room. I couldn't figure out whose behavior confused me more, Ashley's or Howie's.

After that night, Ashley and Howie began spending more and more time together. My aggressive pit bull now had silky, soft fur. In addition to regular baths, Howie was also getting deep-conditioner treatments and regular brushings. Sometimes Ashley and Howie would just disappear outside together, to go on special "sniff walks." Walks where Howie was allowed, encouraged even, to linger and sniff as much as he wanted. Something he was absolutely forbidden to do with me because that kind of dillydallying made me completely crazy.

I was still in the picture, but in a third-wheel sort of way. My work schedule didn't seem to bother Ashley, since she was sleeping in with Howie. Howie didn't bother to get up with me either, now that he was snuggled up under the covers with Ashley, anticipating a leisurely morning sniff walk. That is, if Ashley didn't surprise him with an early morning trip to the dog park. Ashley had recently outfitted the back of her hatchback with a plush dog bed so that Howie could ride around town with her in complete luxury.

Right under my nose, my dog had abandoned me for Girlfriend Land.

# PART TWO

# AMPUTEE DREAMS

The first time I saw Cosmo as a double amputee, he was sitting up in his hospital bed and writing in a diary. At first, seeing him in bed, I was completely blown away by how small he seemed now with both legs amputated at the thigh. And then I noticed the diary. It had a soft leather cover.

Cosmo had been a tall man before the second amputation. Now he was just a little over four feet long. I fixated on the journal instead.

Cosmo had been cut in half, but it was the journal, I decided, that was singularly disturbing. Cosmo was an outdoorsman. A hunter. A fisher. Not the type to keep a diary.

Cosmo was like me. Gritty.

There was a trophy case in front of our clinic with framed celebrity photos, coins from visiting generals, and autographed footballs. Cosmo had joked before the surgery that he was going to put his "worth-less piece of shit leg" in the trophy case.

"Give it to me," I had shot back with similar gallows humor. "I'll hang it in my living room like a hunting trophy."

But there was nothing funny about seeing Cosmo with both of his legs gone. I was completely unprepared for the physical shock of seeing him as a double amputee. If I hadn't been holding on to the door, I would have fallen over.

Standing there, I could smell the chlorine coming off my skin and see the veins cours-ing their way down my arms. Cosmo's hospital room was small and hot, and in there, I was totally surrounded by the chemical stink of myself. I felt for a mo-ment completely guilty. While Cosmo had been lying in his hospital bed getting regular doses of Dilaudid through an IV the night before, I'd been in the pool powering through a 4,500-meter workout. Something Cosmo would probably kill to be able to do.

And then I had spent the rest of the night writing, like I now did every night before bed, telling myself I was doing it for "mental therapy" because I am not the type to keep a diary either.

I desperately wanted to ask Cosmo what

he was writing about in that nice leather journal, but at the same time, I didn't want to back him into a corner. Instead I inhaled the comforting smell of chlorine. And for a brief second, I considered explaining myself to Cosmo. My weird passion for training for a swim race that was, at its best moments, completely agonizing.

The 4.4-mile Great Chesapeake Bay Swim is one of those events you hear about only if you are crazy enough to participate in it — like the Iditarod in Alaska and Burning Man in Nevada. From Annapolis, you cross the neck of the Chesapeake Bay by following the twin spans of the Bay Bridge. There, underneath the bridge, you encounter strong currents, waves, and wind. Jellyfish and driftwood and other swimmers kick you in the head.

To keep the currents from sweeping you away from the bridge spans and out into the middle of the bay, you have to constantly swim on a diagonal. Swimming in such a contorted fashion guarantees immediate back, neck, and shoulder pain, and turns the rest of your race into a nonstop stream of mental bargaining. Promises to yourself, the water, the wind, and any possible higher power, that if you make it to dry land you will never, ever again participate in such a foolish and risky event.

Except you will.

There are no screaming spectators cheering you on across the bay. There are no marching bands, no pep talks with fellow swimmers, and no friends waiting for you at the last mile to help you swim it in. It's just you, the water, and that relentless, pounding current. To willingly return to the start, year after year, and walk into that cold briny water knowing you're going to spend the next two or three hours swimming blind and deaf to everything but the occasional glimpse of sky and bridge takes a different sort of person.

It takes a trait I was surprised to discover in myself.

And now, six Bay Swims under my belt, it is a trait I can instantly recognize in other people. I had instantly recognized it in Cosmo in the ICU, that streak of recklessness and persistence. It made him feel familiar to me.

In 2003, a determined swimmer caught up in the currents refused to get in the sweep boat picking up struggling swimmers. He was later plucked out of the water by the Coast Guard, arrested (for being belligerent), and disqualified.

I have to say, I greatly admired the spirit

of this lone swimmer. While he was selfishly breaking a rule established by the race directors for the safety of others, I enjoy thinking about him, surrounded by strong waves and screaming race officials, refusing to get out. It is something I can easily see Cosmo doing. Except now he was in that hospital bed, completely tamed, writing in a big leather journal.

If Cosmo was aware of how different he appeared as a double amputee, he didn't show it. But he seemed changed on an entirely different level, too. He was smiling and laughing. Truly happy for the first time in the twelve months I'd known him.

While I patted myself on the back for being the special breed of person who could handle the environment of the amputee clinic with no ill effects at all, suddenly, after several years, nightmare after nightmare began to blast me awake. Maybe it was the shock of seeing Cosmo that first time as a double amputee that did it.

Every night I had another terrible dream. They were about family members — my parents, my sister — sitting in wheelchairs with missing limbs. Sometimes I was the amputee. Sometimes it was Ashley. I'd sit up suddenly in the dark, sweaty and sobbing from the dream.

Amputations had become my new reality, day and night.

The nightmares continued, and outside work I began to suspect that anyone I saw was an amputee. I didn't realize I was consciously doing this until one Sunday afternoon in downtown D.C., while I was sitting on a bench in the sun with Howie and a couple of friends. We were aggressively people watching. My friends looked at the person's face, and probably their butt, but I was singularly focused on legs and arms, straining to see the telltale edge of a prosthesis.

We watched a man with a limp go by and I told my friends I thought he was an amputee with a poor-fitting socket, when in reality he probably just had knee pain.

Later, a woman bent down to pet Howie. She held one arm behind her back and I wondered aloud later about her "high upper-extremity amputation." My friends were horrified by such an extreme blunder and talked me into taking a week off from work. Ashley forcefully agreed with them and, backed into a corner, I reluctantly submitted my time-off paperwork.

The first day of my forced vacation passed fitfully. I spent the day moping around, trying to read the newspaper in between rechecking my barren refrigerator for anything edible besides the glass of water and the box of baking soda that were sitting in there. The clock slowly ticked along. I knew, back at work, time was scarce for my co-workers, who were busy treating over a hundred amputees. I'm sure they didn't appreciate the extra burden of having to divvy up the long list of patients on my schedule. And it wasn't like I had taken the week off to fly to London or another exotic location. I was seven miles away, sitting in my barren condo like a rat in a trap.

After the first fretful day, I considered going back to work early, before spontaneously deciding to remodel my 1970s-themed condominium.

The fact that I had never remodeled anything in my life did not slow me down one bit, because outside work I was a complete Home and Garden Television addict — which therefore made me an expert.

HGTV is a cable channel devoted to home remodeling. It runs twenty-four hours a day. No matter what time you flip to the HGTV channel, there is always an incredibly beautiful person happily ripping out an old toilet or blowing fiberglass insulation into a crawlspace while wearing designer jeans and joking around with a handsome carpenter friend.

No amputations. No crying. No colostomy bags. It was mesmerizing.

While the rest of my neighborhood was up-and-coming, my condo development had definitely been heading south. Reading the monthly mimeographed condo minutes was like reading a police crime blotter, and if you wanted to get held up anywhere, the parking lot of my condo was where it would happen.

It was easy for me to imagine showing off a brand-new kitchen to my friends. But it's not that fantastic to be spending Saturday night marooned in your kitchen, splattered with wet cement, and sending a frantic email to the do-it-yourself forum on a laptop spotted with paint.

What especially bothered me about this scenario wasn't the fact that I could quite possibly ruin my kitchen floor, but that I felt and looked like a homeless person. This would never happen on HGTV where, no matter the project, shirts always stay neatly tucked in. No one on HGTV ever sits on a wet paintbrush or gets cement in her eye. No one on HGTV is ever filmed stupidly trapped in her kitchen because a refrigerator is stuck in the door frame.

I imagined that remodeling my condo would somehow turn me into a carefree, nightmare-free, HGTV-like personality, but instead it was just literally breaking me down. Every waking hour of my vacation was devoted exclusively to working on my condominium. The bathroom, kitchen, and bedroom were all half dismantled, so I was sleeping in a sleeping bag in the living room.

The last weekend before returning to work was a forty-eight-hour sprint spent cutting molding, patching drywall, and refinishing my cabinets. I barely slept, ate, or answered the phone. Outside of the time I spent on various DIY online forums, and brief visits with Ashley, who had made several trips to Home Depot for me, I hadn't had contact with any other humans for a full week.

But it was done.

Instead of feeling elated like I anticipated, I felt deflated. I sat on my couch on top of gleaming wood floors and glossy white floor molding and didn't know what to do with myself. All my tools were stacked carefully in the closet, alongside sacks of grout and cement, cans of paint, glue, and spackle. Outside in the parking lot I could hear my neighbors screaming at one another and car tires squealing as some gangster shot at someone down the street.

The next morning I got dressed and went back to work. The blue paint in my hair did little for my complexion but highlight the dark circles under my eyes. Nothing in my life had changed. Except one. I hadn't had a single amputee dream for an entire week.

After my condo remodel, I had one more amputee dream, and then none. In my last dream, we had a new amputee. He was just a head, and was whizzing around the clinic on a special skateboard that he was able to control via a suck-and-puff straw similar to the ones quadriplegics use to control their wheelchairs.

As he zipped into the clinic on his skateboard, my coworkers leapt to their feet and applauded him.

"Look at you! Look how great you are doing!"

"I am!" he enthusiastically agreed. "I *am* doing great!" he said before scooting out of the clinic and down the hallway, a lone head on a skateboard.

When I told my coworkers about my dream, they smiled. "You're right," they laughed, "that's *exactly* what we would do."

While I didn't have any more amputee dreams, the damage had been done. I started to view Walter Reed with some suspicion. It was changing me, and I didn't think I liked it.

Luckily, Ashley stepped in. She liked to travel, something I rarely did.

We went to Switzerland, where I enthusiastically counted five people with broken legs and three people with broken arms in the very first week.

"People sure are clumsy here," I'd say to Ashley, who instantly got irritated when I'd point out yet another cast to her. Ashley preferred looking at the alpine vistas, not at another unfortunate person propped up on crutches.

We went to London, where I saw six midgets in six days, including one on a double-decker bus. Ashley enjoyed the architecture and cosmopolitan feel of London, but I was on a survey for what I felt was the unique disability of the area.

And on our frequent weekend trips to Baltimore, I was on high alert for any kind of person in a wheelchair. "Look. Look," I'd say, and Ashley would absolutely refuse to turn her head. She said it was my way of being unable to get away from work.

I kept a running tally in my head, and when I got back I recited my list of seen injuries and disabilities to my coworkers. I skipped right over the places I visited and the people I met, and got right down to the nitty-gritty. This hardly seemed strange to them, and they asked thoughtful questions.

"How about amputees?" they asked. "How many? What kind of prosthesis were they wearing? These people in wheelchairs, did they have any lower-extremity function?"

Of course I noticed the amputees. I was always looking for amputees. And when I saw one, I was always disappointed by how few of them had a prosthetic leg. Or if they had a prosthetic leg, how unnecessarily terribly they walked on it. It was all I could do not to directly confront them on the street.

It seemed as though the longer the wars went on, the more my coworkers and I related to one another and the less we related to people outside our clinic. Which was why Darcy and I decided to sit for the orthopedic specialty exam. Studying for it would be a way for us to reconnect with standard physical therapy. In physical therapy, the OCS (orthopedic credentialed specialist) is a much-sought-after credential that requires passing a rigorous and difficult eight-hour exam.

At the time we took the exam, Darcy had eleven years of experience and I had eight, but we hardly considered ourselves experts in anything. We had spent the last five years on the battlefields of Walter Reed, after all.

It took us several weeks to fill out the twenty-three-page application. We each paid our thirteen-hundred-dollar exam fee. And waited to see if we would be approved to sit for the exam.

We both were.

Darcy was surprised we made it through the approval process. After all, at Walter Reed we hadn't rehabbed a torn ACL or rotator cuff in years.

"Does multilimb loss and traumatic brain injury really count as standard physical therapy?" Darcy asked me in an email.

We started a somewhat haphazard method of reviewing everything we had learned in and after PT school. We began, randomly, with the elbow.

We both thought we would enjoy studying for the exam, but instead, as the exam date got closer and we were still agonizing over the elbow, it started to seem less like a good idea and more like a guillotine hanging over our necks.

I never realized how draining my job was until I started taking it home with me every night in the form of detailed notes on various lower-extremity fracture patterns and spinal cord injuries. Darcy wasn't getting much studying done at home either, so we took to carrying our books into the clinic every morning. During the mandatory 0700 staff meeting, the morning military huddle, we'd hide in the back and try to get through a couple pages.

Walter Reed, I learned, is not a good place to surreptitiously study for a board exam. I was always losing my book, leaving it in the parallel bars or behind a pile of prosthetic legs. In the chaos of the physical therapy clinic, trying to review a note card as you're walking briskly across the room is a good way to get hit in the head with a medicine ball or trip over a wheelchair.

In the end, Darcy and I gloomily hunkered down and braced ourselves for a humiliating exam experience.

Cosmo had once told me that he tried to keep his mouth open when he was ambushed so that the blast wouldn't shatter his teeth. It was an offhand comment, but it had completely floored me. I studiously never asked my patients what happened to them. I read the medical details, how many units of blood they were transfused, when their amputations had occurred, whether they had been conscious on the scene, et cetera, in the medical chart. But I didn't want to force them to rehash, yet again, the worst day of their lives. After all, outside our clinic they were stopped and asked to tell their story dozens of times a day by every well-meaning stranger who wanted to thank them for their service.

But I never forgot Cosmo's comment.

I was worried that the exam would be graded on a curve. When Darcy and I walked into the room to spend a day taking an exam completely out of our reality, I checked out the other clinicians. I was hoping they'd look stupid, but they looked like regular physical therapists to me. Trim. Athletic. Khaki pants. They looked calm and organized. I could easily see them treating one tennis elbow, one sprained ankle, every thirty minutes, all day long.

The computers powered up and I braced for the first hit. I kept my mouth open.

To our surprise, we both passed. We were specialists in our field. After all those years of feeling like a castaway, I was now formally considered an expert. For a few days Darcy and I gloated. When we passed each other in the hallway, we would greet each other with, "Hello, OCS." And then we'd laugh like crazy.

Because, really, the joke was on us. Earning your OCS, if you were a military PT, resulted in a monthly OCS bonus on your paycheck. And for those clinicians working at civilian practices, having an OCS designation certainly would command a higher salary. But not for us. Except for some extra initials we could add behind our name, nothing was going to change.

The army had paid for a study course for the military PTs who were taking the OCS exam with us, but Darcy and I had been on our own. Luckily, though, our military counterparts reached out to us. One of them gave us a copy of her study guide and notes. And another suggested which textbooks we should read. A few months later, after we had proof that we passed the exam, we got reimbursed for the cost of the exam fee. I was ecstatic and treated the return of my thirteen hundred dollars as a bonus and immediately ran out and bought a new bicycle. Darcy just shook her head and was quick to remind me that I was just respending the money I had already spent.

In the end we went back to the usual: wrapping stumps while simultaneously discussing trashy reality TV shows. I wondered about the other physical therapists who had taken the exam. Had the exam changed them? Were they massaging a tennis player's shoulder with a little more pizzazz now? How was that higher salary they were enjoying?

On my walks home, I scanned fellow

pedestrians' legs for telltale signs of artificial extremities while trying to decide if I should tile my kitchen backsplash.

Darcy went back to watching celebrity videos on the Internet and emailing the links as mandatory "homework assignments" to the rest of our coworkers.

And after spending a year in horrible nonstop pain, Cosmo was suddenly racing down the hallway to the PT clinic in his wheelchair, recklessly zooming around corners on the edge of one wheel. Life was his again. He had been released from his shackles. With his mangled leg gone, he didn't need help from anyone. He could easily hop in and out of his wheelchair. He could do all those things we take for granted. Take a shower. Get in and out of bed. Sleep through the night. Live without pain.

I'd smile when I'd see him careering down the hallway. And imagine his pus-filled leg in our trophy case, and then I'd wonder to myself, what was in that diary?

The nightmares, for some reason, have never come back.

# Bad Boy Meeting

Because Cosmo had both of his legs amputated above the knees, he would start learning to walk on short prosthetic legs we called stubbies or shorties. These are legs without a knee component, consisting of just a socket sitting on top of a foot. Tiny little legs that, for some soldiers, are just a little over a foot tall.

With stubbies, the beach shorts our patients favored stop just above their tennis shoes. Unless you know better, you wouldn't know these soldiers were amputees at all. Instead, they look like a group of stocky midgets tottering along.

Walking on stubbies is hard work, but easier to get your balance than being perched way up high on full-length prosthetic legs with hinge-like knees.

In the beginning, to help patients learn to balance on stubbies, and to make it easier to clear the toe, we sometimes turned the feet around. With the feet facing backward, the patient doesn't have to worry about falling backward — only forward — where they can catch themselves with their hands. But if it isn't awkward enough to find yourself topping out at four feet tall, having your feet turned backward has the potential, based on a soldier's level of self-esteem, to turn an awkward situation into a humiliating one.

Luckily, walking on stubbies with feet turned backward lasts only a day or two. Then the feet are turned around. As the patients' balance continues to improve, the pylon on the stubby is lengthened and they don't seem so midgetlike, only tragically short. And then once their balance is good enough, knees are added to the prosthetic legs. After having gotten used to seeing your patient as a short, stocky man, it is thrilling to suddenly have to look up at his face when he stands up on his full-length prosthetic legs for the first time.

While many patients are eager to take their prosthetic leg home with them and show it off out in the community (preferably at a bar filled with pretty college girls), the soldiers in the stubby contingency aren't going to be caught dead out in public. As a result, they spend a lot more time in the PT clinic, walking endless laps. They are so short when they pass the computer desk you can't even see them.

Cosmo was trying out his stubbies for the first time when a group of hair-dyed congressmen walked into the clinic. Cosmo's feet were facing backward to help him balance, and standing up, he was exactly four feet tall.

One of the congressmen came over to introduce himself to the patients. When he turned around and saw Cosmo standing there in stubbies with feet facing backward, he completely lost it and started to cry.

Cosmo has a finely tuned sense of humor and didn't miss a beat.

"I think he thought I was a goddamn midget for real! And that I was too fucking stupid to know that my legs were on backward."

Then Cosmo scrunched his face up, crossed his eyes, and with exaggerated effort grunted out the word "Duh!"

I couldn't help myself and exploded into laughter.

After the congressman left, whenever Cosmo and I were around each other, we'd entertain each other by acting stupid.

Darcy would tease her soldiers by calling them girlfriend and sister. But Cosmo and I were the only ones who'd talk to each other in our own personal idiot voices. Being an idiot, after all, was something I felt I could relate to. Tottering on his stubbies, Cosmo would screw his face up and grunt out "Duh!" every time he passed me. On his approach I became alert with anticipation, and the minute Cosmo started crossing his eyes, I'd fall out laughing. Wildly inappropriate, but it gave some comic relief to an otherwise awkward situation. A big man who would normally tower over me was literally cut off at the knees.

If the other staff members heard me and Cosmo laughing, they didn't understand it. They just watched us from afar.

I kept trying to convince Cosmo to do some "stubby time" on his own outside the PT clinic, but somehow he'd always manage to sneak his stubbies into the closet when I wasn't looking. I can't say I really blamed him.

We had the same conversation so many times it started to turn into a comedy routine, involving various what-if scenerios of Cosmo actually wearing his stubbies outside the PT clinic. It started to resemble *Green Eggs and Ham* by Dr. Seuss.

*I will not wear them with a goat, I will not wear them on a boat.*

"Are you kidding?" Cosmo would say, crossing his eyes and deliberately letting a little drool leak out of the corner of his mouth while I started giggling. "I can't wear these stubbies out of here. I'd get backed over by cars in the parking lot."

Or the next day, "Kids would follow me around and think I was a midget."

And the day after that, "People might cry. Remember that congressman? Duh! Duh!"

If there was a patient who had my heart, it was Cosmo.

I appreciated Cosmo's insight into himself and, of course, congressmen. Cosmo was brutally honest. And in spite of everything, he made me laugh and laugh.

With a clinic full of young soldiers and marines who wanted to be challenged, we left the standard physical therapy exercises behind for exercises we gleaned from the back of various men's health magazines or that we thought up on a difficult commute home. These exercises came with ominous names like Burpees and Cock-Up Drills. In the afternoon it wasn't unusual to see a group of patients struggling though a circuit consisting of Mountain Climbers, Windshield Wipers, Boat Bailers, BOSU Burpees, and the Inchworm before climbing up and down onto a two-foot-tall box until they dropped from exhaustion.

A patient didn't have to be high level or high speed to start these drills. Just as long as they were careful and didn't hit their head when they fell. Loud thuds were common, usually followed by a pause and then a shout, "I'm okay!"

These circuit courses were Darcy's specialty. In the summer of 2010, we had enough patients in stubbies that Darcy made up special circuit courses directed specifically at them. Darcy was not afraid of pushing anyone and could make anything sound like a good idea — even a circuit course ominously named the Stubby Tsunami.

The Stubby Tsunami usually consisted of eight stations. The patients would do ten to fifteen reps at each station, followed by one lap around the clinic's indoor running track. It easily took forty-five minutes to complete. If they wanted to be punished more, they could try the entire thing two or three times.

Darcy's Stubby Tsunami reminded me of the Nordic course in that year's Winter Olympics, where fit young men on cross-country skis shot at various target stations in between doing laps. It was the Stubby Olympics. The clinic was the Olympic

Stadium. The physical therapists were the audience. Using their canes like cross-country ski poles, the patients spread out along the course. The track was lined with streaks of sweat, and of all people, Cosmo was the one leading the race. It was hard for me to not jump in the air and scream in total jubilation.

Except once the novelty of walking on stubbies wore off, Cosmo immediately reverted back to his old rebel self, coming in late, not wearing his legs, hanging out in the smoking shelter, and sneaking out whenever my back was turned. I was devastated by this sudden change in motivation. I couldn't decide if I was sad for him or mad at him or mad at myself, which made me frustrated. I frequently queried myself: *Who was letting who down?*

I could see Cosmo hiding out in the back of clinic where he thought I couldn't see him, jawing with a few other soldiers. He never came on time, and when he did, he'd sneak in the back door so I wouldn't notice.

But of course I'd see him sneak in. I'd watch Cosmo from across the room, noting with irritation that he didn't have his legs on. I'd scan the room for them, noticeable for their bright orange running shoes, clenching and unclenching my hands in preparation for our usual morning interaction.

Our conversation would begin with me announcing, "You are _____(hours/minutes) late."

Or the variation, "What time are you supposed to be here?"

Or finally, the desperate plea, "Can you just let me know when you're in here?"

I believe my last suggestion inspired Cosmo to install an air horn on his wheelchair. He glided into the clinic one day, as usual not at his scheduled appointment time, slid up behind me, and blasted the horn. I jumped about three feet into the air.

"I'm here," Cosmo said, spinning his wheelchair in a circle for effect.

I started to rip this nonregulation horn off his wheelchair, but Cosmo grabbed my hands, insisting that he needed it. "I need this fucking horn to clear the motherfuckers out of my way. Not you! None of those downtown fuckers in front of Starbucks will clear off the fucking sidewalk." Sidewalks in D.C. can be really narrow and I imagined no one would notice a guy in a wheelchair, unless of course that guy is Cosmo and he's blasting an air horn.

I decided to drop the air horn matter and pick up on our usual conversation — the disappearance of Cosmo's prosthetic legs.

"Where are your legs?"

"I forgot them."

"How is that possible? Didn't you think, for a second, that you might need them to, I don't know, practice walking?"

"I'm just forgetful, I guess," Cosmo said coolly with a smirk.

The reality was that Cosmo had been up all night with nightmares, something I frequently forgot and something we rarely discussed. His way of managing his PTSD was to play violent video games, *Call of Duty* and *Halo,* a strategy I thought ridiculous. But for Cosmo it was social. Something he could do with his army buddies, no matter where in the world they happened to be. They could hunt down and kill enemies together over the Internet.

I was no psychologist. The nuts and bolts of physical therapy, the focus on the physical, was what I knew. I would never be able to counsel Cosmo. The only thing I had to offer was the routine of me.

This, more than anything, bothered me about myself. I could never give emotional guidance. I was too blunt. Too rigid. Too singularly focused. The only thing I could offer you was consistency. No matter what was going on with you, I would be there to give you a hard time about why you were late.

Cosmo had weathered the loss of his intact leg with considerable aplomb, but back in the Fishbowl, not much had really changed. Rehab moves at a much slower pace than the few weeks it takes a new amputation to heal shut, which left Cosmo and me at an impasse. Now that Cosmo was mobile and up and at 'em, we never seemed to *do* any actual physical therapy. Instead we spent our appointment hour bickering and complaining like an old married couple.

Every morning I made a resolution not to pick on Cosmo, but then he'd show up at 1400 instead of 0900, or he wouldn't have his legs, or he'd ask permission to go to the smoking shelter for ten minutes and never return.

Once when Cosmo didn't show up, I decided to go outside and eat my lunch early. There were some tables outside and it was a nice day. I carried a sandwich from the cafeteria and a plate of French fries and sat down at one of the picnic tables. When I looked up, I realized I was directly across from the smoking shelter where, of all people, I could see Cosmo sitting inside visibly cringing. I could tell he was hoping I couldn't tell that that was him in the smoking shelter.

I *knew* it was him.

I took my time eating my lunch, chewing my sandwich extra slowly and never taking my eyes off of him.

The army has an electronic medical chart system. At the end of the day when I'd go to write my notes, I'd select the patient and open their treatment note. If, however, the patient was Cosmo and he didn't show up for the day, I could highlight it and check the no show box.

The No Show missile was the only one in my quiver. Before No Showing Cosmo that day, I looked down the hall and gave him an extra five minutes to make an appearance, call, or text me. And then I hit missile launch. I imagined a rocket blasting off from the center of the MATC clinic and arcing gracefully over Walter Reed's cherry-tree dotted campus, before making a dramatic descent toward the Mologne House Hotel.

I'm not sure exactly what the mechanism was, but getting a No Show unleashed what I imagined to be a dozen angry platoon sergeants into the culprit's hotel room. In reality, it was probably just Cosmo's nurse case manager. But if Cosmo got too many No Shows, his platoon sergeant would have him physically escorted into physical therapy for the rest of the week.

Launching a No Show missile at the Mologne House guaranteed one thing — a phone call from Cosmo within five minutes. He had somehow programmed his cell phone number into the hospital's No Show system. Not only would Cosmo's sergeant at the Warrior Transition Brigade get an automated phone call of Cosmo's missed appointment, but so would Cosmo.

Cosmo didn't say hello when he called. He dispensed with all pleasantries and launched right into what he felt was a huge error on my part.

"Did you just No Show me?"

"Did you come in today?"

"I was there."

"I didn't see you."

"Well, I looked around for you and left."

"That's funny, because I haven't left the clinic all morning."

"Well, I couldn't stick around and try and find you. I had something *important* to do."

"Oh, yeah? What?"

"I had a TBI appointment."

"I'm looking at your appointment list right now and the only appointment you had today was me. And you were a No Show."

"Fine. If No Showing me makes you feel

better, go ahead."

I was convinced Cosmo was a pathological liar. It seemed that he lied one hundred percent of the time. On a personal level, I find lying to be exhausting because it just leads to more lying. The energy that Cosmo seemed to put into his constant lying over his whereabouts just wouldn't have been worth it to me.

Once, in exasperation, I had blurted out, "Cosmo, don't you think life would be easier for you if you weren't spending all your time thinking up new excuses?"

Cosmo looked me right in the eye and scoffed, "What are you talking about?"

One day while Cosmo was vigorously explaining why he was three hours late for his physical therapy appointment, he opened his mouth wide enough for me to catch a glimpse of his teeth. They were black with decay and visible rot. The ones that weren't actually black were covered with a thick layer of mossy plaque.

"Jesus, Cosmo!" I gasped.

Cosmo realized his mistake and snapped his mouth shut.

"Open your mouth."

He narrowed his eyes at me, but opened his mouth.

"What happened?"

"I fell in with the wrong crowd when I was on tour."

"What?"

"No one I hung out with liked to brush their teeth."

"Come on, you're kidding me!"

Cosmo, as it turned out, hadn't brushed his teeth during the entire year he had spent in Afghanistan. And given the current mossy condition of his teeth, I doubted he brushed his teeth during his stay at Walter Reed, either. I contacted Cosmo's nurse case manager, who sent him immediately to the dentist.

I wish I could have been there when the Walter Reed dentist got a look at the inside of Cosmo's ugly mug. It must have been dramatic because Cosmo was immediately scheduled for a "deep cleaning" over a course of several days. The deep cleaning was so intense they sedated him. It was Cosmo's first legitimate missed physical therapy excuse. I gave him the entire week off.

He came back the next week. From across the room, I saw him hanging out by the water fountain with a few soldiers. It was the middle of the afternoon. Hardly his 0900 appointment slot. Cosmo gave me a smirk and we started back up where we left off.

"How long have you been in here?"

"I've been waiting for you to notice me."

I looked closely at Cosmo. The edges of his mouth were imperceptibly turned up and his eyes twinkled. The normal accusatory tone in his voice was gone.

Once a week at work we had a meeting about soldiers and marines who concerned us, with representatives from each of the disciplines in our patients' Walter Reed lives: PT, OT, social work, physical medicine, the nurse case manager, and the Warrior Transition Brigade. The official name of the meeting was the multidisciplinary meeting, but in the clinic it was better known as the "Bad Boy Meeting." It was a place to highlight soldiers who were missing their appointments, doing drugs, being disrespectful, or who were flat-out AWOL.

Cosmo was a frequent headliner in the Bad Boy Meeting.

But after attending my first Bad Boy Meeting about Cosmo, I realized that he wasn't just missing my appointments, he was missing everyone's. At least he popped into the clinic enough to keep me on my toes, while others at the meeting hadn't seen Cosmo in weeks. And compared to some of the other bad boys, Cosmo's tardiness was minor and routine, practically a lovable trait.

A few of the other bad boys had done some really bad things. One soldier, not combat injured, had flipped out and pulled a gun on a school bus full of children. He had lost his leg in a car accident and had been sent to Walter Reed for amputee rehab. Another one was wanted for pedophile charges back home once he was medically discharged from the military. In the meantime he was dragging out his recovery in our clinic, No Showing for his medical board appointments so they would have to be rescheduled for a later date.

I resolved that, in light of his relatively minor offenses, I would be easier on Cosmo. But it was more easily rationalized than done. I worked on my frustration through what I came to see as an unofficial Bad Boy Meeting — weekly bike rides with Maj. Tavner and Capt. Dumont.

By the end of the week, we all needed an opportunity to blow off a little steam, but probably no one more than Capt. Dumont, who spent so much time at work she had memorized the birthdays, home states, and "Live Days" (date of injury) of every one of our amputee patients.

We met at Walter Reed at 0800 on Saturday mornings. Riding up the hill toward the

MATC, I usually saw Maj. Tavner and Capt. Dumont standing outside the building straddling their bicycles. Capt. Dumont would look impatient, probably because she'd shown up on military time — fifteen minutes before we were supposed to meet. Although I couldn't entirely rule out that Capt. Dumont might never have left work the day before. She would give me a sullen stare while beside her, Maj. Tavner would smile and wave enthusiastically.

Once I'd showed up, we'd blast through the neighborhood outside of Walter Reed and down into Rock Creek Park, where we'd stand up on the pedals and ride fast and hard for three- to four-hour stretches. This is a long time to ride fast, especially considering the quality of our bicycles, which were rusted out and look like they were bought at yard sales in West Virginia.

Maj. Tavner was fast and entertaining to bike with. She was well informed, not just on our current patient caseload, but on unusual subject matters like edible root crops in Africa, the effects of poverty on self-esteem, and why certain people get PTSD and others do not. Maj. Tavner was a philosopher cyclist as much as she was a great physical therapist. Ride with Maj. Tavner and you always learned something.

But eventually the topic always drifted back to work, and our bike rides quickly turned into what they really were — a moving group-therapy session. Over the course of several hours we'd work our way through our patient lists. Who was having a hard time? Who was giving us a hard time? Who did something really nice? And who did something that kept us awake for a few nights?

On Saturday mornings, while the rest of D.C. was slowly waking up, a high-speed Bad Boy Meeting in Rock Creek Park was taking place.

We'd ride fast and ignore all bike trail rules, frequently riding two or three abreast. People yelled at us and then dove out of the way. We'd ride and ride and ride, crisscrossing back and forth over the city. Based on which soldier or marine was highlighting our conversation, our speed varied from a gentle, laughable conversation pace to, more frequently, a full-on chase during which we shrieked back and forth to each other over the noise of the wind and grinding gears.

Capt. Dumont and Maj. Tavner did most of the talking. While complaining is one of my better-known traits, during our bike rides I'd back off a bit, not wanting to interrupt Capt. Dumont and Maj. Tavner from their rare opportunity to vent. And vent we did, even the normally tight-lipped Capt. Dumont.

We'd ride from the northern suburbs of Silver Spring to the southern suburbs of Arlington and into Alexandria, barely covering half the patient list. We'd continue on, pedaling across D.C. to Bethesda, Silver Spring, and Takoma Park. Sweat would fly out of the holes in the sides of my helmet, and my voice would be hoarse from yelling.

Sometimes we'd stop briefly and discuss whether we should take a break. But we never did. We had more complaining to do. The kind that could not be done tastefully in a Bethesda coffee shop.

In Bethesda, we'd straddle our bikes for five minutes and debate getting ice cream, before plowing ahead to Silver Spring. Upon arriving in historic Mount Vernon after a hard twelve-mile uphill push, we'd consider taking a tour before ruefully turning our bikes around in the parking lot and plunging back down the hill toward a distant Washington, D.C. I might not mention Cosmo once, but it was immensely helpful to realize out there, twenty miles from Walter Reed, that I wasn't the only one struggling with a difficult patient.

# TBI

It wasn't quite 0700, but there were already a few patients working out in the PT gym when I walked through with Casey, my new student intern. One of the patients, a heavily tattooed marine walking on a C-Leg (a sleek silver prosthesis we started all our new AKs on) came walking briskly up to us.

I braced myself for our usual morning routine. For the past month, ever since he had gotten his C-Leg — which has a microprocessor in the knee and a sensor in the foot to automatically tighten the joint for additional stability or release it for smooth walking — Juan had very politely asked me the same question, word for word, every morning. Sometimes he'd ask me throughout the day.

"Question," Juan would say, holding up one finger.

"Yes?"

"Do you see how I'm walking?" He was

lurching over to the side of his prosthetic leg when he walked. This was known technically as a Trendelenburg gait pattern, a common gait abnormality seen in above-knee amputees because they have lost the attachment site of some of the hip-stabilizing muscles that used to attach below the level of their amputation.

"Why do you think I'm walking this way? Is it my socket?"

"No. I think it's probably something you're doing."

"Do you think that maybe it's a little bit my socket?"

"Well, it might be a little. But mostly, I think it might be you."

"Really? Don't you think a new socket would help?"

"Maybe a little bit. But mostly it will get better when you get stronger on that leg and can balance on it better."

"You think that will help?"

"Totally. It will totally help. We can work on it together."

"Thank you."

"I'd be happy to, Juan."

For me, it's not unusual to have the same scripted conversation with the same person every day and sometimes several times in one day. But having Casey standing there taking it all in made me acutely aware that she was going to witness this routine question-and-answer session between me and Juan every morning for the next three months, the entire course of her internship.

Juan was extremely smart and composed. He had a fast-paced job in the military, and ultimately, after his recovery, he went to work for a powerful defense contractor. But part of the problem of being in an explosion is that it can give you a mild traumatic brain injury (TBI). Not enough to cause obvious damage, but enough to make things seem slightly askew.

To work on his one-legged balance, I lined up some cones on one side of the clinic for Juan to practice stepping over. The concept of the cone drill is not difficult to grasp. You tap the cone with your foot and then step over it and tap the next cone. It's just a PT trick to get you to balance on your prosthetic leg.

As I demonstrated, I said aloud for clarity, "Tap and step over."

Juan was a total workout freak and was chomping at the bit to get going on this drill.

"Got it."

"Okay, let's see."

He tapped the cone but didn't step over it.

"Okay, that was good. But this time, let's tap and step *over* the cone."

"Oh, yes! I forgot."

"That's it. Tap the cone. Oops. You didn't step over. You stepped to the side. You need to step over."

"Oh yes. I got it."

"Okay. Okay. That was really good. But now, let's step over. See, watch me. I tap. And then I step *over*. Not to the side. *Over*."

"Oh yes. I see what you mean."

I could have the tap-and-step-over conversation with Juan for an hour and not get rattled. It is the hallmark of a very mild brain injury, a concussion type of injury, where nothing really seems wrong. Except in certain situations. Juan can follow directions easily, until they involve more than one step. And then difficulty will arise. Similar to how I might behave after a long and sleepless night. I would have trouble with the cone drill for sure then, too, and I might tend to perseverate on one or two seemingly minor things. Like maybe, my shoes feeling like they might be too tight.

It's totally normal and I knew in a few months Juan would be completely fine. But Casey, who had been thrown into this conversation without any background information, watched with obvious alarm. Her eyes swiveled back and forth between me and Juan, trying to figure out who exactly was the crazy one.

"Tap it and step *over*!"

"Do you see how I'm walking?"

Walter Reed was usually a very competitive internship. The students who were selected by their schools to go to Walter Reed frequently had scratched their way to the top of their school's selection list. Some of these alpha dogs arrived at Walter Reed ready to teach the staff physical therapists something, instead of the other way around. They gave us a smug once-over on their arrival, as if they were liberating a Neanderthal from a cave. But that definitely did not describe Casey, who arrived with big black circles under her eyes and hair electric with apprehension.

"I've got to tell you something," was the first thing she said to me. "I don't do well when people criticize me in public. I mean, I'm okay with criticism. I just don't like it in front of a lot of other people."

I thought that was comical. Did she expect me to dress her down in front of an entire battalion?

"I mean, one of my classmates found out I was coming here and she told me in front of the entire class that it should be her and

279

not me."

I laughed, thinking how funny it was that Casey was nervous to be coming to Walter Reed, because I had been wracked with a similar amount of anxiety about having agreed to take a student. Luckily, I had managed to quell my apprehension by thinking of my new student as not a student but as a *personal assistant*. And in any case, it was clear Casey was definitely not there on a mission to teach me about physical therapy. Instead she dutifully followed me everywhere. It was like having a film crew following me while I awkwardly narrated what was happening around us.

In 2010, we lost four full-time staff in the amputee section. They were not replaced. I'm not in administration, so I can't speculate why their positions weren't filled. But I imagine the reason would be government red tape and Base Realignment and Closure Commission hiring restrictions.

It unfortunately coincided with the surge in Afghanistan. We were simultaneously swallowing our old coworkers' caseload and absorbing more and more new patients. When we really needed all hands on deck over at Walter Reed, Walter Reed was in the process of moving to Bethesda.

Our clinic, which had been busy before, was now bursting at the seams. All the mat tables were full, the arm bikes were all in use, patients were sharing parallel bars, and the leg press machine had a visible queue of patients waiting their turn to use it. Every available piece of equipment seemed to have a line in front of it.

It was frustrating for the patients. And it was hard on the staff. Soldiers would joke about having to call in advance to "reserve a mat table," but even though they meant it as a joke, I'm sure it bothered them. And to stay on top of our rapidly accumulating paperwork, the staff was coming into work earlier and earlier. We worked through lunch and left late. There wasn't a minute in the day when we weren't working.

And when you are working that hard, you can't sleep either. I was treating patients all day long, and then in my mind all night, too, as I waited impatiently for sleep to rescue me. I would lie awake in bed feeling like there was a clamp around my head, getting ratcheted tighter and tighter.

This was the clinic Casey stepped into as a young, optimistic student. A clinic overrun with war casualties and stressed-out clinicians. Little did Casey know she would be cast into the role of mentoring her mentor. After we had reviewed all of our patients' charts and planned out everyone's treatment, after we had finished stretching out three different patients, disinfected their mat tables, got another one back in his wheelchair, ran a pair of legs over to prosthetics, waited impatiently for someone else to get their legs on, in those empty minutes when we had no one around who needed our help, I would confide in Casey: "Casey, I couldn't sleep at all last night. I feel like I'm on a treadmill without an off button."

While I might have fantasized about having my new student function as my personal assistant, I had instead quickly turned Casey into my own personal shrink. Casey would listen thoughtfully, like a true professional, to my medley of physical, stress-induced complaints before proffering her sympathetic advice. "I hear you. What you are going through, what everyone here is going through, is just so difficult. But just try to remind yourself it is temporary. You are doing the best job you can do."

Our congressionally ordered closure was less than a year away. Soon the patients would be transferred by army ambulance buses to a new hospital built on the grounds of National Naval Medical Center in Bethesda, Maryland. Arriving with them would be most of the clinical staff, the saber that Maj. Walter Reed had once carried, and the name — Walter Reed. The new hospital would hoist its flag and rename itself Walter Reed National Military Medical Center, and seven miles away a very unusual thing would happen. The gates at the old Walter Reed would close.

In anticipation of the BRAC move, the employee parking lots on base were closed down, one at a time. And people who had garage access were systematically kicked out.

In order to find parking on base you had to get to work earlier and earlier, to the point that the only way you could guarantee a parking spot for yourself was to arrive no later than six a.m. Even though I usually rode my bike, I was so tired, the last thing I wanted to do was pedal a hilly route to work in the dark. So in addition to working through lunch and staying late in the amputee clinic, now we were slogging in an hour earlier, just to find a parking space.

Then came the command decision that we would now be working mandatory weekend shifts. Thanks to the BRAC move, all of our weekend contract employees had been terminated. For me, the overtime pay was in no way worth the stress of working twelve days in a row.

My coworkers were dedicated and professional. They were upset about the work conditions, but for the most part they kept it to themselves and readjusted their lives. Because in spite of all the frustrating aspects of the BRAC, Walter Reed was a difficult place to leave. For many of us, we couldn't pull ourselves away. We believed in what we were doing. We were fighting the good fight. And I had an advantage. I had Casey.

One weekend after Casey joined us, I attended a party given by a distant relative who was part of the Coalition Provisional Authority in Iraq, a job I thought she may have gotten because she was the daughter of a prominent neoconservative. In spite of disagreeing with her politics, I think my relative is otherwise a very nice person. But unfortunately her friends fell into a common category of people that are hard to avoid in Washington, D.C. — young professionals swollen with self-importance. These were people chock-full of ambition. They moved to D.C. on an aggressive campaign to move up the ladder. Meanwhile, I had abruptly moved to D.C. with my inflatable mattress, a garbage bag full of clothes, and a bicycle because my way of getting over someone was just to suddenly leave town. In an ocean full of ships steaming aggressively toward some distant horizon, I had floated into town eight years earlier as an unmoored dinghy, bobbing aimlessly around and waiting for the typhoon to hit.

I was apprehensive about spending an entire evening trapped in a room full of people I usually judiciously avoided. But strangely enough, I enjoyed the party. Unlike the last party I'd attended, when I'd shown up with a six-pack of cheap beer, I carried a bottle of respectable red wine, nice shoes, and a lot of anxiety — but also a plan.

I had spent the Metro ride downtown trying to think of a good way to handle what I anticipated would be an over-the-top Washington, D.C., name-dropping affair. And I'd come up with a strategy that had been one hundred percent inspired by Jim.

Earlier that week the stress of seeing so many patients had started to seep into our tight-knit clinic. It started at lunch while we were all trying to catch up on our notes. One of my coworkers went through her caseload aloud, highlighting her superior intelligence by repeatedly describing her patient load as being much harder and more complicated than anyone else's. The rest of us, the beaten and downtrodden, sighed and tried to tune out this obnoxious behavior. But Jim grinned and said, "You are a real inspiration!"

Jim's compliments were rarely sincere, but he said them in such a pleasant way that you couldn't get angry with him.

A few days later it was a little after six in the morning and I and all of my dour coworkers were already at work in our new reality. Jim was sitting off to the side flipping through the newspaper and reading selected headlines aloud to the rest of us, in case we had forgotten that there was a world out there outside our clinic.

One article particularly entranced Jim. It was about free gifts you can give to your friends. The number one gift? Jim challenged us to guess, but there were no takers. The number one gift was, "A genuine compliment."

Jim read this aloud, and I laughed, "I guess that leaves you out!" And Sgt. Hernandez looked up from his computer, big black rings under his eyes from not sleeping, and chimed in, "Yeah, Jim. You are the most unsincere person I know."

Jim was thrilled by this noncompliment and beamed around the room.

"I guess I am!" he said with a smile, and then added, "Good for you!"

■ ■ ■ ■

When I arrived at the party, everyone was standing around a table drinking champagne and eating smelly, oozy cheese. It was interesting to be at a party where I was fully surrounded by right-wing think-tank strategists who I felt were responsible for our caseload of new amputees. Not only were they in some way involved in the suffering of patients that made me grind my teeth in my sleep, they appeared to be proud of this — or at least they were proud of their perceived power. There was constant name-dropping and meaningful handshakes while people introduced themselves by their first and last name, as if they were running for Congress.

I introduced myself by my first name and didn't mention where I worked. Instead, I listened as the conversation turned to the war and the guests discussed traumatic brain injuries like they knew what they were talking about. One of them had gone to Walter Reed to visit the troops that week. He'd probably been one of the blurred faces in the window that had watched me work. "I toured the Traumatic Brain Injury Ward at Walter Reed this week," he bragged loudly to the rest of the room, before going into some sort of layperson soliloquy on the statistics of traumatic brain injuries coming out of Iraq and Afghanistan. I was amused by the stilted way he pronounced each of the words, instead of using the acronym TBI, which you did if you really were getting your feet wet. The thousands of TBIs like Juan who had passed through Walter Reed had just helped catapult his career higher.

Warmed up by the champagne, I mingled and talked with everyone. When the conversation inevitably veered to how important they happened to be, I shut them down with an immediate and overly friendly, *"Good for you!"* Maybe the champagne helped. There was absolutely no malice. With Jim in my head, I heartily congratulated them on their success, smiling at their stunned faces, and clinking my glass to theirs before wandering off to pour myself another celebratory glass of champagne.

Balancing some cheese on a cracker, I laughed openly at their reaction. *Good for you!* It was what they had been angling for. But not exactly in the way I said it.

That Monday at work, I could hardly wait to tell Jim about my success at the party. As I anticipated, he puffed up and began preening with pride that I had concocted a strategy entirely based on him.

I met Casey, and as we walked into the clinic, we saw Juan.

"Question," Juan said, holding up one finger.

"Yes?"

"Do you see how I'm walking?"

"Um, yes."

"Why do you think I'm walking this way? Is it my socket?"

We continued to work together through the morning, and Juan truly made some good progress, even if he didn't actually step over the cone.

"Hey, good for you!" I told him. And meant it.

# C-Legs

We usually kept our bilateral AKs in stubbies until they were consistently wearing their legs six hours a day, able to get down to the floor and back up without support, step on and off a twelve-inch box, walk over uneven surfaces like grass and mulch, and go up and down average hills. Most important, they had to be consistently walking to the MATC from the Mologne House in their stubbies.

Cosmo had thrown up a roadblock there. He wore his stubbies but only in physical therapy, where he could walk sturdily around the level floors of our clinic. He could step on and off boxes, do push-ups, and walk up and down the ramp and stairs, but it didn't look pretty, and he sure wasn't walking around outside on his own.

Under great duress, he had walked in his stubbies with me twice to the Mologne House. It helped that most of the patients coming in on the medevacs now were triple amputees. So no one even noticed a bilateral above-knee guy walking across base in stubbies.

It's much harder to make the progression to full-length prosthetic legs if you haven't spent enough time in stubbies. One marine described walking on two prosthetic knees as "walking on stilts with hinges." If you haven't mastered the necessary skills in your stubbies first, it is way more difficult to acquire them when perched on top of knees. The balance requirement is much more intense. Not to mention you need to learn how to control an artificial knee and ankle joint that you cannot feel.

In the end, totally worn down by Cosmo's resistance to practicing in his stubbies outside the clinic, I decided to bump him up to full-length prosthetic legs with knees anyway. Later I would regret it. Maybe that was the mistake.

At Walter Reed, all the new above-knee amputees learned to walk on an advanced computerized prosthetic leg known as the C-Leg (and later, the updated version of the C-Leg, the X2). A computer chip in the C-Leg controls the stability of the prosthetic knee through a relay of signals between the sensors in the leg and the hydraulic cylinders in the knee.

When we land on our foot, the muscles around our knee prevent the knee from buckling underneath our weight. In a basic noncomputerized prosthetic knee, it is inherently more difficult to balance because you have to be able to throw your residual limb forcefully backward inside the socket to keep the knee from collapsing underneath you, should you stumble. This requires a lot of strength and lightning-fast reflexes — and remember, you can't feel your foot, so it's not like you get a heads-up that you are going down.

But in the C-Leg, if Cosmo stumbled, the knee stiffened up and provided support. He didn't have to kick his stump back into the socket to keep the knee from suddenly collapsing underneath him. And he didn't have to swing his stump forcefully forward to swing the lower leg out. The microprocessor would do that for him.

I'd stashed Cosmo's new legs in our "leg closet," which is where we kept a new walker's legs until they were safe on them. Walking into this closet took some getting used to. It was packed with legs: C-Legs. Power knees. RHEOs. Pliés. X2s. Mechanical knees. Running legs. Legs in bike shoes and dress shoes, legs in flip-flops, legs in combat boots, and legs with high heels (for one of the female soldiers). My favorite pair of legs had Rollerblades on the ends instead of feet.

In spite of the cheery roller-skating legs, the leg closet completely creeped me out. It reminded me of a tomb. But it didn't seem to faze Sgt. Hernandez, who frequently disappeared into the leg closet during his lunch hour with a pillow and a sheet to take a nap. Hovering behind him in my usual highly caffeinated state, I would get anxious just watching the door click shut behind him.

Since Ottobock invented the C-Leg in 1997, other microprocessor knees have been released. Össur, a prosthetic company in Iceland, released the RHEO in 2005 and the Power Knee in 2006. And Freedom Innovations, a California company, invented the Plié in 2007. And in 2009, Ottobock released the updated version of the C-Leg, the X2, billed as a "back to combat" knee. It has a stair-climbing mode, can be fully submerged in water, can walk backward, go from walking to running without reprogramming, and can negotiate steep declines. Best of all, it holds a charge for five days. It's powered by a rechargeable lithium battery in the shaft of the leg that can be charged just like a cell phone.

After getting used to the C-Leg, almost all of the above-knee amputees at Walter Reed try out the different computerized and mechanical knees before settling on the one that seems to be right for them. In the end, their go-to knee won't necessarily be a computerized one. Even though that is the latest in technology, many of the soldiers don't like the restrictions of having a computer controlling the artificial knee.

It took some time to find a patient's legs in the leg closet. I scanned the sockets until I saw the pair that matched the thighs I had become so intimately acquainted with in the year and a half Cosmo and I had been working together. I unplugged them and ran back to the clinic.

We started by learning how to walk in the parallel bars. The C-Leg's default mode is to keep the knee locked until the user shifts seventy percent of his or her body weight onto the toe of the C-Leg. Hitting "toe load" signals the microprocessor to unlock the knee and advance the foot forward. Most new C-Leg users require a lot of cueing to hit toe load. Usually they are hesitant, because it requires them to trust that the new leg is going to be there for them. It's a catch-22. If they don't shift their weight fully onto the prosthetic foot, the knee won't unlock underneath them and advance the lower leg forward. But it is also the position where they feel they are most likely to fall.

Except during his first time out, Cosmo was already charging across the parallel bars. He was more than halfway across the parallel bars and approaching the ramp at the end when I realized what was happening. "Hey, hey! Look at me!" Cosmo cheered himself on. "Fucking awesome! Fucking bad ass!"

I darted behind him, ready to grab him if he tried to step outside the parallel bars, but Cosmo reached the end and twirled around coming face-to-face with me. "You got some sort of problem?" he asked me, and I sighed in spite of myself.

There was no reason to cue Cosmo how to hit toe load, I thought as I watched him strut in the parallel bars. He was already doing it. His impulsivity and lack of fear had taught him how to use the C-Leg even before I could.

But it would be a whole different ball game when we left the parallel bars. The parallel bars give you artificial stability. Outside the parallel bars, even if you are hooked to the zip-line in the ceiling to keep you from falling, and even using crutches or canes, trying to stay upright while balancing on two artificial ankles and two artificial knees is extremely difficult. Your hip muscles are working overtime to stabilize your stumps inside your prosthetic sockets (even more so if you talked your prosthetist into giving you advanced, wobbly-bobbly feet) and your trunk muscles are stressed out trying to stabilize your trunk over your hips. You can't feel the floor. Without good muscular control, step wrong and you'll catch your toe on the floor or accidentally hit toe load and down you'll go.

We walked sideways in the parallel bars and then backward. Taking a step backward was something that required a lot of focus in the C-Leg, and in other prosthetic knees that released the knee via a toe load trigger, because the motion of placing the leg behind you could easily cause you to accidentally land on the toe, unlock the knee, and drop to the ground. I wasn't about to move Cosmo out of the parallel bars just yet.

We moved ahead to my next standard in my arsenal of drills, the cone drill. We had a lot of high-tech equipment in the physical therapy clinic, like, for example, a seventy-thousand-dollar antigravity treadmill, the AlterG. It has an air chamber that could unweight you to as little as twenty percent of your body weight, suspending you above a cushion of blowing air, making it possible to run on a fractured leg. But it also gave you what the patients zealously described as a "power wedgie."

We had a computerized perturbation platform, a climbing wall, and a million-dollar virtual reality treadmill that tilted up to three feet in any direction in space and reacted to a soldier's movements by speeding up or slowing down. We also later got two Olympic-sized balance beams.

This top-of-the-line equipment was nice to have, but in most cases, like the climbing wall and balance beams, it was totally ridiculous. I wouldn't trust myself on the balance beam, let alone a new bilateral amputee. Most of our patients, who were used to much more sophisticated video games, scoffed at the virtual reality treadmill and thought it was "boring." They called it "Pong." The perturbation platform took too much time to set up, and unless you wanted to learn how to walk on a boat or wow everyone in the middle of an earthquake, didn't have a lot of carry-over. And with the exception of those few who seemingly had the proverbial "crotch of steel," no one was lining up much to get on the AlterG.

Which was why no piece of equipment got

more use than our set of five-dollar plastic cones.

Patients who were missing just one leg practiced stepping over the cones, and then progressed to lightly tapping the cone with their intact side and stepping over it while balancing only on their prosthetic limb. Patients who were missing both legs practiced weaving through the cones. Both drills, done with the support of the parallel bars, could be tricky. But done with no support at all, they were completely unnerving.

Once I saw the most battle-rough Army Ranger become completely undone when faced with the daunting prospect of stepping over the cone outside the parallel bars for the first time. With his muscular chest and arms, crew cut, and skull tattoos, he was a guy you might be afraid of. But there he was, standing on the rubberized track and harnessed to the zip-line facing a small, cheerful yellow cone and looking absolutely terrified. His physical therapist stood totally oblivious beside him. "Sergeant! Just tap it. Tap it!"

Cone drills were done forward, backward, sideways, in a zigzag pattern, and sometimes, since this was a military clinic, while carrying a fake machine gun. There was no end to the type of cone drills we could do.

In addition to the cones, we also had the equally cheap floor ladder for agility drills. This was a ladder we had made ourselves by affixing electrical tape to the floor. We used to have a real floor ladder with rope and plastic slats, but we got rid of it after a congresswoman caught her high heel in one of the rungs and almost bashed her head open right in front of us. The ladder was also frequently in use.

We had about twenty cones. I made sure I took only seven. Woe to the therapist who greedily set up all the cones for his or her patient to practice with. Laying the cones out every eighteen inches in the parallel bars, I had Cosmo practice walking sideways while swinging his prosthetic legs around each cone. Punishment for knocking a cone over was ten push-ups.

Except I accidentally backed into a cone, knocking it over. "Fuck, yeah! Ten push-ups! Ten push-ups now!" Cosmo demanded gleefully. I ignored him, or I'd be doing push-ups for every single patient on my schedule, and I had twelve guys coming in after Cosmo.

Instead, I called for a spontaneous "skin check." Cosmo's sockets were new — his prosthetist was still in the process of making them fit more comfortably — and not every new amputee has good sensation on the bottom of their stump. Besides, Cosmo looked like he was ready to take a break, I needed to give him an out. He was breathing hard and sweat was rolling down the side of his face.

Cosmo pulled off his prosthetic legs and rolled the silicone liners off each of his stumps. A good quarter cup of sweat came pouring out of each one onto the floor.

Cosmo's skin was pink and a little sweaty. Perfect. He seemed a little disappointed. I think he was anticipating the look of horror on my face if he'd pulled a bloody stump out of his socket. Still, he lingered in his wheelchair, taking advantage of my skin check to rest. His T-shirt was drenched in sweat.

Later Cosmo asked for permission to take a smoke break. I wasn't surprised when he didn't come back.

Walking on prosthetic legs is a huge energy expenditure. Besides balancing on them, they are heavy. A bilateral above-knee amputee will expend sixty to three hundred times more energy just to walk at half the speed of his or her able-bodied counterpart. Which is why my patients might hear me gleefully telling them, "You'll never have to pay for a gym again!"

No matter how high tech prosthetics become, you still have to balance in them, and lift them up and down. And they certainly don't walk for you. In fact, if you walk badly in a cheap leg because you blew physical therapy off, you will walk just as terribly in an expensive leg.

Once, a high-level government official came to Walter Reed to test out the new X2 microprocessor knee. He had been walking on the first edition, C-Leg (what one of my male coworkers referred to as the "Cadillac of knees"), for ten years, but he hadn't done enough physical therapy. As a result, he had a very pronounced "funny walk." Lurching forward with his nose far ahead of his hips like he was leaning forward to smell flowers, he took a quick step with his intact leg, and then carefully brought his prosthetic leg level with his intact side, another quick step with his intact side, and then a slower step, bringing the C-Leg level with it.

I recognized his gait immediately. The wedding march! He didn't have the skill or strength to balance on his C-Leg very long, so he wasn't going to risk anything by balancing on it long enough to step past it with his other leg. Instead he wedding-marched around.

In spite of having a thirty-thousand-dollar prosthetic knee, he stiff-legged it around the clinic like he was wearing a peg, never allowing the top-of-the-line knee to bend. Or as we would say at Walter Reed, he was "walking like a pirate." This was alternatively called "going retro," "bringing it back," or "totally vintage." Strung together in a sentence, you might hear, "What's up, Captain Hook? You're totally retro today. Does your socket hurt? Are you touching bottom? Are you bringing it back? Going vintage?" No one else might understand us, but our patients sure did.

He was at Walter Reed because, unbeknownst to me, he was a high-level DOD official chosen to receive the new X2. One of my patients had tested out an initial prototype of the X2 a few months earlier, so I had some experience with the knee, which was why he had been sent to me for some pointers. Only, he'd been sent over with no introduction. I had no idea who he was, why he was getting the X2, or why I had been summoned over to watch him walk.

I watched him walk and then laughed. "Where's the wedding?" He said he was hopeful the new X2 would help him walk better, and I retorted with a chuckle, "You walk like you're walking on a peg. So it doesn't matter if you have a new knee or an old knee, you won't walk any differently."

He was aghast and left to get his new high-tech knee. Forty-five minutes later, he came wedding-marching back up to me. "See? Totally retro," I said. But the way he walked wasn't unusual for an untrained amputee. "Don't stress," I said. "Let's try something." I tied a long, thick piece of Thera-Band (an elastic cord frequently used in therapy) around his prosthetic leg and had him walk while I physically restrained it on the ground, forcing him to balance on it much longer than he would have liked.

To encourage him to stand up straight and power his prosthetic leg past his intact side, I leaned back and pulled as hard as I could on my end of the Thera-Band. It was completely crude, and his aides looked totally appalled as he huffed and puffed around the clinic dragging me behind him like a water skier. What was worse were my poorly chosen words of encouragement as we went around and around the track, and I shouted, *"No! More! Wedding! March!"*

But when I took the Thera-Band off, since he was still used to pulling against my resistance, he took symmetrical steps around the clinic, swinging his prosthetic leg out in front of the other leg for probably the first time in his life. It wasn't the new knee. It was just the fact that he was still anticipating pulling me along.

"See, now you are walking pretty," I said smugly. "You just need to drag a manhole cover behind you for a few days and you'll walk fine."

I found out later who he was and had about a week of sleepless nights while I waited to get canned for my galling lack of respect. I never got fired, and a few months later I received a Certificate of Appreciation from this nice man's office. Maybe he appreciated the pointer, or more likely, he appreciated someone finally being totally upfront with him, something that his position had probably prevented.

I'd just treated him like anyone else, and I was used to operating inside the confines of our clinic's fairly crude locker-room mentality. Once our patients were up and walking on their prosthesis, we dropped the Florence Nightingale acts. Their days of being greeted with applause the first time they nervously pushed themselves into the MATC without help were long behind them. Now we monitored their arrival time and gave them a hard time about what they were doing when they weren't in physical therapy.

"You're late, sister! I hope you have a good excuse."

I could be a total dictator. It's not that my patients were walking badly, they were just not, as I like to put it, "walking pretty." With ten to fourteen soldiers and marines on my daily schedule, "Walk pretty!" was my signature war cry.

While aesthetically it is better to have a "pretty walk" than a "funny walk," the real reason you want to have a pretty walk is that it will spare your remaining joints from the additional stress of having to compensate for a lifelong lurching gait. This is especially important for our amputee soldiers, most of whom are in their early twenties and have many decades ahead of them. Not counting phantom limb pain, low back pain is the number one complaint in all amputees. I experienced a touch of this after spraining my ankle one weekend. On Monday, my ankle still twinged a little — but what was really killing me was my back after walking funny for two days.

Older amputees seem to have numerous weird orthopedic injuries. They get multiple joint replacements — shoulders, hip, knee. They get spinal arthritis. Tear their rotator cuffs. Fall down and break their arms. Not because they have bad luck, but because they walk funny. Once you can safely stump around short household distances, insurance companies aren't going to keep paying for the necessary rehab to help you walk pretty. But they will later pay, without hesitation, for you to have your knee and your hip replaced, your spine fused, and your torn rotator cuff repaired.

Everyone had their own strategy in the clinic to tackle what my coworkers and I referred to as the "Amputee Pimp Walk."

Sgt. Hernandez hammered it out of them with good old-fashioned strengthening, complete with systematic and obtainable weekly goals.

Capt. Dumont set up full-length mirrors at each end of the clinic, and her patients walked back and forth between the mirrors for fifteen minutes before their treatment session.

Darcy's patients were easy to find, you just followed the trail of sweat. They were getting killed with cardio.

Jim's patients were almost always enjoying a long walk, a piece of cake, and good conversation.

While assembled on the side of the clinic, my patients would do agility drill after agility drill.

We freely bounced and stole ideas from one another. If someone did something that seemed to work, we'd use it with our patients, too. For a while there, our clinic resembled a fashion runway, with a half-dozen soldiers walking back and forth between full-length mirrors.

But no matter what the method was, the goal was the same: to get our patients back to the highest and best level of function, and at Walter Reed, with the luxury of long-term physical therapy and the best prosthetic care, we were able to do that.

We were always aghast at how badly civilian amputees walked when we saw one out in the community. If I was with one of my coworkers, we'd stop on the sidewalk visibly recoiling in horror.

"Did you see that?" we'd whisper back and forth to each other. "He's walking like he's a hip disartic" — a person who has lost his leg at the hip joint — "and he's only an AK!"

# WAR VICTIMS

With the surge in Afghanistan, we were not just overrun with patients — we were also overrun with clowns. Two local clowns had taken to showing up more and more frequently in our clinic. While the clowns blew their bubble pipes and swaggered around in extra-large red shoes, my coworkers and I rushed frantically back and forth across the room treating multiple patients.

Darcy, normally perpetually happy, had to leave the floor for five minutes and take a break after a clown deliberately sprayed her in the face with a water pistol. "I swear, I almost punched him in the mouth," she said when she came back into the clinic, flushed with unusual anger.

The next morning we got five new amputees. "That's practically a full caseload," Jim said with some alarm. "Did we get a new physical therapist, too?"

Two days later we got another five new

amputees. Ten in a week. Eight of them were triple amputees. I held my breath waiting to see what Jim was going to say, but this time he didn't say anything.

And I was assigned a special patient: a high-ranking officer with a sprained ankle who was insisting on being treated in the amputee clinic. My major with the sprained ankle had been going from physical therapist to physical therapist. She was the perfect *Washington Post* patient, the kind of patient who needed to be placated before she started calling congressmen and reporters to complain about her treatment. She had been boarded at Walter Reed for two years, refusing to leave, while seeking validation for the most minor of injuries in a clinic where no one even had an ankle.

Walter Reed, besides treating actual combat injuries, also unfortunately functioned as a large workman's compensation facility. We had many, many soldiers sent to Walter Reed with legitimate and painful injuries that prevented them from being able to fire their weapon, wear heavy armor, or run. But we also had soldiers seeking treatment at Walter Reed for exaggerated injuries. They were almost always pain complaints, since it is impossible to prove that someone doesn't have pain. There were dozens, probably hundreds, of soldiers being boarded at Walter Reed for minor injuries. Some of them really worked the system. One patient stayed at Walter Reed long enough to get married and have two children!

It was one of the luxuries of working in the amputee clinic. No one could fake an amputation. But then I got the major as a patient. With a caseload of mostly double and triple amputees, I was surprised to find myself rehabbing a two-year-old ankle sprain.

Out of the ten new patients in the amputee clinic, I knew immediately that the major was the one who would never get better. Because I've discovered that no matter what the situation is, in life there are always people who view themselves as a victim, and victims never get better.

In situations like these, I always remember my interview for physical therapy school. There were six interviewers and me. For an hour they put the screws to me, asking me difficult questions and questioning my answers — mostly, I think, to see how I would react. Some of the questions I had predicted: *Why did I want to be a physical therapist? Why should they pick me?* Some of them were simply strange: *What person from history would I most want to be?*

And then they asked me a seemingly innocuous question: *How would I react if I had studied hard for an exam and then received a bad grade? What would I do?*

I said I wouldn't do anything.

"But you studied really hard for this exam."

"Well, I guess I didn't study hard enough."

They weren't satisfied with my answer and we went back and forth.

"What would you do?"

"I wouldn't do anything."

"Nothing? You got a bad grade and you wouldn't do anything?"

"No."

"Would you talk to your professor?"

"No."

"You wouldn't do anything?"

"I would study harder for the next exam."

After the interview I kept drifting back to that question. What would I do if I got a bad grade? How would I react? Compared to the many more difficult questions and scenarios my interviewers had asked me, this seemingly minor question was the one that puzzled me the most.

Later, in my first year of PT school, I was surprised to see some of my classmates, always the same ones, argue with the professors over a few missed points on an exam, a question they missed, yet somehow this was the professor's fault — not theirs. It was the interview question being reenacted for me.

That interview taught me a life lesson, because now I understand the question: They were screening me. They were screening me to see if in difficult situations I would play the role of victim or pick myself up and do what I could do. It is a character trait that, after eleven years of clinical practice, I can instantly pick out in people.

It didn't take me very long. The small outpatient clinic I worked in after graduation in downtown Baltimore was on the fifth floor of a large medical office building. During my first week, I walked out to the waiting room to meet my afternoon patient. He was a workman's compensation case referred for low back pain. Slouched down in one of the waiting room chairs and listening to his iPod, he didn't look like he was in a lot of pain. But as soon as I called his name, his face wrinkled up into a pucker like he had just eaten a lemon. As we walked back to the examining room, his gait dramatically deteriorated. By the time we got to the examining room, I was worried for his safety as he careened off the walls of the clinic and used furniture and exercise equipment to propel himself forward. I helped lift him onto the table.

I was scared. His physical deterioration had happened so rapidly. While he lay panting on the table in agony, I gently lifted his right leg up to test his range of motion and he took a deep breath in and screamed at the top of his lungs. Startled, I dropped his leg, evoking yet another blood-curdling scream, at which point I decided to immediately end the exam.

With an arm around his waist, I walked him carefully back to the waiting room, where the patients in the waiting room sat bolt upright in anticipation. They watched us shuffle toward them with nervous eyes. I felt terrible and wanted to call an ambulance. But he refused an ambulance and instead decided to reschedule his appointment with me. *Huh?*

While he was with the receptionist discussing different appointment times, I ducked out of the clinic and ran down the five flights of stairs to the lobby. I was sitting in one of the overstuffed couches in the lobby when he came walking smugly and strongly out of the elevator. He was just about to stride right past me when I jumped up, threw my arms in the air, and yelled, *"It's a miracle!"*

He never came back. And from that day

on, whenever I had a questionable patient presentation, I always went down and sat on that couch in the lobby and waited. The security guard loved it and would get all fidgety in anticipation. But my boss didn't love it when word got back to her about my new evaluation tactic, and she put an immediate end to my "It's a Miracle" test.

Ever since that day, I've been tainted. I know it and I regret it and I try not to judge. But in spite of my best efforts, I know I maintain a shred of skepticism, which is why, so many years later, I am still working with amputees. Because no one can fake an amputation.

But even in the amputee clinic, it has been helpful for me to realize that there are some people who will never get better. Not because of their injuries, and not because of their physical therapist, but because of themselves. They will always be a victim.

It can be very easy to beat yourself up when patients don't live up to their potential. You try every trick in the book. You rally them. You rally yourself. You consult others. You get frustrated. They get frustrated. You stay up late at night thinking about it.

For me, it has been a comfort to drift back to that interview and try to accept that, no matter what the situation, there are people who will simply never take responsibility. It's never their problem. But if I'm not careful, it becomes my problem. I blame myself.

In addition to my major, I had three relatively new patients in the clinic. One only a week out from his injury, loaded down with lines and tubes, was matter-of-factly doing sit-ups on the mat. Another one, with both legs amputated and both of his arms broken, was carefully wiggling himself out of his wheelchair and onto an adjacent mat table. My third patient was trying out his prosthetic leg for the first time in the parallel bars. Because he was missing a hand, he couldn't use crutches and just had to be brave. I held on to his bicep in case he lost his balance and, mostly, to keep myself calm.

In the corner of the room, doing balance exercises where I could see her, was the major. She was pleasant and enthusiastic and always eager to show me how hard she was working. I knew that in four months my three other new patients would have made great progress, but the major would still be saying she had ankle pain.

Her old physical therapist from the outpatient clinic walked into the amputee clinic one day and completely freaked out when he saw the major in our clinic doing her ankle exercises. He started yelling at me. What was she doing in there? He had discharged her. She had refused to do anything he gave her to do. What did I think I was doing?

I said I wasn't doing anything different. It didn't matter whom she saw, him or me. She wasn't going to get better. She wanted to be a war victim. And she wanted to be in the amputee clinic.

Behind the major, the clowns were clustered around a marine who was missing both of his hands. They had brought in an Apple iPad, a computer they thought he could use, except the touch screen didn't react to his fake hands. The patient didn't care. There are a lot of more important things he can't do with his fake hands.

But the clowns didn't understand. They would not give up. They got frustrated. When a physical therapist walked by, the clowns shot him in the back of the head with a water gun.

No one laughed.

The next morning in the 0700 Tuesday staff meeting, the talk turned to the anxiety-provoking Saturday morning employee field trip to Mount Vernon, George Washington's historic estate. Everyone was wiped out

316

from the nonstop work, and being forced to tour a historic site on our day off was not helping our stress level. Every few months, a semi-mandatory department outing was planned. Not for the patients, who have choices in such matters, but for the staff, who are peer-pressured from all levels to attend.

Usually these were fun events. Happy hours at the Quarry House Tavern or barbeques at the colonel's. A few times we went to a baseball game, where everyone relaxed and sat back in the stands with a beer and a chili dog.

But we also went on a few fairly strenuous outings — to the ballet, the opera, and once, a Southeast Asia cultural fair at the Kennedy Center. Jim championed these outings because he was on a perpetual quest for culture.

Jim was the *Social Secretary* — a position he frequently said he was going to quit, except he was the one who'd created the position of Social Secretary and appointed himself to it, so it's not like he could just fire himself. Lately Jim had been flexing his Social Secretary muscle and aggressively pushing the Mount Vernon trip through, like a president pushing an unpopular bill through Congress. Under the guise of democracy, Jim held a vote a few staff meetings back and everyone who was in favor of going to Mount Vernon had raised their hands. Three people. Sold. Thirty-seven of us did not raise our hands, but now we were all going.

One of those three hands voting yes had belonged to Jasmine. Beside her, I shook my head in disbelief. Twelve years outside of the cadaver lab and we were still the Odd Couple.

The Quarry House was easily the hands-down favorite for official and unofficial staff outings. A local dive bar, the tavern had a distinctive putrid smell: part mildew, part litter box. The stink was especially strong in the front bar. Which was why Quarry House regulars skirted quickly to the back room, leaving newbie coworkers standing in the front wrinkling their nose. A group of regulars went to the Quarry House so often that they jokingly referred to it as "the Office."

We sure weren't going to the Office this time.

In the staff locker room, after we first checked under the stall doors for shiny commander boots, a low-level hysteria about the Mount Vernon trip started bubbling to the surface. Instead of driving, we were all going to "cruise" there on a boat from Alexandria. This had seemed like a harmless and fun idea until it leaked out that there wouldn't be a return boat for a full six hours.

The occupational therapists who shared the locker room with us seemed to be enjoying the physical therapy drama a little too much.

"Is it true?" they asked, stirring the pot, wide-eyed in contrived innocence. "Are you guys really spending an entire Saturday touring Mount Vernon?" And then a small snicker escaped their lips.

On the morning of the trip, everyone morosely met in Alexandria expecting to board one of the dinner cruise ships. But instead we were corralled onto a small fishing boat. The only place to sit was in the downstairs cabin, on a couple of aluminum benches.

But the smell of gasoline pushed almost everyone out on the deck. There wasn't room to stand outside. So we stood single file, hanging on to the side of the boat and shouting back and forth to one another over the wind and spray. It was bouncy and loud, but the way the sun reflected off the green water was stunning. And to our disbelief we saw two bald eagles flying above our boat, seemingly on their way to Mount Vernon themselves.

Downstairs in the cabin, Jasmine seemed to not mind the gasoline smell and was looking out the window at the green water of the Potomac. Maj. Crazy sat next to her, clutching a bag of popcorn and looking upset.

"I thought we were going on a cruise," Maj. Crazy complained bitterly. "This is *not* a cruise. I thought they would be serving breakfast. Instead I had to pay two dollars for this bag of popcorn. And it's stale."

Once we arrived at Mount Vernon, everyone warily climbed off the boat. We were clutching paperback novels and magazines, grimly prepared to spend six hours stranded at a historic site. In my backpack, in addition to a sandwich and a bottle of water, I had brought a detailed list of bus schedules in case anyone wanted to spend two hours getting home on public transportation with me.

But the time went by faster than we thought, and in the end, there was no better place to be than sitting on the grass beside the Potomac River with a few coworkers sprawled quietly behind you. No hospital monitors beeping, no crying mothers, no clowns with their iPads, no patients without hands. It was just quiet and green and smelled like water and flowers.

We could have been home frantically doing laundry and grocery shopping and getting ready for another week of casualties. Instead, we were at Mount Vernon, George Washington's beautiful riverside home, where during years away at battle he understandably yearned to return.

# THE REAL THING

I was outside with Cosmo on the uneven grassy hill behind the clinic. Cosmo was perched way up high on his C-Legs, and I had a belt around his waist so that I could hold on to him while we carefully negotiated the terrain. It was difficult and scary. Cosmo was a lot bigger than me, so if he fell, all I'd be able to do would be to slow his descent. That is, if he didn't completely hammer me into the ground.

Cosmo stopped for a second to rest, leaning onto his canes, sweat running down the side of his face.

"So, I'm never really going to be able to go hiking again, am I?" he said. His question surprised me and for a few seconds I didn't say anything.

"It would be really difficult," I said, feeling sheepish. We weren't in Utah or Yellowstone. We were in Washington, D.C., walking down a sloping, overgrown, gravel parking lot.

"I thought that when I got my C-Legs I would be able to do all those things."

I'm not a big fan of never. But I didn't say that. Instead I admitted truthfully, "Nothing is as good as the real thing."

A lot of people are under the impression that there's nothing technology can't do. A lot of people — I would say most people — think that the new computerized and mechanized legs are bionic. That you can strap them on and they will walk for you.

I am sure that a technology-captivated young man like Cosmo certainly had those hopes. His only outlet, outside of physical therapy, were his video games where, in a computer-simulated environment, he could truly be a bionic man.

But the real world is much less forgiving. Even with the most advanced prosthetic legs, if you are a bilateral above-knee amputee, walking requires a lot of energy and a lot of strength to balance on your nubs on top of artificial knees and ankles and propel yourself along. And you have to do your homework. You have to be doing all that in stubbies first.

There are bilateral above-knee amputees who eventually walk, even run, everywhere. But there's another goal that eludes them:

to be back at the level they were before they got hurt. And most of these amputees have an advantage of being small and slight of build. The lighter you are, the easier it is to move yourself around. But for a large man, with a heavy, muscular torso, it is much more difficult.

I used to joke with my patients that if my father lost his legs it wouldn't affect him. He'd still be sitting in his armchair in the kitchen, micromanaging my mom and blasting the volume on the TV. Most amputees in America are elderly diabetics. In a way, being an amputee might have been harder for my patients, because they were not sedentary people. Not walking was hard for them. They did not want to be trapped inside.

I know the day we went outside and into the sun was the day I lost Cosmo.

Cosmo walked smoothly inside the clinic on his C-Legs. He got the knees to bend consistently and didn't catch his feet on the floor. But in the real world, outside of the amputee clinic, there are curbs and uneven sidewalks. There are hills and holes in the ground. There are rocks and roots. There are crowds and cars and runaway dogs. Even a supposedly level sidewalk tilts on an angle toward the street.

Why expend all that energy to go a hundred feet when you can easily zip by in a wheelchair?

Cosmo stopped doing physical therapy. He would pop by once a week; I'm sure, just to keep from getting in trouble with his case manager. I let him get away with it.

"Did you get caught up working on your Nobel Prize–winning research?" I asked him when he showed up again after missing a week of PT. I said it because I knew it would make him laugh. Cosmo laughed. He looked tired.

"What time did you go to bed?" I asked. Cosmo knew I found his bedtime to be fascinating, because he went to bed right around the time I woke up for work. "Xbox?" I said, even though I already knew the answer.

Cosmo was very strong and could have gotten to a level where he would be a community ambulator (someone who could walk around in his community). But it would have required a lot of time and work. And let's be honest. It wasn't his goal. It was mine.

I wanted Cosmo to be an ambulator.

I wanted Cosmo out in the world.

Instead, Cosmo retreated into an online world. A virtual world where he was whole again. Where he could link up, via Xbox live, with his old army buddies and be in the real army again. Thanks to the Internet, video monitors, and high-definition computer graphics, Cosmo was a soldier again, staying up all night and going on missions with online friends.

In a way, it was an escape I could understand. Online he was strong and fast and skilled and could go everywhere his friends could go. If he got hurt, it was just a game. Real life was much more frustrating.

When I'd get home from work I'd retreat to a screen, too, usually falling asleep in front of the TV. I considered buying an Xbox and trying one of the games Cosmo talked about. I wondered if it would have the same effect on me. Would it be more fun for me to run on a computer screen than through a suburban neighborhood?

Somehow I doubted it. Because running for me is about the feel of it. It's the discomfort I enjoy. And I enjoy it, I'm sure, because it is temporary.

But the discomfort that Cosmo felt wasn't temporary, it was permanent. He was not me. He was a very practical person, while I, with my compulsion to enter long-distance swimming events, can sometimes be prone to extremes. We talked about it one day when I suggested Cosmo use his legs instead of his wheelchair the next time he went to the mall.

"Are you fucking kidding me? Do you know how long it would take me to walk across the fucking mall in these fucking things? I wouldn't make it to PT in the morning."

"You wouldn't make it to PT in the morning anyway."

"Whatever. That's a fucked-up idea. Why the fuck would I want to do that?"

"I don't know. Maybe to practice walking? Just a crazy idea I had."

"Crazy idea is right. I tell you, I can blow any of these walking fuckers — even the BKs — across the mall, across this fucking base even, in my wheelchair. It's easy. Why the fuck would I want to fucking kill myself like that just to prove some dumb fucking point?"

Cosmo went home for a month on pass. While he was gone I fretted to myself about him. Was he stuck in his house all alone? Was he lost to a virtual life?

But Cosmo came back. He looked exuberant. He had gone on several trips, including camping in the Rockies. He found a wheelchair-accessible cabin. And went on a helicopter ride.

I was so relieved. He was out in the world.

We talked again about walking. Cosmo wasn't interested. He was okay with his life the way it was.

We had an anthropologist in our clinic once. He was a silent presence, there for the sole purpose of research. I didn't understand his position, except that he was studying us in some way. I asked him once what he had figured out about us, and he told me that we were forcing our goals on our patients.

The fact that he summed us up in one sentence was entirely uncomfortable for me. On the inside I felt immediately small and defensive. Of course we were going to work on walking. It was the amputee clinic. That's what we did. We weren't vocational rehab. We were physical therapy. But I didn't say that. Instead I muttered something about him being in the PT clinic and not Social Work and stalked away.

But I reflect back on that often and I can see in many situations that he was right.

The highest compliment my coworkers and I can give one another is how well someone's patient happens to be walking. It is a thrill. And if a patient doesn't walk well, it's almost always because they are "difficult." Doesn't listen to what you say.

Doesn't do the work. Doesn't come to PT.

But Cosmo wasn't always a difficult patient. In many ways he was the patient I identified the most with. We just didn't have the same goals.

And even though it wasn't the result I was aiming for, I am really proud of him.

# IT'S NOT ABOUT THE BIKE

I was alerted to Jim's participation in the Marine Corps Marathon by a text message from Maj. Tavner early on a Sunday morning. She was riding her bike down to D.C. to cheer him on, did I want to join?

I was surprised to hear that Jim was participating in the marathon, since Jim's only marathon training, as far as I knew, consisted of him speed walking to the cafeteria and back. I was more than curious and eagerly agreed to meet Maj. Tavner on the bike trail.

Pedaling through the fall foliage of Rock Creek Park, Maj. Tavner breathlessly filled me in on Jim's spontaneous Marine Corps Marathon entry. "He's doing the hand-crank."

The hand-crank bicycle is a three-wheeled recumbent bicycle that you propel using your arms. It is designed for people who have little or no lower-extremity function.

Every few months, the New York Achilles Track Club brings down hand-crank cycles and helps our wounded warriors enter local running events. Their mission is to create a community of able-bodied and disabled runners experiencing the sport of long-distance running together. This may include running, walking, or in some cases, use of a hand-crank bicycle. In addition to providing hand-crank cycles, the Achilles Track Club also provides able-bodied volunteer escorts — which was how Jim was quickly entered into the Marine Corps Marathon the night before.

"Who is he escorting?" I wanted to know. The patients we knew who were doing the Marine Corp Marathon were all experienced and enthusiastic hand-crank cyclists; this was the third and fourth marathon for many of them. In spite of their injuries, all of them, former marines, were in excellent shape.

Jim, on the other hand, was not. With the exception of about five minutes of prerace instruction on how to shift the gears and brake, Jim had no experience on hand-crank cycles and hadn't ridden even a regular bicycle in fifteen years.

I was immediately worried for Jim. "This is a crazy idea! He is going to have a heart attack out there."

Standing at the seventeen-mile mark of the marathon course, Maj. Tavner and I waited anxiously for the first of the hand cyclists to zoom around the corner on their way to the finish line. The hand-crank cyclists are much faster than the runners. We watched and cheered as we recognized patient after patient fly past us in a barely recognized blur on their way to the finish line.

Jim was not with any of them.

Darcy joined us just as the first group of runners began to zip past us. More and more runners began taking up the race-course, until the road was fully filled with marathoners. It was exhausting to continuously scan the course for Jim among the thirty thousand racers. We hadn't seen a single hand cyclist or wheelchair racer in several hours. Was it possible Jim had died out there?

By the three-hour mark, our concern for Jim began to sour.

"I bet he's standing in line at Georgetown Cupcake."

Maj. Tavner was the only one not to lose faith in Jim.

We called his cell phone several times, before flopping down on the curb and watching the slower runners plod past us.

We were discussing whether we should cut ahead to the finish line and look for Jim there, when I saw him on the far end of the road, a lone hand cyclist dwarfed by a sea of runners. We jumped up and down screaming, *"Jim! Jim!"*

Jim smiled when he saw us, giving us a gracious wave before being swallowed up again.

Running beside Jim was a tall woman in a red Achilles Track Club T-shirt. She appeared to be escorting Jim along the course. Was that possible?

After Jim cycled off, Maj. Tavner and I got back on our bikes for the usual hurly-burly ride home. After a shower, I flopped down on the couch when my cell phone beeped. It was a photo message from Darcy.

The text read simply, "Jim mile 20."

But the picture said so much more. In the picture Jim was *walking* and pulling his hand-crank bike behind him!

The next day at work, Jim enthusiastically described his adventures.

When we asked him about the runner who appeared to be escorting him, he smiled and sighed. "That was Saint Margaret."

Saint Margaret was a local triathlete who had volunteered to escort a disabled runner with the Achilles Track Club.

This was Margaret's first experience volunteering with the track club, but as it turned out, the disabled runner she had been paired with had been much faster than she was, so Margaret dropped back and decided to assist Jim, who looked like he could use some assistance.

Jim was, of course, in no way disabled and, unbeknownst to Margaret, was a volunteer just like her. But Jim enthusiastically welcomed her company, chatting happily with her about the different restaurants they were passing along the race route.

Margaret, who came from a long line of veterans, was proud to be escorting what she thought was a wounded soldier. As she ran beside her injured veteran through the spectator-packed start of the Marine Corps Marathon in our nation's capital, she became extremely emotional.

People cheered for Margaret and they cheered for Jim. The patriotic screams of the crowds were overwhelming — especially through Georgetown, where she struggled to push Jim up the hills. She is a small person, but Jim isn't.

She was pushing Jim up a particularly steep hill, when she felt a pair of hands on her back. Another runner was helping her.

Before he ran off, he leaned in, squeezed her shoulder, and said, "It's not about the race, it's about the *human race*," causing Margaret to burst into tears.

Her tears were short-lived, because Jim, arms tired, suddenly announced, "Margaret, you are about to witness a miracle." And he stopped the bike and stood up.

If Margaret was surprised to see Jim walking sturdily along, pulling his hand-crank bicycle behind him, she didn't say anything. After Jim had rested his arms sufficiently, he got back in his cycle and continued cranking as Margaret ran lightly along beside him.

Jim and Margaret passed her husband at the six-mile mark. Still stunned, she recovered enough to yell quickly, "I've got something to tell you!"

The spectators, seeing Jim appearing on the course in his blue track suit, red helmet, and red, white, and blue hand-crank bicycle, screamed with gusto. He was, as far as people could tell, the last of the injured veterans on the course.

Luckily, "Saint Margaret," as Jim had started calling her, had a good sense of humor. Fully aware now that Jim was an able-bodied volunteer, she began to anticipate Jim's "moments of healing" and the reaction from the cheering crowds.

In between moments of healing, Jim pedaled gratefully along the 26.2-mile course, relishing the cheers of thirty thousand spectators. "It was *amazing!*" he told us the next morning. "I felt like I was in a tunnel of screams. I'll never experience *anything* like that ever again."

The runners on the course had also enthusiastically cheered for Jim and, as they passed, cleared a path through the crowd of runners ahead of him.

"Wheelchair racer! Wheelchair racer coming through," they'd yell.

Only one runner didn't yield to the "wheelchair racer," and Jim and Saint Margaret accidentally knocked him over. It was at the eighteen-mile mark and they would have ordinarily stopped, but they were too close to the finish line.

In Darcy's photograph, at mile twenty, Jim is walking and enthusiastically waving at the camera. Walking slightly behind Jim and laughing shyly is Saint Margaret. On either side of them are spectators, wordlessly staring.

Of all people to pass them at that point in the race, it would be the colonel. She was not happy to see the spectacle of Jim miraculously walking. Not happy at all. Careering toward the finish line, she quickly yelled out one disapproving sentence as she flew by: "Jim, *what* are you *doing*?"

The next day, Jim entertained his patients with endless retellings of his adventures in the Marine Corps Marathon with the glow of a satisfied long-distance runner.

After lunch, an air force general stopped by our clinic to visit the troops. He was in town because he had run the marathon the day before. It was a yearly tradition for him and he described it to Maj. Tavner as she escorted him around the clinic.

This year's marathon had been particularly hard for him, but what really kept him going, he said, was seeing the injured soldiers on their hand-crank cycles. One soldier in particular had inspired him. And as he described him, we realized in silent horror that he was describing Jim — Jim, who at this point in the general's story, was a few feet away, obliviously typing on the computer.

"He was really having a hard time," the general told us, and described how sweat was coursing down Jim's face as he struggled over the final hill before the finish line. "I didn't think he was going to make it."

But with hundreds of screaming spectators lining the route, Jim managed to get himself over that final hill and surge across the finish line — the crowd exploding into a deafening roar of approval.

To the general, it was a display of courage he would never, in his lifetime, forget.

But luckily he'd forgotten exactly what Jim looked like.

When the general left the clinic, Jim went back to entertaining the patients and the staff with yet another retelling of his marathon day experience. Darcy's pictures of Jim were proudly displayed. And later that evening, we all, including Saint Margaret, received a personal thank-you email from Jim.

Saint Margaret had so thoroughly enjoyed her marathon experience with Jim that she wrote to the Achilles Track Club, volunteering to start a D.C.-based chapter. As for Maj. Tavner, Capt. Dumont, and I, we had continued biking until it got cold.

Unlike Jim, we didn't have any spectators enthusiastically cheering us on.

# Pigeon in the Pool

In his room on Ward 57, Jasper Pigeon startled when we opened his door. He jerked up in his bed, arms flailing and eyes blazing. I took a step back and muttered to my intern Casey, "Geez, how long was he in Theater?"

Pigeon was twenty-three, long, and pale — practically an albino — unusual for someone who had just come from deployment. Even though he was from Ohio, he spoke with a thick Brooklyn accent. The discrepancy prompted me to keep asking him where he was from. "I told you!" he'd spit out. "From Ohio."

He'd lost his leg above the knee, half of his other foot, and the tip of his middle finger. The doctors weren't specific about his hand injury, so I asked him about it and he held up his middle finger with the missing tip and said, "I can still do this."

"You'll be a good D.C. driver," I said.

After we left, I heard the occupational therapist, who had walked in after us, asking Pigeon about his hand. I pull Casey over and we watch Pigeon give the OT the finger.

A few days later in the clinic, Pigeon looked at me and said, "I was twenty-one when I killed my first man."

His comment took me by surprise. This was something physical therapy school doesn't teach you. I paused for a moment and finally said, "That must be hard to forget."

Pigeon studied my face for a long time. I imagine he was trying to decide between yelling at me or agreeing with me. After a while, his face relaxed and he admitted it was hard to forget.

I breathed out in relief and walked over to familiar territory, the parallel bars. But inside I berated myself — *Was that the right thing to say?* — because we took no classes on psychology or motivation in PT school.

I made a mental note to ask Casey what she would have done. "How do you think I handled that?" I'd ask later. Casey always gave good advice.

Before Casey and I took Pigeon back to Ward 57 that afternoon, I asked him if we could change his bandages.

Pigeon assented, and lay down on one of

340

the therapy mats while I unwrapped, cleaned, and rebandaged his stump. Then he rolled onto his stomach so I could take the bandage off the back of his thigh, except as soon as I touched his thigh he became furious.

"I don't want anyone touching my ass."

"I'm down by your knee, Pigeon, not your butt."

"You're awfully close."

"Pigeon, I swear, I'm nowhere close."

"I don't think you should be looking at my butt."

"Pigeon, I'm not looking at your butt. Look, why don't we just ask your nurse to change your dressings when we get back up to your room?"

"Oh no you don't! You said you were going to change my dressings. Now you're trying to get out of it."

"I can do it. But maybe you'd be more comfortable having Nursing do it?"

"See? There you go. You are trying to get out of *doing your job.*"

"Okay. Okay. Relax. Relax. I'll do it."

"Everyone in this room can see my ass."

"No one can see your ass. You're all covered up."

"My ass is hanging out and everyone can see it."

"No one can see anything, Pigeon. You're all covered up."

"Everyone can see *my ass*!"

With perfect comedic timing, Darcy — who had been watching the scene from the nearby parallel bars — interrupted, "Josh can't see." On cue, her patient Josh laughed and added in a deep voice, "I can't see your ass, man."

Pigeon let loose a hail of expletives. "What the hell is wrong with you people? You fucking lunatics! I'm fucking telling you to stop and you are still parading my goddamn asshole in front of everyone in this fucked up room." Casey and I bundled him into his wheelchair and rushed him back up to Ward 57.

I sure didn't need to make a mental note to ask Casey about this one. I could barely wait to get back down to the clinic and get her opinion on what had just happened. In the meantime, I tried to calm myself by imagining diving into a pool. A deep and quiet place. I briefly visualized myself in the cold water, and then went back to the task at hand — rushing Pigeon, who was screaming obscenities at us, back up to Ward 57.

Over the next several months, Pigeon was released from inpatient care and learned to walk around on a prosthetic leg in his daily sessions with us. Yet he stayed unpredictable. Quiet one minute, explosively angry the next. But mostly he was sad.

One thing was clear: Pigeon thought the typical strength progression we took with prosthetic patients was beneath him. He wasn't interested in our standard amputee protocol. He wasn't going to do cone drills or treadmill walking. Used to the days of thirty-five-mile ruck marches, obstacle courses, and eight-mile runs in full armor, he yearned for that feeling of full-body fatigue. His was a simple and frequently repeated request: to "get smoked," i.e., totally exhausted.

Pigeon wasn't the first one to ask to get smoked, but he was the hungriest for it. He'd sneer at the ladder drills, but if I offered him a drill culled from *Men's Health* magazine with the word "challenge" or "man" in it, he'd show a glimmer of interest. One day I saw him sitting morosely in the corner instead of doing the 25 manmaker challenge (a cross-fit exercise combining push-ups, prone dumbell rows, a squat-clean-thrust and standing lunges) I had given him to do. When I walked over to see what the problem was, Pigeon squeezed his belly fat and showed it to me.

"Adele, look how fat I'm getting. I've

never been fat before." And then he said a sentence that made me want to cry. "How did I go from being a total stud to this?"

Our soldiers are thin and wiry when they're carried off the ambulance bus. They lose more weight in the hospital as they rotate in and out of the OR every other day. Pigeon lost so much weight in the hospital that his cheekbones stuck out like shelves. One time when he stood up in the parallel bars, his pants fell right off of him.

But gradually the side effects of the medications start to appear. Pain medications, sleep medications, antidepressants, and nerve pain medications all have the unfortunate side effect of weight gain. It's the same on all the soldiers — right around the middle. The sudden appearance of love handles on a soldier who prided himself on his two-mile run times and ability to do a hundred push-ups in a row is, in some ways, more alarming to him than the loss of his leg.

But phantom limb pain in particular is, in the words of Dr. C, a real "show stopper." While you as a person are perfectly aware that your limb is gone, your brain never quite gets it. It will always think that the leg is there. After all, the nerve endings in the brain that were mapped to your leg are still intact. They have no idea that your leg isn't there. When those nerve endings don't receive any incoming messages from the missing leg, they start filling in the blanks themselves, creating a "phantom" sensation. If you didn't know better, you'd think you still had that leg. You could, after all, certainly still feel it.

Phantom sensation is frequently also phantom pain, maybe due to the traumatic nature of the limb loss; no one really knows. But if the foot you no longer have is in a prolonged cramp, has an itch, or a stabbing or burning sensation, there is nothing you can do about it. It's not like you can stretch your toes out, scratch the top of your foot, or pull your foot away from whatever is burning it.

There are some tricks to managing phantom pain. Wearing a prosthesis helps because you are giving your brain what it is searching for — a leg. Another trick is to straddle a mirror with the reflection facing your intact side. With the use of the mirror you can see two legs instead of one, and give your brain the visual it is searching for — that lost leg. If your foot is itching, you can look in that mirror while scratching your intact foot. To your brain, looking at two feet in the reflection in the mirror, it looks like you are scratching the foot that isn't there.

But in our clinic, with just about everyone missing two legs, mirror therapy wasn't something we could do anymore. While Pigeon still had part of his other foot, he hated looking at it: "It looks like a hoof." He sure wasn't going to do mirror therapy. In the end, the easiest solution was always medication. But the side effects were not pleasant.

Pigeon wanted to sweat. He wanted to get smoked. While I'd never done a half mile of burpees, before things got so crazy at work I was always training for some sort of endurance event, something long and suffering — a triathlon, a swim across the Chesapeake Bay, a century ride. I knew full-body fatigue. There was no better feeling in the world then to collapse in the grass after a long run, sunburned and soaked in sweat, with your pulse beating a slow and steady rhythm and your body and mind in a zenlike trance.

But I sure wasn't doing triathlons anymore. Not at the end of 2010, when my patient caseload shot completely through the roof.

I could understand Pigeon's alarm, because the same thing was happening to me. I had substituted beer for long-distance swimming, and now I was growing my very own little round belly. In fact, it was happening to everyone, all around the clinic.

A few months earlier, I had been up on Ward 57 working with one of my patients when his commander walked into his hospital room. They hadn't seen each other since before his injury.

Before his accident, this soldier had been a huge, muscular man. When I treated him in the ICU, I always liked to look at his pre-injury photographs. Photographs his wife had taped above his bed.

People looked so bad in the ICU. Swollen and bloated. Lines and tubes running out of their bodies. Machines ventilating their lungs for them. Thankfully there were those pictures above his bed, reminding us that he was a young, handsome, athletic soldier. A husband and a new father.

There were many days we thought he would die. But there he was, day after day, a testament to his own strength. His body had changed tremendously. He was a half of his former self, missing a leg at the groin and the other at midthigh. His left arm was amputated close to the armpit, and the other one had been heavily skin grafted.

I was curious how his commander would respond to him.

But the two men exchanged pleasantries, man to man. They talked about sports and wives. And then the commander left.

After he was gone, my patient looked at me and said, "He really looked like shit."

I laughed. "Wow."

"No, seriously. He got fat. He totally let himself go."

The commander hadn't even gotten hurt. But when you lose a leg, or two, it's hard to exercise. You gain a belly and sometimes a lot more. Especially at Walter Reed, where we were surrounded by trays and trays of homemade chocolate chip cookies.

Thanks to the generosity of the administration and local athletes, our patients were constantly being introduced to unusual sporting events that they couldn't do. Like rock climbing. The centerpiece of our clinic was our larger-than-life climbing wall. It was two stories tall and whenever there was a news feature about the amputee clinic, the cameras always zoomed in on the climbing wall. It was easily the most photographed piece of equipment in the entire hospital. Yet weeks, sometimes months, would go by without a single patient ever climbing it.

When new patients saw the climbing wall, their eyes lit up and they got immediately excited. I knew what they were thinking: *Hey, losing two legs must not be that bad if I'm going to be able to climb this wall. I'm going to get new legs and I'm going to climb this and do everything just like I did before.*

I was guilty of facilitating this kind of deception. The climbing wall was the very first thing I showed new patients, too. I did it because it cheered them up. And it was a lure. A way to get them to buy into physical therapy. But for all its usefulness in rehab, it might as well have been an ice-skating rink.

Pigeon was frequently limited by his prosthetic leg. His amputation was so high up on his thigh, it was hard to get a good socket fit. The socket frequently slipped off his stump, and sometimes it rotated on him when he walked. But swimming was something I thought he could do, since it mostly involved floating and you didn't have to worry about falling. In the pool you don't need fancy equipment. You don't need special water. You don't even need prosthetics. Just goggles and some bravado.

Outside of work I'd begun training again with a recreational swim team a few nights a week. We practiced at a community pool close to Walter Reed. One day I called and asked the pool manager if it would be okay if we brought some of the patients. I thought he'd say no, or at the very least, charge us, but he said that would be fine and that it would be free. So the next week we borrowed a van from Disabled Sports USA and drove five guys to the pool. Pigeon was the first to sign up.

I'm no swim coach and have no idea how to teach anyone to swim, but I'm a physical therapist, which in the patients' eyes puts me on the same level as Genghis Khan. So when I suggested everyone get out of their wheelchairs and into the pool, no one argued with me. It was shallow, only four feet deep, so if you had a leg you didn't necessarily have to be able to swim. But for the others, the ones who had no legs at all, my only strategy was for them to cling to the wall and venture across the pool in any way they saw fit.

We learned some surprising things: It is impossible for a person who is missing both legs to sink; you can do back flips off the side of the pool using just your arms to spring you into the air; and even if you are a triple amputee missing both legs and an arm, you can pull yourself easily and gracefully a half-dozen times back and forth across the pool with your one good arm.

I figured the pool program would gradually lose its appeal, but the next week when we brought the van around, eight patients waited along with Pigeon. And then eleven.

I consulted with the coach from my swim team and she volunteered her services. She didn't have a car, but took two trains and a bus to meet us in the middle of the day. She was a strict and serious coach. Pigeon would hang on the side of the pool, his injuries submerged under the water, listening seriously to her feedback, before pushing off to swim another lap under her guidance.

The soldiers learned modified flip turns and racing starts. They did drills and races and worked up to five hundred and then to two thousand yards of continuous swimming. Having a coach gave some legitimacy to our program. For two hours once a week, the soldiers stopped being patients and were transformed into a swim team of sorts.

We were still a motley crew at the pool. I was convinced our time there was limited. In addition to their obvious battle injuries, most of the patients had big, semi-offensive tattoos. They were loud and boisterous and left their prosthetic legs and arms lying around the pool deck. In between sets, they'd splash and dunk one another under the water and generally create inappropriate pool chaos.

But no one ever got mad at us. Instead, a strange thing began to happen. People started to swim with us. They'd get out of their lane and enthusiastically hop in ours.

"Man!" they would say, swimming up to the nearest soldier, "you are doing a good job. You keep on swimming! You can *do* this!"

One day we got to the recreation center and the elevator going down to the pool was broken. I thought that some of the guys could bump down the stairs on their behinds, but it was two flights. Would they have enough energy to lift themselves back up the stairs later?

We were getting ready to leave when the pool manager and two of the lifeguards came running up and wordlessly began carrying our most injured guys down the stairs. It happened so fast, I didn't get a chance to second-guess it. An hour later when we got out of the pool, they were standing at the stairs waiting for us. I had seen a lot of goodwill in my years at Walter Reed, but nothing on this level — physically reaching out and carrying another person. In my world of heroes and superheroes, I put those lifeguards right up there with firefighters and ambulance drivers.

The pool was a great place to revel in

goodwill for a while, but most important to Pigeon, the pool was a place where he could finally experience full-body fatigue again — hanging on to the side of the pool after swimming intervals for an hour, totally and utterly smoked.

Pigeon completed his medical board in nine months and was officially discharged from the army. He had killed his first man at twenty-one, but now he was heading off to college. Before leaving for the airport, he stopped by the clinic to say goodbye. I was standing behind some moving trolleys and didn't see him walk in. He sneaked up and bear-hugged me from behind, sweeping me completely off my feet as he carried me across the clinic.

"Let me go. Let me go!" I squirmed. I couldn't see who exactly had me, but I recognized Pigeon's obnoxious cologne. The inpatients who were lying on the therapy mats laughed as they watched me getting toted around.

This was in no way okay. When Pigeon set me back down on my feet, I let loose a shrill stream of high-pitched accusations. Pigeon looked down at me with self-satisfied amusement, watching me stomp my feet and rail at him.

"You are not allowed to just walk up to me and pick me up!"

"Whoa! Calm down. Calm down. I did not pick you up."

"What do you mean? You most certainly did."

"You leapt into my arms. You couldn't control yourself."

"That's crazy," I muttered, still angry, but starting to laugh a little bit in spite of myself.

"You saw me, a blond *Adonis,* a total *stud,* and couldn't help it." He smiled down at me. "It's okay. I don't blame you."

I made a mental note to call Casey later and discuss the scenario with her. Her internship with us was over, and she was working on a rotation at a slow-moving outpatient clinic in Florida, treating low-back-pain patients. A place where a patient would never dare grab her and carry her around like a bundle of firewood.

Pigeon shook my hand and stepped out the door. I watched him walk down the hallway, a tall, lanky man in blue jeans and an Old Navy sweatshirt. He could have been anyone.

# THE DONOR

Five days after donating bone marrow, I returned to work, limping like a new, untrained amputee. To my own shock and horror, I was walking just like my patients did when they thought I was nowhere around. And just like them, I was entirely resistant to the idea of using a cane. Instead of calling attention to myself with an "old man stick," I preferred to wobble painfully down the hallway. That was, if I absolutely had to. Like some of my patients, it was just easier to stay in a chair and not walk at all.

Planted in a chair near the back of the room, I was aghast to overhear Darcy talking on the phone with Juan, who had called to say he was running late.

"Oh, wait until you see Adele. She is walking just like you!"

Having a limp is okay, probably cool, if you are a desk jockey working from home, but poor publicity if you are a physical therapist.

Thankfully, my patients were nothing like me. They didn't walk behind me with a hand on my hip nudging me onto my sore leg. Or make me practice walking back and forth on the foam balance beam. Best of all, they didn't pull out my favorite trick, which was to saunter casually past them in exactly the same sloppy way they happened to be walking.

My patients didn't do any charade jokes. Instead, they brought me a chair and asked if I wanted to borrow their cane.

And they asked about my pain. Which, compared to theirs, was a total joke.

When I woke up in the recovery room, it was the first thing I thought about. The nurse asked me to rate my pain on a scale between zero and ten, just as we made our patients do at Walter Reed. I said my pain was a one. He said that was impossible. So I revised my pain to a two. I had just had two liters of bone marrow sucked out of my pelvis in a four-hour procedure under general anesthesia. It was definitely uncomfortable, but compared to the patients I was used to visiting in a recovery room thirty-eight miles away, I had no pain at all.

When you are in the Harry and Jeanette Weinberg Building at the Johns Hopkins cancer center, you are surrounded by cancer patients. It is sort of like being dropped onto another planet, where everyone is bald and connected to some sort of beeping IV pole. But hidden among the cancer patients were people like me. Donors. Selected because we are the healthy genetic match of our sicker versions in the Weinberg Building.

I was not an anonymous donor. I was my father's donor.

Before my father got sick, my sister used to accuse me of being exactly like him. She was waging a constant improvement campaign aimed at the two of us — from giving us new sweaters to trying to convince both of us to have our cars towed immediately to the junkyard.

Recently, in spite of my father's illness, my sister was appalled to find out he had been thrown out of Teaism, a trendy New Age teahouse, for lounging around in one of their booths while drinking a Starbucks coffee. The tables at Teaism are reserved for paying customers drinking expensive, loose-leaf tea blends and eating organic vegan scones — not people like my father, who wore flannel shirts and carried their important papers around in a plastic grocery bag.

While my sister, Nicki, was horrified, I thought it was hilarious, and our conversation veered to our usual topic.

"You just think it's funny because you are *just like him.* It's *exactly* the kind of thing *you* would do," Nicki always tells me.

I joke back, "The transformation is almost complete," which is what I'd always say in my defense when Nicki caught me doing something that my father would do — like trading in the REI sweater she gave me for several cans of propane gas and some dehydrated food in preparation for doomsday, an obsession that my father and I shared. My father might have built a bomb shelter in his basement, but I had enough dried food, water, and gin to get Howie, me, and now Ashley through any kind of nuclear holocaust.

Besides survivalism, my father and I had the same adventurous taste in food. My dad, who was always getting put on a forced diet by my mom, would escape to my neighborhood on the weekends. It was an immigrant neighborhood, full of small ethnic restaurants. Restaurants where you frequently had to shout out your order through thick bulletproof glass. With my dad, I ordered plates of saucy duck feet; had big bowls of pho piled high with basil leaves, mystery meat, and bean sprouts; stood in the outdoor line for smoky Peruvian chicken; and got take-out Styrofoam cups of Horchata. But frequently my father would cut out the hassle of finding me, and would just hang out in my neighborhood himself on the weekends. He'd say to my sister later that evening, "Have you been to the Wheaton library near Adele's condo? I went there after I had lunch at the Anh Binh around the corner. They have a new lunch special." And Nicki would call me. "I think Dad wants to be you."

My mother is from a small village in Switzerland, the first person in her family to leave her medieval town. Or as my mom likes to say, "I come from a long line of peasants." In spite of not knowing any English, she applied to work in America on a whim after seeing an advertisement in a Swiss newspaper seeking foreign lab technicians to staff American labs. The America in question was Saint Louis, which, in the late 1960s, was a crime-infested horrible place. But my mom just found it wonderful. And in the lab, hunched over some slides, she found my father, who was, with his black hair, olive skin, and goofy red turtleneck, "exotic."

My mother is the funniest person I have ever met. Her self-deprecating stories have made me laugh so hard I have gone into full-on laugh-induced body spasms, where I can only writhe around bent forward at the waist, capable of moving only my right hand. "Stop. Stop," I'd squeak, holding my hand up in front of me like a protective shield. But my mom would just keep right on talking. Meanwhile my father would watch the two of us from across the table with a lopsided smile, trying desperately to figure out what was happening, because my father didn't understand funny.

I never could figure out what the attraction was between my parents. How could my hysterically funny mother marry someone as serious as my father? Until the day my mom motioned me over to listen in on my father's telephone conversation with a local bakery. "I saw your bread being sold at the farmer's market today for three eighty. Yeah. No, I didn't buy any because I had already bought some from your store, and do you want to know how much you charged me? Four dollars! That's right. Twenty cents more!"

My father was, my mother announced at that moment, the funniest person she had ever met. She motioned in my father's direction. "I mean, listen to this! It's his sport!"

When my father found out his cancer had

returned after a one-month remission, he held a family meeting. Not about the cancer. But about a clause he had discovered in his life insurance policy.

"If I die at work, Mom will get a hundred grand," Dad told us. And then he turned to me, "No matter what happens, you have to get me to work."

I could tell my sister was about to cry. Thankfully, I had inherited my mom's sense of humor. "Do I have to actually get you into your office, or can I just dump you out in the parking lot?"

In spite of herself, my sister started to laugh a little. My dad ignored us. "I'm sure the parking lot will be fine. Just make sure you get me there."

I had matched my father on several preliminary blood tests, but it was my sister, who is in no way like my father, who surprised everyone by being the better match. But she was six months pregnant with our family's first grandchild, so I was queued up as the backup quarterback for the transplant.

Even though I was coming off the bench, I was determined to be the game changer. I cleaned up my act. Stopped drinking so much, went to bed on time, and started taking vitamins.

Every few weeks I was up at Johns Hopkins for another series of tests. Most of these were blood tests. While my blood passed, I as a specimen failed horribly, even embarrassing myself by fainting in the hospital lobby after going through a series of eighteen different blood draws.

But in the end, I made the team. My father's cancer-prone immune system would be replaced with a newer, healthier version. Mine.

My father spent the week before the transplant undergoing high-dose chemotherapy and full-body radiation. This was done to completely kill his bone marrow so that he could receive mine. What my dad had to go through scared me. But it didn't scare my dad. Mr. Doomsday was entirely unusually optimistic about the transplant. It was his one shot at survival. While sitting beside him, I was secretly pessimistic. I worried that, instead of my father dying of cancer, he'd die of an infusion of me. But I kept it to myself.

"Of course it's going to work," I told my mom and my sister and Ashley before they wheeled me back to the operating room. "This is *me* we are talking about."

I joked that I'd ask the doctor to deliver my bone marrow to my father in a champagne flute. And I fantasized aloud that instead of us sharing traits, now he would receive some that were just my own — a sense of humor and maybe a love of open-water swimming.

But what we did was risky.

Getting pushed into the OR in my hospital gown and blue party hat was one of the saddest days of my life.

In the OR, while I lay on my stomach unconscious, two liters of bone marrow was mined from my pelvis. For all my grandstanding, I turned out to be a poor bone marrow specimen. Instead of bone marrow, all they were finding was blood. I ended up spending close to four hours in the OR, instead of the expected forty-five minutes. And I lost so much blood I spent ten hours in the recovery room, instead of the normal one or two.

The transplant was done via an IV directly into my father's bloodstream. They ran a two-liter bag of bone marrow upstairs from the OR, once they had finally dug it out from me, to the room where my father lay eagerly waiting. The transfusion of my bone marrow into my father took about forty-five minutes. We spent the next thirty days waiting to see if the new bone marrow would migrate to my father's empty bone cavities and begin to repopulate them.

My father was supposed to stay indoors until his new immune system — the one he got from me — was fully functioning. A third of all bone marrow transplant recipients die in the first thirty days. But my father was feeling great and celebrated his first day post-transplant by treating himself to a Mocha Frappuccino.

I wasn't heading out for a Mocha Frappuccino anytime soon. I got out of breath just walking to the bathroom, and had a noticeable limp for six weeks.

I had five days before I was due back at work. At home I spent most of my time lying on my stomach, feeling not at all like myself. Sitting up made me feel like I was going to pass out.

If I was Cosmo, I would have been reliving my combat days by playing violent video games alone in my room and then having nightmares for half the night. I probably would have slept through my physical therapy appointment, received a No Show missile, and been woken up by an angry platoon sergeant. Instead, I had the luxury of being at home surrounded by my dog, my things, and people who loved me.

My father was still in the hospital. I couldn't visit him because I wasn't well enough to drive. I tried not to dwell on it. I was going to recover. Hopefully, so would he. At least we still had both our legs.

Two days after the harvest, thoroughly sick of being sacked out on the couch, I decided to rally myself. It was time, I decided. It was time to get out of bed and start physical therapy! What I needed was a short, obtainable goal. I decided I would take a walk outside to the stop sign on the corner.

It was a nice day out as I stepped gingerly into the sun. The pain in my buttocks was incredible. On crutches, I shuffled carefully down the sidewalk, trying not to activate my gluteal muscles in any way. They had told me prior to the harvest that they would drill one, maybe two holes into my pelvis to suck the bone marrow out. In each hole they would do one hundred needle aspirations of bone marrow. But they had trouble finding enough bone marrow for my father in my pelvis, so instead of one or two drill holes, I had ten drill holes. They had done more than a thousand needle aspirations. Before leaving the house, I had caught a glimpse of my behind in the bathroom mirror — it looked like a salad strainer.

Halfway down the block I gave up. I was completely out of breath and feeling woozy again. As I leaned against a parked car, everything felt soft and far away.

On request, I had once accompanied Pigeon to one of his surgeries. At the time, he was still behaving like a complete hand grenade. He was frequently snappy, unpleasant, and unfriendly. I was surprised when he stopped by the staff desk one afternoon and asked, in his Ohio-Brooklyn accent, if someone would go to his amputation revision surgery with him. It was a question posed in the air, seemingly directed at me and the two other therapists I was standing beside.

"Does anyone want to watch my surgery?"

I didn't volunteer. I hate watching surgeries.

Pigeon asked again. And after a long pause and several firm elbows in the ribs by Darcy, who was standing next to me, I "volunteered."

I still wasn't sure if I would go. I figured Pigeon wouldn't know if I was there or not.

But in the end, I was in the OR. Gowned and gloved up. When they brought Pigeon in, a wave of sadness broke over my heart. I'd seen other people being escorted to the OR by their family members. But Pigeon was staying at Walter Reed by himself.

I was just one of the many masked people in the OR when they brought him in. He was doped up and woozy, his head nodding while he struggled to stay conscious. He looked completely, utterly helpless.

I'd never seen Pigeon like that. I was scared for him. "Is he okay?" I asked the anesthesiologist. "Are you *sure* he's okay?"

The surgeons asked Pigeon to slide over onto the OR table. But before he did, he looked groggily around the room. "Is my PT in here? My PT? Is she in here?" He said it several times, in a drug-induced slur. "My PT. Is my PT here?" The Brooklyn accent, I noticed, was gone.

I said, "Pigeon, I'm here. I'm right here."

Pigeon slid over onto the OR table then and lay back. The anesthesiologist put a mask over Pigeon's nose and mouth and he stopped moving.

When they had brought me into the OR for the bone marrow harvest, it looked just the same. Except this time the patient was me and I knew my family was waiting right outside the double doors. They pushed my stretcher next to the stainless-steel surgical table. I remembered Pigeon woozily scooting himself across, after first checking that I was in there. Making sure that someone would be in his corner.

I asked my surgeons if they would like me to scoot myself across, and the anesthiologist laughed good-naturedly. "That won't be necessary."

And that's the last thing I remember.

I had my eyes open in the recovery room for a while before I realized I was awake. I was looking at the curtain at the foot of my stretcher when a face interrupted my line of vision.

"Look at you! Look how well you are doing! You're awake!"

I smiled, pleased with myself. I *was* awake.

Later, my nurse Vincent asked me if I'd like to try sitting up a little bit. I nodded, and sat up a little bit. I was pretty much still completely reclined, but I got rave reviews from Vince. "Look at you! Look how well you're doing! You're sitting up! You are doing so well!"

I was totally groggy and out of it, but inside I glowed. *I was doing a good job.*

If my coworkers were enthusiastic, they had nothing on Vince. He cheered when I ate some ice chips and later when I had a sip of juice. Everything I did was Fantastic! Amazing! Great!

When I went back to work, I tried to channel Vince's enthusiasm toward my own patients. My patients looked at me funny, but eventually seemed to get used to it. They even seemed to like it.

The other thing I brought back was a special picture for Pigeon. Pigeon had asked me to take pictures of him when he was in the OR, so I asked the OR nurse to do the same for me. I gave Pigeon a picture of me with a tube down my throat and my eyes taped shut.

The transplant we had done was experimental. There was no time to find a perfect match. So the transfusion had been done with me, a half match. The doctors thought that part of my father's bone marrow would recover and would work in synchronicity with mine. But the only bone marrow to repopulate my father's bones was mine.

In the beginning, shortly after the transplant, before my bone marrow began to multiply, I noticed my father behaving strangely. He had started borrowing books from me. *Funny* books. Later he began emailing me comedy videos he found on the Internet. The first few I blew off as a fluke. But by the time the sixth and seventh comedy video arrived in my in-box, I became alarmed. I could not picture my father ignoring his research to watch inane You-Tube surfing dog videos. Was he not feeling well? I privately called my mother to discuss it. While we were on the phone, I could hear my father *laughing* in the background. He

369

was watching *Doc Martin,* a British comedy I had also recently started watching. My blood pressure revved up. My dad *never* wasted his time watching television.

His blood counts were still very low then. The doctors weren't sure if my bone marrow would take. And then I remembered my pre-transplant prediction and realized, when I heard my dad laughing again at the TV, that my bone marrow was growing just fine.

Over the next few months, my father changed blood type, from A+ to O+, my blood type. He became a chimera, a person with two sets of DNA. His body was genetically his, but his blood was one hundred percent mine.

*The transformation was complete.*

My dad and I became partners in optimism. We would joke over the phone to each other that he would be able to commit the perfect crime now. And we celebrated together how it was really working. We were beating this. We were winning.

When the cancer came back, my father and I were the only ones who weren't worried. My bone marrow was much more aggressive. It would aggressively go after the cancer, and also, it would go after my father. My immune system attacked his liver and his lungs, keeping him fatigued and out of breath. But my immune system also kept him alive. It produced normal levels of red blood cells and white cells and platelets, and it kept the cancer at bay.

I was surprised when my limp came back. It was exactly thirteen months from the day of the transplant. When the pain in my pelvis started to wake me up at night, I worried that it was a type of phantom pain and I wondered to myself if anonymous donors also experienced bone pain when their bone marrow recipient began to die.

I was sleeping on the couch in my parents' living room. My father was just a few feet away, sleeping on a twin bed we had pushed in there for him. He couldn't get up the stairs anymore. Something I had blithely referred to as a temporary setback.

As my blood continued to die off, his fingernails turned black. He couldn't get out of bed. He couldn't breathe. He couldn't walk. He couldn't talk. The sharp pain in my hip kept me from walking or sitting normally but I was still convinced that he was going to get better.

When he died, no one was more surprised than me. No one, except maybe my father. He wasn't planning on dying. He had my super bone marrow in him.

I watched him dying, completely aghast. He couldn't leave me now. I had a new water purification system I needed to show him. We still had one more season of *Doc Martin* to watch and discuss, and a new Jamaican roti stand in Wheaton to check out.

The transformation had happened.

We were going to beat this.

# VISITORS

Unlike other celebrity visitors who turned their visit to Walter Reed into a publicity tour, Tim Gunn, the popular gay designer from *Project Runway,* made a trip to Walter Reed to visit only one patient, Regina, who had lost her leg at thigh level during her fourth deployment to Iraq. Regina's family had contacted Tim Gunn personally because she was a fan of his show. Coincidentally, so were several of the therapists on staff, especially our guide to all things celebrity: Emma.

In the days leading up to Tim Gunn's visit, Emma would sidle up to me with barely contained excitement and say something incomprehensible like, "Two days!" And then do a little dance.

I didn't watch *Project Runway.* "Two days to what?" I'd ask.

"Tim Gunn!"

My female coworkers were addicted to

*Project Runway.* They watched it every week, sending text messages back and forth to one another during the commercials. Tim Gunn was frequently quoted in the clinic, and during breaks, my coworkers enthusiastically discussed snippets of that week's show. *Project Runway* was their religion, and as far as they were concerned, Tim Gunn's visit was the Second Coming.

The day before his visit, my coworkers were shiny with nervous excitement. In between patients, they broke out into spontaneous *Project Runway* discussion groups. They were discussing what outfits they should wear for Tim Gunn and enlisting the help of the group.

I happened to wander by in the middle of yet another heated group wardrobe decision. *Linen pants or khaki pants?* Upon seeing me, the linen pants discussion was immediately sidelined in favor of a campaign to convince me to wear my green velour tracksuit to work on Tim Gunn Day.

The green velour tracksuit had been a misguided Halloween costume I had worn to work earlier that year. I had been inspired by Chanda, one of the physical therapists in the inpatient clinic. Every morning after getting her list of inpatients, she would spin past our clinic. She wasn't seeing any patients in the amputee clinic. She dropped by only to model that day's outfit.

Chanda's outfits consisted of a wig, clothes, and personality. She is very versatile and could model a host of different looks, ranging from a bold 1970s power strut with Afro wig, flared pants, and platform shoes to a prim librarian in bob wig, pleated skirt, and conservative buttoned-up blouse.

I liked to think that Chanda came down for me personally because I was her biggest fan. As soon as I saw Chanda, I would break out into an immediate smile. She wouldn't stay long. Fifteen seconds at most. Sometimes, to my delight, she would shout, "I'm bringing it back!" from the doorway on her way out and I would laugh appreciatively and throw my fist in the air, too.

I loved all of Chanda's personas, but especially her short, unruly Halle Berry, because I coveted that particular hairstyle. I have short hair, too. It's wavy and unruly, but unlike Halle Berry, it doesn't look stylish. It just looks like I slept in a wind tunnel. I tried to explain this to Chanda once, but it came out awkwardly. But she didn't judge. She gave me an understanding nod and a modest Halle Berry smile.

Chanda owns eighty wigs and her fashion modeling was something that only she could pull off. I knew if I ever showed up at work in a wig, I would get fired on the spot.

For most of us, our work uniforms were exactly that: uniforms. The military wore BDUs (battle dress uniforms) or dress greens. The civilian staff was decked out in khaki pants and collared shirts. The inpatient team wore green or gray scrubs. The one day we were allowed to deviate from our normal workwear was Halloween, when it was perfectly okay to come to work in a mechanic's uniform with a smudge of grease on your face and a wrench in your shirt pocket.

I usually don't dress up for Halloween, but the year of Tim Gunn's visit, I decided I would go out on a limb and get a costume. I wanted to keep it subtle and low-key. Inspired by Chanda, I showed up at work in a 1970s green velour tracksuit with old-school green Puma running shoes. The entire outfit, including the shoes, cost me five dollars. I was patting myself proudly on the back when I walked into the staff meeting and realized, to my horror, that I was the only one in costume.

Even Chanda was dressed down.

In the staff meeting, they were introducing our new department chief — something we had apparently been briefed on in advance, if only I had been paying attention. We took turns standing up and introducing ourselves. Out of the forty people in the room, I was the only one wearing a green velour tracksuit. The clinic chief nodded politely as each employee stated their name, rank, and position. When I introduced myself, I got a special curious stare.

If Chanda had shown up in a green velour tracksuit on the day our new chief started his position, she could have totally pulled it off. But I wasn't pulling anything over on the new chief. Chanda would have looked cool, but I looked ridiculous. Something my other coworkers noticed immediately and turned my day at work into a nonstop tunnel of good-natured hoots.

The green velour tracksuit became something of a legend after that. As a joke, I'd wear it to happy hours and parties. I just made sure I never wore it to work again. And I certainly was not going to parade around like a clown in front of a famous TV fashionista in a thrift store tracksuit.

My female civilian coworkers decided in the end to go with black slacks and sweater cardigans, while my female military coworkers got out their dress uniforms. I wore blue pants and a Christmas sweater. Our male coworkers ignored the entire event. In spite of the staff's busy wardrobe prep, we forgot that Tim Gunn was not coming to visit us. He was on his way down to visit Regina.

It's hard to be an amputee. But it is especially hard to be a female amputee. Outside Walter Reed, the women amputees get twice as many stares. While it might be tough and cool to have an obvious battle injury as a man, it's not always that way for the women.

Luckily, in our clinic, the women soldiers fit right in with the guys. Although from time to time, we were also guilty of treating them differently. Like the time I excused one of my female amputees from physical therapy for a week after a disastrous haircut — something I know Cosmo wouldn't have gotten an excused absence for.

Requests for a prosthetic leg outfitted for high heels was something the male soldiers wouldn't dare ask for, either. This special "glamour" leg was built on request for one of the women soldiers, a military police officer whose convoy had hit a buried IED outside Baghdad. The foot of her custom glamour leg pointed daintily toward the ground, enabling her to wear heels. Not ordinary high heels, but stilettos. The leg made its debut in the clinic during our busiest hour, 1030. A patient strutting into the amputee clinic on five-inch heels, short shorts, and a matching purse immediately brought all activity inside the clinic to a screeching halt. But only for a second. The guys took it in and then went right back to what they were doing.

Tim Gunn's visit couldn't have been better timed. Regina was on the cusp of losing her motivation. Male or female, everyone gets to that point, some sooner than others. It frequently happens when a soldier is finally able to walk around on their prosthetic leg. They can walk. Now what? They're walking, just not like they did before. Compounding Regina's loss of motivation were her recent socket fit issues. Her socket was too tight and wearing her leg was uncomfortable. She contemplated calling off Tim Gunn's visit entirely.

But on the day of the visit, Regina came in early. She was wearing gray sweatpants, a long-sleeve T-shirt, bright red lipstick, and a pair of large fake eyelashes.

Tim Gunn didn't do the usual parade around the clinic, shaking hands and posing for pictures like most celebrity visitors. He walked in by himself and introduced himself only to Regina.

Regina is not normally a shy person, but upon shaking Tim Gunn's hand, she became instantly shy. Instead of talking, she threw herself into her physical therapy program with a vengeance we had never seen. I caught a glimpse of her out of the corner of my eye, doing dozens of sit-ups while Tim Gunn watched her. Regina may have been showing off for Tim Gunn, but he was watching her in obvious awe. It was a mutual admiration society.

I was surprised to see Tim Gunn blushing. He was so clearly out of his element; he seemed likeably shy. Regina did box step-ups in the parallel bars, dazzled Tim Gunn with perfectly executed ladder drills, and later, towed Tim Gunn around the clinic behind her as he held on to resistant bands wrapped around her waist.

He spent the entire day with Regina. They went out for lunch to the hospital cafeteria, and then came back to the physical therapy clinic to work out some more. In between drills, Regina sat next to him in a sheen of sweat and happiness.

Before Tim Gunn left, he came over to the staff area. He seemed genuine when he told us he admired the work we did. It was rare for celebrities to acknowledge us, let alone pay us a compliment. With that one heartfelt comment, my coworkers and I got quiet. I think his compliment affected all of us the same way. He made me feel proud of myself, something that I frequently forgot to do when the going got tough, and it got tough a lot.

And then, with his hand on Regina's arm, Tim and Regina left to hit up the department stores downtown. There weren't going to be any velour green tracksuits in Regina's future. They turned and waved at us from the doorway. In their wake, the clinic glowed warmer than ever before.

In addition to celebrity visitors and politicians, we also frequently had disabled visitors who came to cheer up the patients as a mentor or peer visitor. We had, practically on staff, Korean and Vietnam war amputees who visited on a weekly basis. But we also seemed to be a tour destination for people with missing limbs from all over the world.

We had a woman come who had been born without arms. She was an elegant and powerful public speaker. After speaking to the patients and the staff about her life challenges, she gave a short demonstration of her karate skills, which included swinging nunchakus around using only her feet. Later, she opened a can of Coca-Cola with her toes and demurely took a sip, cradling the can in the arch of her right foot. While it was impressive to see the skills that earned her a black belt, what wowed me the most was watching her drink that can of Coke.

One day in 2008, a handsome young college student showed up at the clinic. He had lost both of his legs at the hip joint from a rare bacterial infection. Because he only had a torso, he was sitting in a bucketlike device. One hook-shaped prosthetic leg extended from the bottom middle of the bucket. Using crutches, he was able to take short, controlled hops on his prosthetic leg.

He talked eloquently about his illness and his life afterward. He described his determination to participate in local 5K races, where he propelled himself slowly along with forearm crutches on that one prosthetic leg. But if he meant to cheer the soldiers up, he seemed to have the opposite effect. The room became eerily quiet, but balanced in his bucket, he continued to smile bravely around the room.

Later, I saw a group of our soldiers clustered around him. They asked him questions about himself and his life. But they avoided asking specifically about his disability, which was similar to how everyone interacted with them when they were new patients at Walter Reed.

For the staff, if we had been paying attention, the college student's visit was a moment of foreshadowing. A few years later, he was someone we frequently wished aloud would come back for a visit, because by then we had several young men with similar injuries. In 2008, we mostly had rows of below-knee prosthetics and new C-Legs propped up against the wall where we kept that equipment at the end of the day. But we'd progressed to stubbies, hip disarticulation sockets, and even three buckets — the same thing that young guy had been sitting in.

The real backbone of our clinic, however, were the regular visitors, older veterans who came to lift the patients' spirits and, increasingly, the staff's. Tom, a Korean War veteran who walked on two prosthetic legs, and his wife, Elle (his former physical therapist), visited every Tuesday and Thursday. They were single-handedly responsible for the mountain of homemade cookies in the hospital.

Elle's fudge was incredible. But her hugs were better. Even though we saw them twice a week, as soon as Tom and Elle walked into the clinic, everyone would stop what they were doing and wait their turn for a hug.

Tom and Elle were everyone's surrogate grandparents. They always seemed to show up in the middle of someone's crisis. If a patient was having a bad day, maybe they'd yelled at their therapist, we'd send Elle in. She'd go over to the sourpuss sulking on the mat table in the corner and give him or her a big hug. Elle was infinitely forgiving and accepting. Later, Tom would walk over and joke around with him, affectionately ruffling his hair — which, by the way, heaven help anyone else who actually reached out and laid a hand on a soldier's head. That was a show of affection that only Tom and Elle could do.

Burt was our long-standing Red Cross volunteer and World War II veteran. He dropped out of college and joined the marines the day after Pearl Harbor was bombed. Twenty-two of his football teammates enlisted with him. In his late eighties, Burt still resembled a former college quarterback. He had bulging biceps and tight hips. In between cleaning mat tables and distributing bottles of water to the patients, he made dozens of trips back and forth between our clinic and the Red Cross office, returning with bags of goodies for the patients and sometimes the staff. Usually these goodies were well received — like packs of gum and motorcycle magazines.

Burt unveiled the items in his Red Cross

bag with a careful lead-in.

"I have a magazine here. It's got very nice pictures and interesting articles."

But every now and then Burt would bring in an item that no one wanted, like socks. When this happened, Burt would get pushy. "Feel them. Go on, feel! Isn't that nice? Soft, right? And luxurious. They're one hundred percent cotton."

Socks were not a big sell in an amputee clinic.

And Burt would complain in genuine broken-hearted disbelief, "No one wants these socks. These are such nice socks."

We used to tease Burt that he should work on QVC — the shopping channel. Burt had no idea what QVC was, but he'd laugh anyway, his eyes twinkling. Later he'd offer you that same pair of socks: "They're Gold Toe!"

During the winter, Burt relocated to Florida. But every spring, we welcomed Burt back to the clinic with applause and cheers. One year Burt brought us a Tupperware container of pristine Florida beach sand. "Feel it," he urged each of us. "It's so soft and fine. Touch it. Look how white it is."

Then there was "Bob the Builder." A Vietnam War veteran, he was the advisor to the construction company, Turner, that built the MATC. After a lifetime of supervising multimillion-dollar construction projects all over the world, after Turner finished building our little clinic, Bob stayed. Semiretired and living out on the Eastern Shore, he continued to commute two hours every morning to Walter Reed.

Bob was the cheering section. He thought everything the patients did was *"Incredible!"* And usually just shouted that one word out again and again. He was instantly likeable.

Bob was a big believer in your ability to do anything you set your mind on. On Monday afternoons, he taught an ongoing business class to the patients — a class he called, with characteristic optimism, the "100 Entrepreneurs Project." He brought in high-level consultants from his vast Rolodex of contacts, and they gave PowerPoint presentations in the conference room to anyone, even the groggiest of new patients, on how they could start their own business. Later, to patients who were interested, Bob would set them up with construction internships. And twice a year, Bob brought in hard hats and took a group of patients on a tour of a local building site — where they were greeted by former Walter Reed patients, who were, thanks to Bob, now construction managers.

One of the physical therapists in the inpatient section, Dan, kept a scrapbook of his time at Walter Reed. It was filled with Polaroid pictures of celebrity visitors, coworkers, and former patients. On every page of the scrapbook, a different person has their arm around Dan. In each photo, Dan is wearing scrubs and smiling. He looks exactly the same, as if the entire book was photographed in one afternoon.

At Walter Reed, even if the brain injury was nonpenetrating, the TBI patients usually had a portion of their skull removed along with the damaged brain tissue, so the brain could swell without becoming compressed by the skull. When the brain swelling had sufficiently receded, the skull piece was replaced and the patient's scalp was sewed shut. In Dan's scrapbook, he had before and after pictures of each of his patients. In the before picture, the dent in the patient's head made his face seem uneven, his scalp hanging down into the empty part of his skull like a hammock. In the after picture, the skull piece had been replaced, yet the patient's smile looked just as uneven as the previous picture.

Scattered between pictures of Dan and

his patients were pictures of Dan with various celebrities. Unlike my coworkers in the amputee clinic, Dan was in no way shy. He was mugging with a man with half a head in one picture and the head of the United Nations in the next.

While I have fond memories of our many different visitors and patients over the years, I never kept a scrapbook. It was something I kept meaning to do, but in the hustle and bustle of our clinic, I never got around to it. So I only have two photographs from my six and a half years at Walter Reed. One is an official White House photograph of me and my coworkers with President George W. Bush. The other, a faded, fingerprinted USO Polaroid of me and Darcy with the cast of *Reno 911!* This Polaroid is easily my most cherished possession. It is a snapshot in time. It reminds me of Cosmo in his wheelchair with the special platform holding his shattered leg. We were different people then. He was serious and in pain. I was young and brash. I still keep that Polaroid in my locker and look at it often.

# GOODBYE

Sgt. Chen came back from her deployment just as Maj. Tavner was queued up on the same flight line to leave. Sgt. Chen seemed different when she came back, more prone to serious comments on our current state of affairs.

Incoming casualties had tripled during the time Chen had been deployed. She'd look around the packed clinic, push her glasses up on the bridge of her nose, and announce to no one in particular, "This place is a total mind fuck."

Chen had gotten away briefly, while we remained, running in place like gerbils on a wheel.

I remember the day Maj. Tavner was promoted from captain to major. We held the ceremony in the amputee clinic. Jim had baked a special lemon pound cake with lemon cream frosting. Standing at attention in front of the American flag, a group of the patients, and the staff, Maj. Tavner cried. Her husband, who was in Iraq, listened quietly over speakerphone. Now on the flight line, Maj. Tavner sent a text message to me asking how everyone was doing.

We didn't say goodbye. We had been saying goodbye for weeks. The day before she left, everyone privately sneaked one last look at Maj. Tavner. We bought her books to read, and I went with her on one last bike ride.

Via text we gossiped back and forth. In my head I could see Maj. Tavner standing on the flight line in her fatigues, waiting to board a transport plane that would take her halfway around the world. I was scared for her. And I missed her.

But things were so busy in the clinic that we quickly went back to work as usual, and Maj. Tavner flew alone, but with several hundred other soldiers, to a distant war.

For Maj. Tavner, it really was goodbye.

When she returned fifteen months later, Walter Reed was closed, the staff and patients dispersed to other military clinics in the area. Six years earlier, the Base Realignment and Closure Commission (BRAC) had designated Walter Reed as one of the bases slated to be closed due to the proximity of two other military medical facilities in the area — National Naval Medical Center in Bethesda, Maryland, and Fort Belvoir in northern Virginia. Our closure date, after ten years of treating casualties in the Global War on Terror was September 15, 2011, four days after the ten-year anniversary of 9/11.

At Walter Reed, we were so busy processing the incoming war casualties that it didn't seem possible they could actually shut us down. It was a reality we thought would never happen. But slowly, while we continued to treat over one hundred amputees a day, BRAC started to close our gates.

Our first inkling that the closing might really be happening was when we were instructed to submit a list of all the personal items that we kept at work to help us with the transition to Bethesda and Fort Belvoir. During a morning staff meeting, Maj. Crazy read his list aloud to us as an example. It contained the usual items you would expect a physical therapist to keep at work: various orthopedic and neurological textbooks, an anatomy atlas, a goniometer to measure joint motion, a gait belt, a pair of scissors, a reflex hammer. But beyond these possessions, Maj. Crazy went into extreme detail, adding the number of pencils and pens in his desk drawer, five paper clips, and the real clincher — thirty-seven cents in change, which he listed as, "one quarter, one dime, and two pennies."

Even though the closure date was less than a year away, I didn't bother submitting a list. Because by September, I told myself, who knew what I would be doing? I wasn't planning on still being at Walter Reed. I had been halfway out the door for the last six years.

When I first started working at Walter Reed, I figured I would stay for a year and then find a new job with better hours and employee parking. But somehow in the chaos of ten-hour days, one year turned into two. At the two-and-a-half-year mark, I was definitely feeling burned out and ready for a new job. But before submitting my resignation, I sat down in the colonel's office and talked to her about what I was thinking. The colonel listened thoughtfully and then suggested I go on a "stay-cation," instructing me to visit a different museum downtown every day.

I was completely flabbergasted by the colonel's corny idea that I use a week of my own vacation time to tour the monuments and museums of downtown D.C. like a goofy tourist. What part of "I'm thinking of quitting for a less stressful job" did she not hear? But, not having any better ideas, I went ahead and did it. The next week I was back at work. After the morning meeting, the colonel asked me to come into her office. We sat down and she asked me about the different monuments and museums I had seen, and then I returned to work.

Three years turned quickly into five and then six. And in 2010, the last full year of Walter Reed's existence, all the other clinicians who could make decisions started to leave. Colleagues we had worked with for years, who had stayed in the area because of Walter Reed, started to think it was a good time to return to wherever they had come from. Our PA moved back to Ohio. Three orthopedic surgeons who had spent years reassembling completely broken young men and women, started the paperwork to get out of the army. Our nurse case manager took off to Georgia. An OT got a job at a hospital in Pittsburgh, close to her parents. PTs disbanded to upstate New York, Baltimore, and California. A prosthetist from New Orleans, who had relocated to D.C. after Hurricane Katrina, went back home. His house, I guess, had finally dried out.

Every week there was another goodbye happy hour. Every week we gathered for pictures and drinks and tearful hugs inside the good old familiar Quarry House. With every departure, we said it was the end of an era. It would never be the same.

Yet the next day, it was eerily the same. The dozens of patients. The tour groups. The visitors. The same menu in the cafeteria. And every other day another medevac full of casualties.

With BRAC breathing down our necks and the closure only a short five months away, a white board mysteriously appeared in front of the administration offices to count down the days until Walter Reed closed. I had walked over to Building One to mail a care package to Maj. Tavner. On the first floor of the original hospital, just past the framed pictures of various presidents, there was a Burger King, a post office, and a mini PX. I was exactly one floor down from the famous suite where Eisenhower spent his last days when I first noticed the white board. I had no idea how long it had been there. But it was obvious that every morning someone wiped it clean and wrote a number that was one day closer to our close date, as if it were a countdown to summer break.

I was stunned and disgusted with the administrative officers and their demoralizing white board, and it suddenly became perfectly clear what I was going to do. I was going to stay. I was going to go down with the ship. Why bother quitting now? I had been at Walter Reed for most of my career.

I had watched my coworkers who had arrived as young officers become promoted to company commanders. My work friends, the ones I'd meet at the Quarry House for half-price cheeseburgers and beer, had, in the time I'd known them, gotten married and had children. I had met their future husbands and gone to their weddings. I had painted their living rooms with them. They had sent me some extremely memorable texts like: "I'm 10 centimeters dilated! ☺" followed forty-five minutes later by a photograph of a newborn infant, a baby I would cuddle in my arms later that same day.

They had been there for me. When my father got sick, Capt. Dumont offered to pick him up in a van and drive him to Walter Reed. Since I started working at Walter Reed, he had always wanted to come see the famous military hospital. It was the perfect blend of history and medicine for him. But when he was healthy he could never take the time off work, and then when he got sick, he was too weak to leave the house. Capt. Dumont had the van and a wheelchair ready for him and was going to personally show him around. Neither my father nor I knew about this — I was so touched when I found out. But in the end I couldn't handle the thought of my terminally ill father finally coming to Walter Reed in a wheelchair, breathing supplemental oxygen as if it was some sort of happy occasion.

And when my father stopped chemotherapy and began hospice care, it was Capt. Dumont who told me what to do. "What are you doing here? You shouldn't be here." She sent me home to be with my father, where, during that long week before my father died in my old twin bed in our dining room, my coworkers checked in on me multiple times a day.

I would have completely fallen apart if it hadn't been for the structure of my job, my patients and coworkers, and the good old-fashioned familiarity of that historic hospital my father had so badly yearned to see.

While Walter Reed was busy dismantling itself, Maj. Tavner sent us handwritten letters from Iraq. At the end of every one, she said she missed us. I'd look around the clinic at Jim, Darcy, Emma, Hernandez, Melody, and Capt. Dumont. How long would we last at the new place? And I'd have a vision of Maj. Tavner coming home again, as the wrecking ball smashed through the façade of our old hospital.

# WE ARE A MUSEUM COLLECTION

All around us parts of Walter Reed were packing up, but the weekly department in-services had to go on. I was still in charge of finding speakers, and with so many people leaving Walter Reed, I was running out of options. There was no way I could have Capt. Jones do a fifth nutrition in-service for the department without risking a complete mutiny. Which was why I asked the National Museum of Health and Medicine if our physical therapy department could come and tour their collection during our Friday 0700 in-service time.

The National Museum of Health and Medicine, with their collection of twenty-five million artifacts, from preserved organs to pieces of Abraham Lincoln's skull, was established during the Civil War as the Army Medical Museum. In 1893, it was Maj. Walter Reed's first post in D.C. and where he first began to assert himself as a medical investigator — proving that enlisted men stationed along the Potomac did not contract yellow fever from drinking the river water. Later, Walter Reed was sent to Cuba, where he led a study on yellow fever showing that the disease was not transmitted by exposure to infected patients, but rather by mosquitoes that carried the virus.

In the years that followed, the staff at the Army Medical Museum followed Maj. Reed's example and continued to remain active in infectious disease research, helping discover the cause of typhoid. But by World War II, the Army Medical Museum's increasing focus on pathology led to its designation as the Army Institute of Pathology, and later, the Armed Forces Institute of Pathology (AFIP). The Army Medical Museum became a branch of the AFIP and was renamed the Medical Museum of the AFIP and, later on, the Armed Forces Medical Museum. In 1989, it received its current name, the National Museum of Health and Medicine.

In 2011, looming behind the National Museum of Health and Medicine was a large, ominous, windowless gray building: the AFIP. Its thick concrete walls had been built in the 1950s to be atomic-bomb-proof. A hundred and fifty-one years after its modest start in the Civil War, the AFIP had become a world leader in the research of obscure diseases. Its diagnostic departments were organized by organ system and included specialty departments in infectious and parasitic diseases as well as environmental pathology. Because the AFIP housed civilian and military specialists on all organ and disease systems under one roof, it was able to provide rapid collaboration on rare diseases. Its vast collection of pathology, including numerous slide and radiological collections, was unmatched.

But in 2011, as part of the BRAC, the AFIP was dismantled and shut down. To close a world leader of disease and pathology at a time when our planet was experiencing an emergence of infectious diseases like SARS, West Nile virus, and recently, the swine flu, struck me as entirely reckless. And maybe for me it was personal, because my father had been an infectious disease officer. As he lay on his deathbed, we never talked about the catastrophe that he was dying. Instead we had talked about what a tragedy it was that Walter Reed and the AFIP were closing.

The National Museum of Health and Medicine was spared by the BRAC and was preparing, at the time I called them, to be relocated. I thought for sure the museum would immediately shoot down my sheepish request to let forty PTs tour their collection an hour and a half before they opened. But instead, the curators surprised me by readily agreeing. Wanting to intrude as little as possible, I suggested the night guard let us in and we would show ourselves around. But that Friday morning, instead of being met by the night watchman, we were met by the museum staff. The entire staff had come in two hours early to open the museum to a group of "special visitors."

They met us outside the museum at 0645 and split us into groups. Different docents led us on narrated tours of the museum exhibits that they thought we would find most interesting — including the amputated leg bones of a Civil War commander, some of the earliest wooden prosthetic arms and legs from the 1800s, and photographs of soldiers walking in parallel bars at Walter Reed after World War I.

A few weeks later as a thank you, we invited the museum staff over to the MATC for a lunchtime tour of our clinic and a behind-the-scenes look at the latest and greatest in amputee rehabilitation. Unlike the thousands of other tour groups that had come through our clinic — congressmen, general's wives, and professional baseball teams — this was the only tour the physical therapy staff organized.

The entire museum staff came, about thirty people. They dressed up for the tour like they were going to a wedding.

Jim was our docent, and as a tour guide he was finally fully in his element. Jim walked the museum staff through our clinic, pointing out the different kinds of equipment and how they were used in rehabilitation. He passed out prosthetic sockets, liners, and legs, and enthusiastically took questions from the crowd. And then he concluded the tour with an invitation to join him for lunch at the DFAC: "Shall we dine?" Shortly before the museum closed for good, they invited us back again for another special early morning tour. It was to be their last exhibit: "Wounded in Action: An Art Exhibition of Orthopaedic Advancement."

Instead of medical devices, surgical equipment, and skeletons, it was an exhibit of artwork that had been created by wounded soldiers, their caregivers, and the orthopedic surgeons who treated them. This exhibit was sponsored by the American Academy of Orthopaedic Surgeons, and the artwork ran the gamut from watercolors to photography to sculptures. I imagine our visit was the only time the museum staff actually got to witness a group of military medical professionals experiencing this particular exhibit.

At the end of the tour, the museum curators announced they had a special goodbye gift for us. They had gone into their offsite storage facility and among their millions of artifacts they had found this piece just to show us.

They reached into a box and carefully unwrapped it.

It was the uniform of the very first army physical therapist.

I watched my coworkers' faces as they examined this uniform in silent reverence. These clothes, this uniform, was from a physical therapist now long dead, who had spent World War I rehabilitating soldiers at Walter Reed, just as we were doing now.

The museum staff looked sad and I realized with a breaking heart why they seemed upset. They knew they were witnessing the end of the story. In a few months, Walter Reed Army Medical Center would shut its doors forever. Our day-to-day would soon only exist as grainy photographs in the back room of their warehouse.

We would join the other Walter Reed

ghosts from previous wars. Our jokes and shouts would fade away, and the echo of our footsteps would mingle with the therapists and patients who walked these hallways in World War I and World War II. We would join our Korea, Vietnam, and Gulf War counterparts. There would be photos of the staff members among us who were in the clinic the day our world changed forever and a new Global War on Terror began: the day the very first victims from the attack on the Pentagon were rushed through our hospital's front doors. The curator looked around the room at me and my coworkers, and then carefully folded the uniform and placed it back in its box forever.

# EPILOGUE

Walter Reed was the longest-operating military hospital in the United States. Over one hundred and two years, it treated patients from every major war from World War I forward, including victims of the attacks on the Pentagon and the recent military conflicts in Iraq and Afghanistan. It was officially closed on September 15, 2011, after the last inpatient was successfully transferred to Bethesda Naval Hospital. In its place, D.C. plans to build new condominiums, a homeless shelter, and some shops.

This book was written from my perspective as a physical therapist in the Amputee Section. But Walter Reed Army Medical Center was much more than physical therapy. The rehab team comprised physical therapy, occupational therapy, social work, physical medicine, orthopedics, prosthetics, nursing, and the military liaisons. The hospital team included not just doctors and nurses, but also pharmacists, dieticians, chaplains, and the cafeteria lady who called everyone "baby." Most important, there were the patients — the soldiers, marines, sailors, and airmen and their families who came to Walter Reed by no choice of their own.

Most of the physical therapy staff was relocated to a new hospital on the grounds of the National Naval Medical Center (known locally as Bethesda Naval Hospital). This new hospital is now called Walter Reed National Military Medical Center Bethesda.

At the new clinic, Jim continues to delight patients, staff, and visitors alike with his adventures. He continues his marathon training. And his most recent pound cake, apple sour cream, was the best one yet.

Maj. Tavner, during the writing of this book, was deployed. In her absence, her husband was promoted to lieutenant colonel. His promotion was held in the Amputee Clinic. Maj. Tavner listened to it long distance on speakerphone.

Walter the service dog was left off the BRAC transfer list, and perhaps as foreshadowing of things to come, was dressed up as a homeless service dog on Halloween with a sign that read "UNEMPLOYED VET DOG.

WILL WORK FOR FOOD. GOD BLESS." He was not transferred to Bethesda.

The colonel was a composite character made up of various officers who worked at Walter Reed during my time there and who have since retired from the military.

Sgt. Hernandez got out of the military. He met and fell in love with a nurse from Walter Reed. They recently got married.

Darcy was the first staff member sent to the new MATC at Bethesda Naval Hospital. She left several months before the rest of us. We joked about the possibility of her arriving there in a covered wagon or maybe dressed as a Pilgrim. She laughed at our suggestions and showed up in khaki pants and her Toyota Corolla instead.

Emma had two children, and continues to be the department expert on celebrity gossip. She talked several staff members into taking the morning of the Royal Wedding off to watch it with her live at 0500.

Melody is working at the new Walter Reed. She continues to enjoy weekends at her vacation house on the cooling lake of a nuclear power reactor in Virginia. Thanks to the active power plant, the water is always warm and Melody swims there year-round. She is frequently joined on holiday weekends by other staff members and present and former Walter Reed patients.

Elijah was transferred to Fort Belvoir.

Dr. C and his Moat Dragon, Chris, both left Walter Reed in advance of the BRAC. Their legends remain intact.

Rumor had it that Jasmine was the alternate juror during the sensational Chandra Levy murder trial. But we will never know. She continues to work as a physical therapist at the new Walter Reed.

Capt. Dumont, for privacy reasons, was a composite character. Shortly after the transfer, Capt. Dumont left Walter Reed for an unknown destination.

Chanda and her eighty wigs made a successful transfer to the new Walter Reed at Bethesda.

Sgt. Chen was recently redeployed to Afghanistan.

Cosmo and Pigeon, for privacy reasons, were composite characters of five patients I treated at Walter Reed. Cosmo became a father. Pigeon is currently in school.

The author is still gainfully employed at the new Walter Reed. She eventually bought a real bed and later moved with Ashley into a house that had a fenced-in backyard for Howie. They have two sons.

# ACKNOWLEDGMENTS

For their inspiration, sacrifice, and dedication — my gratitude and admiration goes out to the staff and patients of Walter Reed Army Medical Center. A huge thank you to the entire team at Ortho/Rehab: OT, PT, Ortho, PM&R, wound care, the chaplains, the social workers, the MATC nurse case managers, and prosthetics. Thank you also to my new coworkers at Walter Reed National Military Medical Center for continuing the mission. And to our patients, thank you for inspiring us to work so hard. I wish you never had to get hurt in order for us to meet you.

I would like to specially thank the rehab coworkers I had the honor and privilege to work closely with during those years: Abdul Brown, Alison Linberg, Allison Hoy, Amy Egger, Andre Speller, Andrea Brooks, Andrea Mahon, Angie Horst, Anne Moore, Arnette Smith, Amanda Urqhart, Audra Winston, Barb Ankney, Barbara Springer, Barri Schnall, Beth Mason, Bill Byers, Bo Bergeron, Bob Bahr, Brad "El Janitor," Bradley Ritland, Bunnie Wyckoff, Caitlin Dennison, Cameo Atkins, Carla Alexis, Carrie Hoppes, Carrie Hausermann, Carrie Storer, Catherine Ennis, Cheryl Howard, Chastity Mims, Choice Gimenez, Chris Brown, Chuck Scoville, Claudia Smith, Coren Point, Cristin Loeffler, Dave Martin, David Peters, Deborah Kerr, Delaine Steel, Delilah Sterling, Elizabeth Painter, Erin Mack, Erin Tuthill, Etaine Raphael, Felix Rijos, Gloria Lejano, Greg Loomis, Harvey Naranjo, Howard Clarke, India Smith, James Abbington, Janet Scardillo, Jasmine King, JD Garbrecht, Jennifer Caye, Jennifer Hundt, Jess Goodine, Jessica Brahmer, Joe Butkus, Josh Davis, Julie Castles, Julie Thake, Justin Laferrier, Karen Lambert, Katie Yancosek, Kelly McGaughey, Kerri Golden, Kerry Quinn, Kim Benson, Kim Capers, Kristen Valent, Kristi Say, Kyla Dunlavey, Laura Friedman, Lauretta Walker, Lawrence Hewett, Leo Mahony, Lisa Hern, Lora Stutzman, Luis Garcia, Lynn Lowe, Marilyn Rogers, Marji Burniston, Matt Scherer, Matthew Helton, Melissa Lewis, Mia Fink, Mr. A., Nicholas Peterson, Nicholle Diaz, Oren Ganz, Paul Stoneman, Pete Lancaster,

Philomena Lai, Regina Sheffield-Wright, Roger Lemacks, Ross Colquhoun, Sara Sutton, Sara Teutupe, Sarah Mitsch, Sarah Simmons, Scott Siironen, Sha'Quitta King, Shannon Coleman, Shannon Lynch, Shon Black, Skip Gill, Solomon Montgomery, Stephanie Beauregard, Stephanie Daugherty, Steve Springer, Sunny Mills, Syreeta Reid, Tamara Tyrell, Tammy Phipps, Terry Cardwell, Tierra Holland, Tiffany Smith, Tomi Adam, Tonja Morrow, Vanessa Haigler, Virginia Gajewski, Virginia Heer, Wendy Abel, Wendy Giles, Willie Holmes, and Yadira Del Toro. If I left anyone off, it was inadvertent. . . . We were quite the team.

Thank you to Elizabeth Painter, Bo Bergeron, Barbara Springer, Lynn Lowe, Chuck Scoville, Shannon Lynch, Leo Mahony, Paul Stoneman, Brad Ritland, and Kerri Golden for their leadership.

There were some fantastic clinicians who played a big role in our section, but due to readability and space constraints were later edited out of this book. Greg Loomis and Julie Castles, I just wanted to highlight you here.

A special thank you to our Amputee Peer visitors and others, especially: Bob "The Builder" Nillson, Jack "Judge" Farley, Jim "Milkshake Man" Mayer, Tom and Elle

"Cookie" Porter, Don "Cane Man" Patterson, Burt "WWII" Oranburg, Jay "Soccer" Frietas, Joe "Hockey" Bowser, and the late Melanie "Red Cross" Strudler.

For their help and advice with the many renditions of my original manuscript and book proposal, I would like to thank: Lydia Nesbit (author of *Shine Shine Shine*), Amy Dawson Robertson (author of *Miles to Go*), and Jenna Land Free (editor, Girl Friday Productions). I would also like to thank David Rozelle (author of *Back in Action*) for his kind advice.

A special thank you to Bob "The Builder" Nillson of http:// 100entproject.org for reading several editions of my manuscript, giving me advice, and constantly talking me off the ledge. Bob, thank you for mentoring me.

I would also like to thank the following people for reading my manuscript and offering guidance: Chuck Scoville, Jack Farley, Susan Hester, Ron Goor, Nancy Goor, Dana Sheets, Paula Pace, Ashley Smith, Etaine Raphael, Verena Levine, Nicki Levine, and the late Richard Levine (who read it through three times back-to-back right before he died, and concluded my coworkers were real heroes).

For taking me on as a scruffy first-year

physical therapy student and spitting me out three years later as a licensed physical therapist, I am indebted to the University of Maryland Department of Physical Therapy and Rehab Sciences. Thank you for training me in the career that I fell in love with.

This book never would have happened if it weren't for the vision of my agent, Howard Yoon. Howard, thank you for taking a chance on me, and never wavering. Thank you also to Howard's co-agent, Anna Sproul-Latimer, for your frank, excellent, and hilarious guidance.

There's a quote out there: "For scientific discovery give me Scott; for speed and efficiency of travel give me Amundsen; but when disaster strikes and all hope is gone, get down on your knees and pray for Shackleton." To my editor, Lucia Watson, what can I say? You were my Shackleton. I had lost hope that this book would ever really come together — and then you arrived. Your enthusiasm for this book blew me right out of the water. Your edits put it together. I trusted you completely and I loved working with you.

My gratitude also goes out to the rest of the Penguin/Avery team — Bill, Gigi, Lisa, Anne, Farin, Meghan, Karen Mayer, and the copy editors, who referred to me as "author."

Thank you to my swimming buddies who unknowingly kept me sane during the highs and lows of this project: Elizabeth Painter and Sue Majewski. Also thank you to Merideth Stakem and Holly Sisk-Roselle for being the original swim coaches at Walter Reed, and the lifeguards and staff at the D.C. Parks and Rec Van Buren St. pool.

To my friends and family who put up with me dropping in and out of your lives, falling asleep in your living rooms, forgetting to return emails and phone calls, and other bad behavior exhibited by me as I got up at four a.m. for several years to compulsively work on a book no one knew about. . . . Thank you for sticking around. Especially: Dana Berliner, Christine Collins, Esther Lehman, Heather Lipin, Dana Sheets, and Ronna Keagle.

A high five to my Ambassador of Cool, Erin Lane, who took me clothes shopping before I went to New York City.

Finally I would like to thank my partner, Ashley Wilder Smith. This book was your idea. Thank you for pushing me. Thank you for giving me the time to write it. Thank you for your constant Adele Levine Improvement Campaign. Thank you for your understanding, and mostly, thank you for

having standards low enough to justify getting set up on a blind date with me!

# ABOUT THE AUTHOR

**Adele Levine** is a practicing physical therapist. She received her master's in Physical Therapy from the University of Maryland School of Medicine in 2001 and her doctorate in Physical Therapy from the University of Maryland School of Medicine in 2005. In 2009, she became a board credentialed Orthopedic Certified Specialist by the American Physical Therapy Association, and has been a Certified Strength and Conditioning Specialist by the National Strength and Conditioning Association since 2003.

Adele Levine worked at Walter Reed Army Medical Center from 2005 until its closure in 2011. She was transferred to the National Naval Medical Center in 2011 (renamed Walter Reed National Military Medical Center), where she continued to rehabilitate war amputees for several more years, and also edited the department newsletter, *The*

*Turnip,* known for such groundbreaking articles as restaurant reviews of the local eatery Fish in the Hood, and suggestions that the new hospital uniform policy include choices of different superhero costumes.

Adele is an accomplished humor writer with more than thirty humor articles published in *The Washington Post.* As a distance swimmer, she has swum across the Chesapeake Bay six times, and once, on a trip to New York City, swam in the Hudson, where a homeless man threw garbage at her. Before becoming a physical therapist, Adele was a purveyor of many dead-end jobs and had several bleak periods of unemployment that she spent rereading old novels and swimming in what she later discovered was one of the most polluted rivers in America.

# Harry Houdini
## Escape Artist

written by
**Patricia Lakin**

illustrated by
**Rick Geary**

Aladdin

**New York   London   Toronto   Sydney   Singapore**

For Steve Geck who offered encouragement, and for Steve Fraser who offered praise and opportunities.
—P. L.
For Deborah.
—R. G.

First Aladdin Paperbacks edition September 2002
Text copyright © 2002 by Patricia Lakin
Illustrations copyright © 2002 by Rick Geary

ALADDIN PAPERBACKS
An imprint of Simon & Schuster Children's Publishing Division
1230 Avenue of the Americas
New York, NY 10020

Book design by Lisa Vega
The text of this book was set in Century Old Style.

Printed in the United States of America
2 4 6 8 10 9 7 5 3 1

Library of Congress Cataloging-in-Publication Data
Lakin, Pat.
Harry Houdini and the shiny coins / written by Patricia Lakin.—1st Aladdin Paperbacks ed.
p. cm. – (Ready-to-read)
Summary: Simple text describes how Harry Houdini, born Ehrich Weiss, worked hard to become a great magician.
ISBN 0-689-85345-9 (Aladdin Library Edition)
ISBN 0-689-84815-3 (Aladdin pbk.)
1. Houdini, Harry, 1874-1926—Juvenile literature. 2. Magicians—United States—Biography—Juvenile literature. 3. Escape artists—United States—Biography—Juvenile literature.
[1. Houdini, Harry, 1874-1926. 2. Magicians.] I. Title. II. Series.
GV1545.H8 L33 2002
793.8'092—dc21
[B]
2001046043

Magician!

Escape artist!

Super-human stunt man!

Who was that and more?

Harry Houdini!

Houdini's real name
was Ehrich Weiss.
He was born in Hungary.
When he was very young,
the family came to America.

4

They settled in Wisconsin.

The family was very poor,

and could not always pay the rent.

So they moved many times.

Finally, they came to New York.

Instead of going to school,

Ehrich and his younger brother

Theo had to work.

But working had its bright side.
Theo's boss showed him
how to make a coin disappear.
Theo showed the trick
to thirteen-year-old Ehrich.

Ehrich was fascinated!

He did the trick very well.

Ehrich had what magicians need—

quick, strong hands.

9

From then on, Ehrich spent his free time learning new tricks. He knew that to be a really good magician he had to be smart, strong, and sure of himself.

Being sure of himself

helped at work too.

One December, Ehrich had a job

as a department-store messenger.

He pinned a sign onto his uniform.

It said, "Christmas is coming.

Turkeys are fat.

Please put a quarter

in the Messenger Boy's hat."

13

Ehrich hid the quarters
in his thick hair,
up his sleeves,
and up his pant legs.

Ehrich told his mother,
"Shake me. I'm magic."
Shiny silver quarters
spun from his body
and danced on the floor!
Mother and son laughed for joy
as they scooped up the rent money.

Year after year,

Ehrich worked at many jobs.

And year after year,

his passion for magic grew.

Ehrich trained every part of his body.

He needed both hands to be strong.

So he spent hours

tying and untying knots.

His lungs had to be strong too.

So he practiced holding his breath

in the bathtub.

He also trained his mind.

He took apart locks and learned

how they worked.

His favorite library book was by
the world-famous French magician,
Jean Eugène Robert-Houdin.
Ehrich added an "i"
to the end of his idol's last name.
Ehrich's nickname, "Ehrie,"
sounded like Harry.
From then on seventeen-year-old
Ehrich Weiss was known
as Harry Houdini.

After years of struggling,
Houdini was finally famous.
In 1912, a New York theater owner
paid him one thousand dollars a week
for his act!
Houdini asked for his salary in coins.

At home, he slowly
spilled the glittering
gold coins onto his mother's lap.
Houdini said that this
was his proudest moment.

But he had much to be proud of
in his career.
People packed theaters
to see his act.
They filled the streets
to see his stunts.

*Click!*

Houdini was handcuffed.

*Clank!*

He was tied up with locked chains
and put into a box.

*Bam!*

The box was nailed shut.

*Splash!*

The box was thrown into the river!

Crowds watched and waited,

sometimes for hours!

Would he escape alive?

He always did,

and without any help!

But how?

Houdini never told his secrets.
And he never stopped
using his head,
his hands,
and his heart.

## Houdini became the greatest magician the world has ever known.

### Here is a timeline of Harry Houdini's life:

| | |
|---|---|
| 1874 | Born as Ehrich Weiss in Budapest, Hungary |
| 1876 | Ehrich's younger brother, Theo, is born |
| 1878 | Weiss family settles in Appleton, Wisconsin |
| 1887 | Weiss family moves to New York |
| 1891 | Changes his name to Harry Houdini and becomes a full-time magician |
| 1892 | Father dies |
| 1893 | Meets and marries Beatrice (Bess) Rahner. She becomes his partner in the act. |
| 1895 | Uses handcuffs for the first time in his act |
| 1899 | Receives star billing from a famous theater owner, and becomes a big hit all over the world |
| 1907 | Jumps into San Francisco Bay, handcuffed, with a 75-pound ball and chained to his ankles |
| 1908 | Creates the Milk Can Escape, where he escapes from a locked milk can filled with water |
| 1912 | Performs his famous Chinese Water Torture Cell, where he is chained and lowered, head-first, into a glass fronted box filled with water |
| 1912 | Performs at the Hammerstein Theatre in New York at a record salary of $1000 per week |
| 1913 | Mother dies |
| 1913 | Performs for former President Teddy Roosevelt |
| 1915 | Performs for President Woodrow Wilson |
| 1919 | Goes to Hollywood to produce, star, and do stunts for the movies. |
| 1926 | Dies on October 31 |